3/82

Shermie Schafer

80.4

FACING DEATH AND GRIEF

George Marshall

CLF Book Service
25 Beacon Street
Boston, MA 02108

If you are an alcoholic, juvenile delinquent, an unmarried mother, an abandoned baby, or just getting old, society is there to cushion your problem. You can get help. But if you are in grief you soon discover that not only are you on your own in your trouble but that few people really know how to help you.

> —*Bernadine Dries and Alice Pattie*
> Up From Grief

Can you say the word dead?
Try.
Death is a fact, a bitter fact.
Face it.

> —*Earl A. Grollman*
> Living When a Loved One Has Died

FACING DEATH AND GRIEF

A Sensible Perspective for the Modern Person

George N. Marshall

℞ Prometheus Books

700 East Amherst St. • Buffalo, New York, 14215

Published 1981 by Prometheus Books
700 East Amherst Street, Buffalo, New York 14215

Library of Congress Card Number 80-84402
ISBN 0-87975-140-1

Printed in the United States of America

Contents

Preface/Acknowledgments

All people will face death, but few prepare for it. This is the current reality. As a result, while we know death is inevitable, most people look upon it as somewhat of a sacred preserve into which the uninitiated should not trespass. Consequently, there is a mystery surrounding death. In spite of the numerous books written on the subject of death, few reveal this mystery and make the facts available to the public, who sooner or later will be consumers of the services of the funeral industry.

This book is written with no ax to grind but has grown out of a lifetime of counseling, of consulting with many ministers, of maintaining cordial relations with innumerable funeral directors, and finally, out of a research project that sought the consumers' viewpoints concerning funeral practices and attitudes. This research involved those that experienced both a traditional funeral and a modern memorial service.

At present, there is no one book that helps the reader through the intricacies in preparing for his own death or that of a loved one and lays out a blueprint or chart for what one should prepare, how to prepare for it, and what to expect. This is the justification for this volume, which has grown out of vast experience in the counseling of the bereaved for death and funerals, in the conducting of funerals, in reading and study in the field, all finally resulting in the research project undertaken. This book, in essence, aims at taking the humbug out of the death situation by removing the mystery and cutting through the complexities and confusions that repel the average person in facing up to what has to be done. Its purpose is to present "What you always wanted to know about death but were afraid to ask"—or face.

Consequently, this volume will explore the attitudes towards death in the overall situation for which one must be prepared, grief, and also the practical matters pertaining to death. It deals with what the consumer has a right to know and expect, how to approach funeral directors, as well as how to deal with memorial societies, one's clergyman or family counselor.

The problem of dying — of what happens in the hospital or the home during prolonged terminal illness — and the ethical, practical, and personal questions with which one must deal are here touched upon. Does one tell the dying? How does one become *honest* and yet maintain the *hope* that is essential until the dying have "made their peace" and are prepared for death? How did our funeral practices and our attitudes toward death develop? A long history from the dawn of civilization until the present is here recorded. What can one count upon from the physician as support and strength in this situation? From the funeral director? What do the church and the clergy have to offer that is valuable? When does one approach the clergy concerning the final arrangements? These questions all need to be answered.

There is a specialized problem concerning the death of children and that of parents. How can one assist children through the mourning process and assist in the reorganization and reconstruction of their lives when the major support has been removed? Help is needed when the death of parents, or the loss of playmates, is thrust upon them. Parents who lose children also need special help in overcoming the intense grief, and possible unfounded guilt, they face.

Today we face many issues concerning death, such as the efficient development of machines that can maintain life so that people have a prolonged period of living, or perhaps a prolonged period of dying. How do we deal with passive and active euthanasia? What are the differences between them? These raise legal, ethical, and humane issues. Other questions considered are eugenics, suicide — often an alternative to euthanasia — concerns such as land for cemeteries, cremation, cryonics — the freezing of the body for future restoration — and ecological problems concerning death. Most people know only a small amount about these issues and find it difficult to totally come to grips with such problems regarding their own individual situation.

Other major concerns include the many legal aspects of dying. Questions over trusts, wills, and life insurance are part of the planning for death. There are the concerns of the dying person who wishes to make provisions for others, as well as the needs of survivors who must be able to survive economically, financially, and legally. What are the concerns that partners should have and how should they be implemented? Through trusts — which kind? Through provisions in wills? Through joint property? Through insurance policies? What happens when an individual outlives all other contemporaries —

the lawyers who drew the will, the witnesses to them — while the bankers and business associates are no longer active in the community? What happens when one moves to a retirement area in a part of the country different from where the major property is? What is involved in competing jurisdictions of courts over state taxes, and how does the individual resolve such problems? Prudent insight can protect those we love.

This book, written by a person who has spent his life as a counselor and advisor in such situations, covers just such a wide range of considerations. In each area of concern, references are made to specific in-depth studies, so that this work is a reference work to many other studies and points of view. Ample quotations from others are cited as authoritative conclusions or the opinions and findings of many experts to whom the author is indebted.

This work includes a case study of funeral and memorial practices and a case study of funeral and memorial attitudes that the author developed under academic supervision, and which should throw light on the individual's concern in making sensitive, intelligent, and acceptable decisions.

While this research material was used as the basis for a doctoral dissertation,[1] its main purpose was conceived in a spirit of fairness to find out if the proponents of either the funeral industry or the modern memorial alternatives were overstating or overselling their own position. For those who are looking for an either-or answer to this question, the following pages should be studied, but the main conclusion may here be summarized as, many people found satisfaction in both the traditional service and in the modern memorial service. It is not a question of one or the other, so far as acceptability is concerned; it is a matter of personal preferences. The public will accept both as does the family, but there are economic and financial, as well as religious matters, to be concerned about in the process, and these are more compelling than often realized.

The intelligent person seeks a sensible approach to the issues of death. There is no one-volume book today with a consistent point of view of one person that offers guidance for the overall comprehension of the nature, pitfalls, opportunities, and considerations involved. This volume is an honest effort to meet this need, devoid of hypocrisy or commercial exploitation, free of humbug, seeking to be completely fair in its presentation of the concerns and rights of the consuming public.

The appendixes and tables included will be helpful for referral purposes as one makes his or her own preparation for death, which this book proposes to stimulate.

Acknowledgments

We are indebted for permission to quote from those who have written in this field, and their publishers, as well as to those whose general ideas laid the foundations for others. Out of their labors we have been inspired to enlarge the area of human inquiry. There are more personal acknowledgments that I, as the author, should make.

Dr. Robert L'Hommedieu Miller, professor of religion at Tufts University for the past quarter century, was of inestimable help in the preparation and tabulation of the Statistical Survey on Death and Grief, which altered preconceived impressions regarding aspects of funereal customs and grief situations, while highlighting other aspects attendant thereon. The Survey is not included in this book, but its results have influenced the point of view presented; in addition, valuable marginal comments and accompanying letters have been freely quoted as illustrative material to enhance the volume. Consequently, the large groups of nearly two hundred respondees from thirty-three states and three Canadian provinces, the vast majority of whom were religious liberals, with a small representation of Catholics, Jews, and Protestants, deserve appreciation. Indebtedness to all is hereby expressed, because their willingness to share their personal grief experiences, trauma, and sense of loneliness and loss created an objective and empirical basis for decision making and preparation to face both the deaths of loved ones and ourselves.

In addition to the several typists who helped in this work, special appreciation is expressed to Sally Ratchford, for original help in outlining the program and undertaking the survey; to Janet Robertson and Dr. Mary Katherine Donaldson, for sympathetic help in the preparation of the typescripts; and to Winifred E. Cole and the corps of loyal staff members at the Church of the Larger Fellowship, all of whom made possible my concentration on this project. Special mention and appreciation is due Howard Spencer of Vernon, New Jersey, whose guidance in the preparation of a pilot independent-study project for CLF on *Death: A Sensible Perspective for Religious Liberals,* which involved twenty-seven of us in the study of many aspects of death, including its sociological, medical, economic, legal, religious, and personal concepts. Out of this project grew my involvement in the research on this subject that led to a doctoral dissertation. Throughout the years, Howard Spencer's guidance and expert skills in independent study programs have been of great assistance. As in earlier works, I owe him a great debt of gratitude.

Dr. Donaldson, besides offering enthusiastic, constructive suggestions, has also prepared a first draft of the index and codified the bibliography, placing me further in her debt.

Finally, I am indebted to my own experience and ability to emote and suffer with many friends (in grief all become friends) and fellow mourners. Through involvement with others I learned the lessons of the Buddha—that suffering is the primary condition of life—and of Schweitzer—that we form an unseen fellowship with those who bear the mark of pain. As their lives and experiences have become a part of my own, my understanding of the human condition has been expanded.

I am further indebted for support to Rabbi Abraham J. Feldman, D.D., who graciously granted permission to reprint whatever I wished from his pamphlet, *In Time of Need,* published in Hartford, Connecticut, by the Weinstein Funeral Home. This was copyrighted by Rabbi Feldman in 1946 and used with his permission. In addition I am indebted to Ms. Rebecca Cohen, President of the Continental Association of Funeral and Memorial Societies, Inc., for her guidance and the use of materials published by the Continental Association.

G.N.M.

1

A Rendezvous with Death

A correspondent wrote:

My mother and grandfather died a day apart during the influenza epidemic, which I have never forgotten although I was less than three years old. My mother, who had been nursing my grandfather, also contracted the disease and died. The two were buried together, following a single funeral service. In that epidemic people dropped like flies after very brief illnesses, since there were no miracle drugs or antibiotics. Funeral directors and gravediggers worked virtually around the clock, and the clergy spent more time in officiating than in consoling, counseling, or preparing families for the proper emotional, psychological, and practical situation into which each bereaved family was thrust. Young as I was, I knew something terrible was happening in my family, although I could not understand it.

Grandfather was very sick and everybody worried about him. My mother was very tired and exhausted and was no longer able to give me attention or be fun. Then the door to grandfather's room was shut, and a strange, elegant-looking piece of shiny, new wooden furniture was set up in the middle of the parlor; the heavy, maroon curtain-drape that covered the doorway was closed, and people walked quietly and whispered when in the parlor. I was forbidden to enter.

Mother, in the meantime, was taken upstairs to bed, sick, and I was never to see her alive again. A second shiny, wooden casket (for that's what they were, although I did not know it) was set up in the parlor, and every now and then an aunt, or my grandmother, or a neighbor would look at me and break out crying, "Oh, the poor boy," and occasionally pick me up and sob for a moment, then embarassedly set me down. It was obvious nobody knew what to say to me. My father would come home and hold me in his lap and against his shoulders, and I knew that he was suffering deeply and quietly.

Then, after a lull of days in which all was quiet, a whispered, morose activity occurred with a flurry. Tall, thin men in black suits began to carry uncomfortable folding chairs into the living room, the hallway, the dining room, and the parlor. The maroon drape over the arch was opened, and I was carried in by an aunt and held up to look at grandfather and my mother, still, oh so still, but looking lifelike and radiant, except that there were copper pennies on their closed eyelids. I squirmed in my aunt's arms and reached down to my mother, picking a penny off her eye and putting it impulsively into my mouth, much to the horror of everyone who saw it. A collective gasp, a unison reaction, audibly shook the room, and voices said, "You naughty boy!" My aunt thrust me around and plunged her fingers into my mouth, nearly choking me, and viciously propelled the penny to the floor. My father heard the commotion, including my sobbing and cries of "Mommy, Mommy." He came rapidly into the room, picked me up, stroked my head, and carried me to the front hall, where he sat down with me on the window seat behind the rows of empty wooden chairs. He tried to tell me that mommy was dead and would never speak to me again in this life.

Shortly afterward, the doorbell rang and people began to come in and take their places in the chairs. Soon the whole downstairs was filled with strangers sitting all around, and then the family joined them. The tall, thin men in black knew everybody and where to seat them; a clergyman in surplice came in, cleared his throat, and began to mumble an unemotional, service, as though what he had to say was meaningless to those seated in front of him. Then the tall, somberly dressed men chose from the audience those who carried the caskets out and placed them in two carriages. Silently, we all followed.

We walked to the cemetery not too far behind the house, where only a few days before I remembered running and climbing up and down the hill. After crossing the bridge over the rivulet, we passed freshly dug holes with huge mounds of earth beside them and continued up the hillside until we came to two holes side-by-side. The party gathered around the graves. The coffins were opened and closed one last time. To my horror I saw my mommy suspended in a wooden box above a deep, fresh hole in the earth. Then, the minister read a prayer and threw a handful of dirt on each coffin. The tall men in black began cranking the coffins — one with my mother! — into the earth. As it sank further and further down, I began to cry and shout in anguish. Breaking

free of my father, I jumped in on top of the coffin, pounding and call-
ing, "Mommy, Mommy!" while the tall men in black retrieved me and
handed me, kicking and squirming, back to my father. He held me in
his arms and walked rapidly away from the people, trying to soothe
me with kisses and the sorrowful affection that he felt. I was enough
aware of the situation to know not only that they were placing my
mother deep in the earth, but that I had disgraced myself and my
father in the eyes of the others; yet, I had acted in the only natural way
I could, and I remember knowing then that my father was probably
the only one there who understood.

It is little wonder that this is the first experience of my childhood
that I remember, and that I have put out of my mind everything
before it. Now, a half century later, I have verbalized this recollection
and written it out for the first time. *

All have a rendezvous with death: some earlier and some later in life; for
some it will come with the death of a beloved person, for others in facing
their own death. The purpose and intention of this book are to assist us in
thinking through the matter of death, both for ourselves and for those close
to us. We need the strength that comes from preparation, the courage that
comes from the awareness that we walk a common path shared by all
humanity, and the insights that come through forethought. The childhood
experience quoted above could not have been prepared for, but all readers
of these words can avoid the precipitous nightmare the writer lived through
by preparing now for facing death.

Throughout history burial customs for the dead and the respect afforded
the departed have been among the most permanent remains; as in the case
of Tutankhamen, much of what we know from earlier civilizations has been
gained by the discovery and study of the dead, their tombs, and the artifacts
depicting life that were interred with their bones. Through such remains we
have learned of their lives, their precious possessions, their faith, and their
concepts of immortality.

Today, changing attitudes on death are evident in many aspects of our society. A moderating climate of religious beliefs reflects new attitudes about
life and death, including the right of the elderly and incurably ill to choose
death by euthanasia.

Technological advances have affected the changing nature of warfare:
soldiers in recent decades have made war on civilians through incendiary
bombings of European cities and nuclear bombings of Japanese cities during World War II. Terrorism, civil war, and strife in the Middle East, Ire-
land, and in Indochina, and the growth of violence and crime in the streets
in American cities have made life cheap and violent death commonplace.

Scientific advances made possible the transplant of organs, such as (originally) corneas of eyes, then ear discs, kidneys, blood vessels, and now hearts. The use of the cadaver for study and research in medical schools and laboratories requires expendable cadavers for anatomical advances. Other technological possibilities are seen in the concepts of the deep-freeze preservation of bodies for future restoration.[1]

The conventional American pattern of funeral customs is likewise changing. Ecological and space problems are hastening a transition to cremation, rather than cemetery burials. The costly and carnal display of the body, embalmed and cosmetically adorned, glorifies the materialistic rather than spiritual qualities of life. Inevitably, changes are occurring due to the technological impact on modern life, not to an increasing religious sensitivity.

Naturally, the problem of death also involves separation and the effect of that separation on the living. Hence we should deal with the problem of grieving and mourning. Death has been the great unseen fact of life, unspoken and not articulated. Removed from the home to the hospital and morgue, new psychological insights are necessary to prepare the survivors for dealing with such severance situations without the sacrifice of healthy human emotions, without otherwise making mannequins, rather than human beings, of people.

There are many reasons to study death. Most are personal, yet it is a universal experience. Only birth rivals it in touching every individual creature. Through death we are brought close to all life, to all living, all formerly living, and all future living.

In modern society discussion of death had been previously shunned, almost as though people were afraid to face the inevitable divide. Yet today, many books on this subject are being published, and courses on death are now presented in colleges, junior colleges, and indeed, even in high schools. A recent psychologists' survey on the subject of attitudes toward death received an amazingly high response: almost as many responded to it as did to questionnaires about sex, the all-time high interest area for questionnaire responses.

There is need for a comprehensive understanding of death as it applies to your own life, to that of loved ones with which you will be emotionally, if not administratively, involved, because death in our society often comes unexpectedly, through accidents and violence. According to the Census Bureau, two million people die each year. One way or another, we and those we love will be included in the statistics in some specific year, as yet unknown to us and our survivors.

Will we be prepared for this event when our time comes, when, as they say, "our number is up"? Will our family or loved one know what our wishes are and be able to proceed without undue stress because of our thoughtful preparations? Can we die with the comfort of knowing we have not left final arrangements up in the air, wreaking economic havoc and emotional nightmares on those we love the most?

A recent reaction when this subject was mentioned was, "How can any red-blooded, active person be concerned with death?" The question was a strange one, coming as it did from a life insurance broker, whose main business activity dealt with insuring for the contingency of death and, therefore, the settlement of estates. His question indicated that he dealt with the hypothetical problem of death in other than personal terms and was psychologically unable to confront the fact that death was more personal and intimate than his actuarial tables, which he lovingly studied before calling on each prospective client. Many people are like this: they can face death in the abstract or in hypothetical terms, but they can't face the fact that it will one day touch them too. Yet we should all recognize that "there but for the grace of God, go I" when the bell tolls.

The thought of life's ending often brings a realization of the loss of those bittersweet, fragrant, rich, enjoyable moments in which we live, breathe, and have our being. It is fraught with a sad and frosty realization: the end of consciousness; the end of life; the end of challenge and strife and the taste of victory; the last moments of warm and loving companionship, ending in the loneliness of a solitary eternity—these all mark the outer boundary of our earthly mortality, of our human community, of our achievement of meaning in this life.

We think of the moments of love and discovery, of the flashing eyes of recognition, of the arm handclasp or the bashful blush, and the joy, the sheer joy of holding, finding, caring, and loving another person. We hear the sound of children's laughter, and the tingling, delightful tittering of love's joyful, thrilling laughter. This all ended? No more opportunities? There is little wonder that death has no attractiveness for most of us.

But often in life there comes the graying experience of aging, with the loss of loved ones, with the slow deterioration of the body, as life's mathematics turns to subtraction, when the active days are past and we long to depart these poor, tired bones and give them final rest. Then indeed we are ready for the flesh to return to the earth whence it came and for our living to become a memory.

Such wistfulness, nostalgia, fear of the unknown, a desire to hold on to what we have in life leads us to put off facing the fact of death, to put off until tomorrow what is not necessary today. "We are the living," the poet wrote, and so we leave death for the dying, but a thoughtful high schooler, in one of those rare moments of disclosure and insight, blurted out, "Why, we begin to die the moment we begin to live!" Life and death cannot be easily separated. They go together, the inverse and obverse, the two sides of the coin. Every breath of life brings us one breath closer to death.

We are, however, prudent, and most of us, conscious of the worth of our property, do make provisions for our estates and go to the trouble of writing wills. We want to protect our loved ones, to see the proper disposition of our wealth so that our families do not squander our life's accumulation in squabbling about it and, perhaps, to see that those institutions in which we believe are remembered by us. This objective situation deals not with our mortal remains, but with our materialistic possessions. While we can still write "Being of sound mind and body, I hereby set forth this last will and testament . . . ," we are able to comfort ourselves with the knowledge that we have lightened the load for those who remain and those who follow after. We should make necessary legal preparations, and in this volume we shall face some of the hidden pitfalls we might meet. An informed person is better prepared to act according to rational insights and standards.

Not only should we be prepared to lighten the load by such legal preparations, but there is need for thoughtful consideration about the proper disposal of our remains and those of loved ones. Confronting this most difficult matter, for many people, is harder than purchasing life insurance, making a will, or setting up a trust. Too often it seems distasteful and unseemly. The body alive is a graceful and lovely creation, but the body dead is cold, barren, and rigid. We would rather not think about it, yet somebody must. If we leave arrangements to the embalmers and funeral directors, the results may be even more dismaying. Death, and our final parting, should be true to the integrity of our own lives and should be a passage reasonably soothing and graceful, on which the heartbroken can look back with pride and satisfaction. At this point the question of pre-arrangements for the disposal of the body and the type of service to be held should enter our discussion. What are the guidelines we need to follow, and how can this final passage from the stage of life be made rational and uplifting? Do we prefer to keep the matter simple and dignified, or do we seek an elaborate ceremonial occasion? Can both be handled without heartbreak and undue emotional stress, or is one method superior to the other? Should the body be present at a public service or for viewing before time? Should cremation or burial be practiced? Should we turn to a memorial society or a funeral director? What are the financial considerations of this necessary and essential duty? We must learn to honestly face such concerns, and this book holds out the hope that it can be done without travail or heartache by facing the making of decisions in times of health.

Others have their recollections of close family deaths, and what they mean to them; of deaths, and of the dying scenes before death. As a minister, I recall other situations.

Mrs. Coombs lay dying of cancer in the hospital. She was in terrible agony, tortured in mind and body because she found no hope in her situation. Then, miraculously, she seemed at comfort and at ease. When I as a young minister next saw her doctor and mentioned how improved she seemed, the physician confidentially answered, "You would rest better, too, Reverend, if you were as shot full of morphine."

Mr. Pritchard was an Englishman working in the United States. He was reserved, sensitive, highly regulated in his own life and careful to control his emotions. He developed lung cancer, which was discovered too late. After agonizing weeks in the hospital, most of his body functions had ceased. He could do little more than lie in bed and groan, while tubes, needles, and machines controlled his bodily functions. He seemed the center of a plumbing system as his life was continued day after day, week in and week out. Mrs. Pritchard would sit by his bed by the hour. "Why won't they let him die in peace, Mr. Marshall?" she would plead; "We wouldn't do this to a dog." But her doctors insisted that it was their duty to keep him alive as long as possible, even for weeks after he was no longer conscious or functioning as a human being.

As a vice president of a major industrial concern, Mr. Walker was powerful, active, and on the go. He had served as president of his church, of the local community fund, and of many organizations and agencies in his community. He was a devoted husband and always solicitous of Mrs. Walker, whose frail, delicate health was a constant source for concern. He had a heart attack and died instantly, intestate. The public relations people at his company came in to assist Mrs. Walker and planned an elaborate, extravagant funeral, as befits a captain of industry, but which denied the human values of Mr. Walker, a tightfisted puritan who believed in integrity and simplicity in his own life. The public display expected of Mrs. Walker was too much for her, and she found herself forced to walk through a nightmare for three days. She felt the final arrangements were not in keeping with her husband's character, but she said, "Mr. Walker always thought I would die first, and so we never talked about his death."

Each of these examples could be illustrated a hundred times over in their nightmarish experiences.

He was a fellow minister and we knew each other well. Like me, he was interested in the subject of death and borrowed my recently preached sermon manuscript from me. Reading it prompted him to preach on death also. He aroused a considerable stir in the press and soon became the leading spokesman in the funeral practices controversy that led to the founding of a major memorial society, which assisted people in planning rational and simple funerals or memorial services. He developed a most deadly malady for a preacher: he lost the use of his voice. As one treatment after another failed, his depression deepened, until one evening he went into the church study, put a pistol into his mouth, and blew his brains out. His young wife, small children, flourishing congregation, and numerous professional colleagues were totally unprepared for this turn of events. Nothing in his life seemed to point toward such a violent action, although the tragedy of a highly articulate thinker unable to verbalize his ideas was understandable.

Then of course, one recalls other deaths, such as that of Emily, a talented, vivacious, high-ranking high school senior tragically killed in an automobile accident. How could her family, friends, and schoolmates possibly be prepared? There was the little youngster killed in a sledding accident the day after Christmas, and the guilt of his father who thought, "If only I had not bought that Flexible Flyer for him!" Meaningless guilt often grips us at the time of death: we see ourselves involved in deaths that were beyond our ability to foretell or prohibit. Little Mary was buried on the day before Christmas, in what would have been her new Christmas frock, because she came down with a lethal virus that was treated by home remedies to no avail before she was taken to the doctor, too late. He could do nothing to save her. Loss, bereavement, and remorse are enough without adding guilt to them.

But not all deaths are tragic. There are people who gracefully fold the mantle of their lives about them and lie down as though to gentle dreams, going without protest—almost in anticipation. Such deaths are often the crowning glory to a gracious life. Innumerable men and women die this way, prepared for life's inevitable summons; yet, so strange is human nature that often the survivors could not understand the ease of his or her departure. "She was prepared for it, but we were not!" they wail. "Good for him, but worse for us," they mutter, little realizing how difficult it is for the survivors to accept the finality of death without an interval of time.

Because of many personal contacts with the principal persons involved, I well recall the death of Dr. Albert Schweitzer, the famed African doctor who died in Lambarene on September 4, 1965, at 10:30 in the evening.[2] He was approaching his ninety-first birthday. Over five years earlier he had said that he could not leave Africa again because of his advanced age: "My Africans would not understand if I left them and died elsewhere. An Africa good enough to live in is good enough to die in." Now on August 12, a number of old friends were invited to Lambarene, including the members of the Association that he had set up to continue the hospital after his death. On August 23, Dr. Schweitzer had apparently diagnosed his approaching end. At supper that evening he announced that he would like to review his plans for the continuation of the hospital after he was gone, and step-by-step he went over how he foresaw the necessary transition. He was alert and concerned over every detail. Dr. Fritz Dinner recalled that his voice was firm and clear. The next morning he didn't get up for breakfast and remained in his room. Three days later he asked for a driver to take him around the hospital grounds. In the lone jeep he was driven to each building and compound. "One could observe that his eyes wandered over the hospital and its buildings as if he took them in, like the last view of his life's work, or—who can tell — as though taking leave," Fritz Dinner recalled. Dr. Schweitzer spent the next week in bed.

His personal attending physician, Dr. David Miller, had been called from the United States, and he reported that Dr. Schweitzer was wholly at peace, conversant with every symptom, and the perfect patient. He knew he was dying and wished to do so quietly. He took no food but drank a little beer to avoid the suffering that comes with dehydration. He spent long hours talking with his daughter, Rhena, about many subjects, including his wishes for the future of the hospital, what to do about his legacy that, due to his fame and numerous writings, would complicate her life, and about the final ideas and thoughts a father wished to share with his daughter. He also talked with Dr. Walter Munz, the Chief of Medical Staff who had agreed to stay on, about anticipated problems or shared helpful knowledge with his successor. Then he went to sleep on Saturday, and at 10:30 in the evening, Dr. Miller announced that Albert Schweitzer was dead.

Radio Gabon carried the news throughout the tropical republic, and tom-toms sent the message inland. A great pilgrimage to the hospital began: people from all walks of life — simple villagers who had long been served by him and his hospital, cabinet members, important professional and business leaders of the new country — just about everybody who could make arrangements came to Lambarene.

At the hospital the Doctor's wishes were to be followed, with no variation from other burial practices. Immediate burial took place, without embalming, in a simple wooden box whose construction had been supervised by Schweitzer himself. A simple wooden cross was erected, like those used for his wife and Nurse Emma Hausknecht, alongside of whom he was buried. The Chief of Staff, Dr. Munz, read the graveside prayers, and Vice President M. Bongo, shortly to become President of the Republic of Gabon, spoke. "We are glad that *Le Grand Docteur* is buried in our earth. Now he belongs to us always," he said.

After the formal service, the people took over and expressed their grief in their own way. Each Sunday for many months the people, often in great flotillas of over a hundred pirogues, came to dance and sing and wail over the grave. Others, on hearing the monotonous sound of the tom-tom, came to join the dancing and to express their own grief.[3] When I read these lines I recalled with a chuckle, as I think Schweitzer himself would, that years before a grateful African elder, following an operation, had held his hand and pledged, "When you die we shall beat the tom-toms for a whole month." The embarrassed doctor replied, "Thank goodness, I won't be alive to hear it." Now the prophecy was true and his death was observed and celebrated in the cultural traditions of two worlds: his own Western, liberal religious tradition and the African tradition. Of his death, another friend, a religious leader who had visited Dr. Schweitzer with me, observed, "He died so gracefully and with such dignity." And the simplicity made the picture complete: it was in keeping with his life, and his integrity was not broken.

The type of observance required at the death of great people or popular leaders often calls for both private family observances and a public ceremonial recognition, as a catharsis for the people. Both of these situations are exemplified in the simple hospital service of Dr. Schweitzer's family and associates, and the continuing native observances held by the Africans in their own style.

One of the most notable dualities recorded in history followed the terrible and nationally wrenching death of Abraham Lincoln, the fallen President, the great solitary leader who had led this nation through a torturous Civil War and was then assassinated. The depth of mourning in the northern United States has been unmatched in our history, and Lincoln has remained one of the great folk heroes of our culture down to the present. Following the state funeral in Washington and the family service in Springfield, Illinois, his open coffin, borne in a draped funeral car, spent months touring the United States, going into many communities accessible by rail in the northern states. Millions filed by, despite Lincoln's written request that his body be donated to science for research, without embalming and burial.

The terrible national catharsis following the assassination of John F. Kennedy in Dallas symbolized the death of youthful hope: something noble, promising, and vibrant clearly had been destroyed when the first President born in the twentieth century, a man of rigorous courage, who dreamed of a "new frontier" for the American spirit, was cut down. The pomp, pageantry, and martial tread of the funeral procession, shared by untold millions through television coverage, were necessary and helpful as a first step in healing the national wound. In the next few years the assassinations of two more youthful, courageous, dynamic leaders, Robert Kennedy and Martin Luther King, Jr., touched the same chord in our national life.

Such people become the property of the national consciousness and their deaths call for social release found, in our society's contemporary culture, through the pomp, circumstance, and personalized editorial commentary of the public media. In the Soviet Union, the embalmed body of Lenin, "Father of the Revolution," is on perpetual display in a glass-enclosed sarcophagus, while in Communist China, the embalmed remains of Mao Tse-tung are publicly exhibited in a glass enclosure, which is viewed daily by thousands of persons.

These public services befit the national statesmen; yet, another service, a private, personally significant service for family and intimate friends, is often called for. Like the public service, it should also express the life values and integrity of the deceased. The two should complement each other: both are valuable and perfectly in order.

For most of us, however, who lack the charismatic nature of a Kennedy or a King, one service alone should convey the integrity of our lives and our values. But some reflection is often necessary: What does our life, and consequently, our death, mean to each of us?

The attitudes with which we approach life condition our attitudes toward death. Perhaps Socrates in his response to the judges, after being sentenced to death at his trial in ancient Athens, approximately five hundred years before the time of Christ, sums it up best.

> If we reflect we shall see that we may well hope that death is a good. For the state of death is one of two things: either the dead wholly ceases to be, and loses all sensation; or, according to the common belief, it is a change and migration of the soul into another place. And if death is the absence of all sensation, and like the sleep of one whose slumbers are unbroken by any dreams, it will be a wonderful gain. If that is the nature of death, I for one count it a gain. For then it appears that eternity is nothing more than a single night.
>
> But if death is a journey to another place, and the common belief be true, that there are all who have died, what good could be greater than this, my judges?
>
> What would you not give to converse with Orpheus and Hesiod and Homer? I am willing to die many times, if this be true.[4]

And the pagan Pericles, in his famous funeral oration for the dead who fell in the defense of Athens, noted that "the whole earth is the sepulchre of famous men, and their story is not graven only on stone, but lives on . . . woven into the fabric of other men's lives."

The fifteenth chapter of Paul's first letter to the Corinthians expresses the classic Christian approach. The later concepts of Christianity have been well expressed by poets such as George Eliot, in "Oh, may I join the choir invisible whose music is the gladness of the world," or, in the words of Robert Louis Stevenson,

> Under the wide and starry sky,
> Dig the grave and let me lie,
> Glad did I live and gladly die,
> And I laid me down with a will.[5]

Accordingly, we see the universality of death, and that people have responded to it in a multitude of ways in various cultures. The heroic element in death, the resigned, the fearful and frightening, has often been preserved in various writings. One might wonder why, if death is so widespread and its experience so inescapable, should we seek for fresh interpretations? The commonplace experience of death, however, leaves much to be desired, decided, improved, and re-defined. The indications of changing viewpoints and outlooks will affect social customs, and this will be borne out in the following chapters.

Death has many dimensions and we should view them. There is the physical termination of a life: for that individual, it is ended. But for those who loved or depended upon that person, there will be grief, and we need help in preparing ourselves to weather the emotional storms and depression that grief causes. Many persons do not know how to deal with the dying person, how to ease his or her acceptance of the approaching end, so that with grace and resignation one can "go gently into that good night." Even while we see a person withering, dying before our eyes, we start to mourn. Before death arrives, we need to understand our roles so as to be prepared to hold on, giving strength and encouragement to the sufferer in the final period, while maintaining our equilibrium.

We also should know how death has been regarded throughout the ages. We need to comprehend some of the modern social dilemmas that have developed in our technological society and the means for resolving such issues. We should know who can help us face death. This volume offers such guidance.

2

The Fellowship of Grief

A correspondent wrote:

> *My first contact with grief on a large scale came when I was working in the admitting office of a small city hospital near Boston during the depression of the '30s. At that time I began to have grave misgivings about the practices of some doctors, many undertakers, and pastors — Protestant, Catholic, and Jewish — in preparing patients and relatives for death and accompanying grief. In fact, as years passed I found their worn-thin Bible passages outmoded, and their calling on families or attending wakes and visiting hours at funeral homes as a more personal approach.*
>
> *Immediately after my husband's death, I was fortunate in becoming a volunteer for a funded, Harvard Medical School research outreach program that helped widows and widowers who were having difficulty in adjusting to a new way of life for which they were entirely unprepared. Here again I ran into the inadequacies of churches to meet the very personal and varying needs of those left behind.**

The person who wrote the above passage found that her involvement in working with suffering persons, first in the admitting office of a small hospital, and then in a university research project touching grief, helped her meet her own crisis. She had learned through the fellowship of grief, common to all, that there are inner resources to see the mourner through adversity.

Dr. Schweitzer wrote of "the fellowship of those who bear the mark of pain," and this fellowship sooner or later includes every person capable of loving, whole relationships, and many who, while not able to love, still knew the meaning, or felt the need, of dependency or reliance upon others. For the day does come when we lose loved ones, or those whose presence gives comfort, assurance, and identity to our lives. Then we know suffering, and with suffering comes grief, sorrow, and a deepening sense of loss.

In this spirit, the words of Jesus of Nazareth are not without their special significance. "Blessed are those who mourn, for they shall be comforted."

Grief is not the special domain of death. We grieve whenever we know a deep, wrenching loss: the loss of a loved one through death; the loss that comes through divorce, separation, severance of any kind, or, the pain felt by young lovers separated from one another or those who know unrequited love. A person whose purpose in life is destroyed by retirement or unemployment may go into deep, traumatic process of grief. Moving to a strange city often creates the condition of grief, and perhaps, it touches children more deeply when they are forced to give up schoolmates, well-adjusted play situations, and familiar surroundings to "begin life over again" in a different environment. In all such situations where a genuine separation is consummated, the grieving process can take place. And because, as some psychologists have pointed out, we expand our lives, our egos, to include all we possess, everything to which we can affix the personal adjective "my," we also have the capacity to grieve over the loss of property, possessions, and wealth. Grief is a natural emotion in which we are inwardly destroyed by the loss of outward relationships, so that for a time we stand alone.

Psychologists have dealt with the many factors that go into grief, some doubting that grief is a single emotion, but rather a compound of various emotions: pity for oneself; guilt for one's failures, real or imaginary; anger over the injustice that has complicated our lives; and fear of the unknown future into which we must now walk alone.

Dr. John Brantner,[1] professor of clinical psychology at the University of Minnesota, in speaking at the Symposium on Death and Attitudes Toward Death in 1972 at the University of Minnesota Medical School, said:

"We don't need to be taught how to grieve, we need to learn how to mourn — to mourn efficiently, mourn effectively, to do our grief work, and in our mourning to re-enter life." The funeral is a good way to let us see what we can expect in ourselves and to observe what happens to other people on such an occasion.

He also suggested that people should attend funerals at which they are not themselves the central mourners. It will improve funerals and deepen our insights if we have this experience when "we are not blind with grief."

Brantner made a distinction between grief and mourning; yet, definitions alone do not create the necessary distinctions. Dr. Edgar N. Jackson, a psychologist and clergyman who served as the director of a psychological counseling service in Westchester County, New York, offered this definition:

"Grief is the intense emotion that floods life when a person's inner security system is shattered by an acute loss usually associated with the death of someone important in his/her life."[2]

As a composite attitude created by a variety of emotions, rather than simply one composed of pity for oneself, grief encompasses guilt for one's failures, real or imaginary; anger over the injustice that has complicated life; fear of the unknown future; dread of the loneliness that now engulfs and threatens to destroy old relationships. It is the feeling of helplessness, panic, fear, and dismay that overwhelms one at some great loss.

Mourning, on the other hand, is a process that enables one to come to terms with grief and structures a response to grief so that it may be overcome, and new, meaningful patterns of living established. Through mourning one finds a way back from hopelessness to hope. Grief is a state of shock, numbness, despair; mourning attempts to deal with this problem.

Lily Pincus[3] dealt with "the importance of mourning," noting that it depends on many factors, such as the circumstances surrounding death and the degree of dependence of the survivors. Hence, the pattern of mourning changes for each individual: the precondition for a person to "complete" his or her mourning must be that each is allowed to mourn in his or her own way.

People grieve because of losses in their lives. Something has been subtracted, and they feel diminished. After the additions of growth in youth, and once one enters the phase of subtractions, where losses increase, there are moments of sorrow. As people lose some things of value, they make alternative adjustments until they come to those moments of finality when simple adjustments do not work. Then a part of one's being seems lost by this deprivation—this is the price we pay when a part of the inner being is invested in another. Yet human experience shows that the richness of personal involvement compensates for subsequent loss and grief.

Emotional reactions cause physiological changes when a person is in grief. Jackson notes that there is a generalized discomfort that indicates malfunction: the muscular system is weak; the glandular system goes askew and works in erratic patterns; the cardiovascular system may react with high blood pressure; there may be hot and cold flashes, rapidity of the heart beat, gasping for breath at spells; the skin may become highly sensitized, causing irritation or rashes. There may also be the loss of appetite, the inability to swallow, stomach cramps, indigestion, diarrhea or constipation. Not all persons go through all these symptoms, Jackson notes, but grief usually brings on some or a combination of them during its intense period.

In addition, the feeling responses, characterized by fears, sorrow, anxiety, uncertainty or indecision, and a loss of energy, may foster personality changes or habit changes: the neat become untidy, the gregarious become withdrawn, the faithful become skeptical, and the cheerful become morose. Futility sets in. Love has been taken away, and we do not want to think of life without love. When anyone dies we all die a little, for we are all diminished by the death of others and reminded of our mortal status. Healthful mourning helps us overcome our normal grief; we can cope with it. Only when grief cannot be assuaged with the passage of time is it abnormal.

Lynn Caine[4] touched the aspect of grief that diminishes the survivor when she wrote, "We grieve not for the dead but for ourselves." She felt that "the widow's grief is the sharpest of all, because she has lost the most." Others have felt that they, too, have lost the most—lovers, husbands, children, and parents. Each dependent survivor feels the acuteness of his or her own suffering and the uniqueness of the loss because of this sense of involvement in one another. As John Donne reminded us:

> No man is an island, entire of itself; every man is a piece of the continent, a part of the main; if a clod be washed away by the sea, Europe is the less, as well as if a promontory were, as well as if a manor of thy friends or of thine own were; any man's death diminishes me, because I am involved in mankind; and therefore never send to know for whom the bell tolls; it tolls for thee.[5]

The deaths of loved ones, of mates, of parents, siblings, and of children are cruel and often difficult subtractions to which one must adjust, so that one's grief ceases to be master. Personality can evolve into a new, ongoing apparatus that creates emotional, cognitive, and spiritual well-being. When grief is brought into perspective, it adds to the experience of all other emotions, and it helps develop our total response to life. A person who has never grieved may not understand the depths of despair, futility, loss, and loneliness that others feel. Unless one has known grief, one has not experienced the full range of human emotions, and it may be necessary to do so in order to be a whole person. After her traumatic experience as a widow, Lynn Caine came finally to see that, "Few people understand that grief can represent emotional growth, an enrichment of the self."[6]

Jackson spelled out what he calls "the wise management of grief" in three steps. First is the painful task of facing the full reality of what has taken place. There is no easy way to face the reality of death in one who was deeply loved. What is called for is courage to endure pain. One must understand that there are no easy ways around the fact of this reality. The second step is to break some of the ties that bind one to the deceased. Jackson notes that this is sometimes referred to as "withdrawing some of the emotional capital from the past." These feelings, loyalties, expectations, and hopes must be reinvested in the present and the future. The third step is to develop ways that make it possible for the survivor to find new interests, satisfactions, and creative opportunities for the days ahead. New relationships must be formed.[7]

Jackson also describes three ways by which people prepare to meet grief.

The first is by education: people learn through their experience and that of others. Courses now taught in high schools, colleges, and adult education programs, including some churches, are helpful.

Secondly, how one copes with death indicates how one copes with life. The British psychiatrist, John Hinton, stated that to a large measure, how persons cope with life determines how they cope with death.[8]

Thirdly, sound community practices at time of death can help. Through funeral and community recognition, Jackson suggested, members of the community can be helped to do important "anticipatory grief work; those most in need of group support can find it; and anyone with unfinished work of mourning is provided an opportunity to accomplish it."[9]

However, these recommendations and preparations do not eliminate the necessity of facing up to and working through a mourning process. A letter pictures one mourner's initial envy of another, who seemed to go right on as though there were no death. The woman wrote that she and her friend were both in the same congregation when their husbands died at approximately the same time. Her friend continued right along in her community, church, and club activities, even taking on new duties. Everyone seemed to admire her courage, spirit, and sense of strength. On the other hand, my correspondent could do very little. She was lethargic by comparison, not able to carry on, but haunted by the comparison she felt others must make between the two of them. She wondered why she was so weak. Today, over seven months later, her friend has had a complete mental collapse and is in a mental hospital; my correspondent has gradually found new strength and purpose, has overcome imperceptibly her grief, and is now living, she believes, a normal life, adjusted to her new circumstances. She was apparently able to make the transition, accepting in time the reality of the death of her husband, extracting some of the investment in the past, and reinvesting in the present and future. First, however, she had to find herself again, in accordance with the guidelines above.

Another point that was made by different writers, including Hinton, Gorer, Kübler-Ross, Jackson, and Pincus, was that every mourner must follow three stages of grief—shock, suffering, and recovery—none of which can be eliminated or avoided. This progression occurs in all kinds of grief. The duration of each state differs with the nature of the grief, the character of the griever, and the depth of deprivation caused by the loss of another human being from the griever's life."[10]

> There is not as yet sufficient information available to determine the "normal" pattern of mourning by adults; but judging by my interviews and the range of rituals and practices reported by historians and anthropologists, it would seem as though most adult mourners pass through three stages: a short period of shock, usually lasting between the occurrences of death and the disposal of the

body; a period of intense mourning accompanied by the withdrawal of much attention and affect from the external world and by such physiological changes as disturbed and restless sleep, often with vivid dreams, failure of appetite and loss of weight; and a final period of re-established physical homeostasis – sleep and weight again stabilized and interest again directed outward.[11]

Bernadine Kries and Alice Pattie also suggested that contemporary social mores provide little help to those in mourning. "If you are an alcoholic, juvenile delinquent, an unmarried mother, an abandoned baby, or just getting old, society is there to cushion your problem. You can get help. But if you are in grief you soon discover that not only are you on your own in your trouble, but that few people really know how to help you."[12]

As Sarah Morris, a widow and a college teacher with her doctorate in psychology and counseling, noted, people meet grief differently, in ways ranging from dazed calm to hysteria. She suggests that the sufferer should not be surprised at the inability to accept the loss and adds in reassurance, "It is normal for you to react to this overwhelming experience in ways that seem abnormal to you. Other people have felt as you do."[13]

Because people find it difficult, either consciously or unconsciously, to accept death and to separate themselves immediately from a person who has died, a state of shock ensues. Ms. Morris describes the second stage of mourning.

> The second phase of mourning is the crucial one, but there is little general understanding of what goes on during this time. . . . It is agreed by psychiatrists who write about grief that each person must go through the important "work of mourning." What this work requires can be quickly and simply stated, but it cannot be quickly and simply accomplished. The work of mourning requires that you, the bereaved, weaken and finally break every emotional tie to the past and every expectation for the future binding you to the person you have lost. Only by doing that can you ever be free emotionally to build a new life for yourself. Some authorities say that breaking the ties is so painful it is amazing that anyone can endure the hurt it requires, and they also say it is amazing that this pain in the lives of those who grieve is taken for granted by others. This work takes weeks, months, and perhaps longer. No matter how reluctantly it is experienced, it must be done.[14]

Using the image of Gulliver tied to the ground by the stakes and ropes of the Lilliputians, Morris suggested that grievers are often bound by the emotional ties to the past – and the expectations for the future. The bonds must be broken if one is to live freely, fully again. Time heals all wounds, and in a practical sense we find that time does act as an agent for healing or for the slow acceptance of the inevitable events that lose their intensity when further removed from the event. Thus, as commonly said, time is the great healer. When the suffering is not assuaged with the passage of time, one lives in bondage to the past, captive to the memory of the departed for extended periods of time. In such an instance, one has passed beyond the limitations of normal, natural grief and needs help from proper counseling services.

When grief is normal and the emotional ties are cut, a remarkable thing begins to happen. The sufferer begins to notice that for short periods the hurt is gone. Healing has begun. One has experienced the loss mentally and is now moving into a time when one can experience it emotionally as well. As Morris says, "This does not mean that you forget, but that you can remember without the emotions of grief tearing you apart as they did earlier."[15]

As emotions are freed, one can become involved in new interests and new activities.

Thus, we all share some common views: life must go on; life is in the living; one cannot return to the past or stop the clock from relentlessly advancing toward tomorrow. Those who attempt to deny these facts suffer more. Grief becomes compounded, and the problem becomes abnormal. One cannot short-circuit the process of mourning. On this all seem to agree, although it does no good to tell the grievers they must go forward; they simply cannot move ahead of their own physical and emotional state. Knowing they need to move, they are powerless until the slow process of divesting themselves from the past and cutting the Lilliputian bonds takes place.

The death of someone close can force one into an acute shock. Pincus writes of it this way, "Usually the phase of acute shock lasts only a few days and is followed by what might be called a controlled phase, in which arrangements have to be made and the funeral faced and endured, and during which the mourner is surrounded and supported by relatives and friends. This period of support and the form it takes vary, not only according to tradition, culture, and social and religious group, but also in the interpretation of the supportive function.[16]

She, like many others, saw that the religious rites and public service provide an important function in keeping the bereaved active and in touch with reality, through the need to meet people, to discuss affairs, and to prepare to face the external world of the community. Traditionally, this was an important aspect of the mourning process. It is important to have to "do the next thing that must be done," which takes one outside of personal misery, so that one lives beyond his or her grief. Jackson states, "Ceremonies have a way of helping us to act out feelings that are too deep to put into words. Through rites and rituals we are aided in facing reality, pouring out our deep and valid feelings and gaining the support of a group of people who give us some of their strength, as we act out our emotions together."[17]

Commonplace knowledge assumes frequently that funeral services assist people in overcoming grief and serving the needs of mourning. Through the public ritual, with the ministrations of religion, one should "make his or her peace" and be better able to go forward and cope with life. This is said about both the traditional funeral and the modern memorial service. Some people feel that the modern memorial service is more psychologically and emotionally able to assist in this process, while many hold that the traditional service, with its pomp, emphasis on death and the meaning of human destiny, with the words from the scripture and the prayers of the pastor, is more helpful.

Yet there is a contradiction to this knowledge in the observation of many students of this subject. Hinton noted that in Western society the religious observance for the dead appears to be diminishing.[18] Jackson has pointed out that we live in a time when there "are strong emotions of death-denying, death-defying culture," which tend to pervert the findings of the careful researcher for general consideration.[19] Gorer noted "the breakdown in styles of mourning in the present century."[20] Hinton, in another place, noted the "decline in modern society of funeral practices."[21]

We shall consider these aspects as we proceed. We will ask, "Are funeral ceremonies constructive or merely residual practices that fail to assist the process of mourning and the acceptance of the mortal loss of loved ones?"

We have illustrated from the experience of others who have written on this subject that there are a multitude of ways one copes with grief, and any number of insights have been exposed to view. These vary from our own outlook on life to clinical observations, religious beliefs, and funeral or memorial practices. All of these are important, and whether or not we have adopted modern viewpoints and outlooks, we must be prepared to deal with the grief that accompanies death and to realize that a wise management of grief will hasten our recovery from the pain and anguish of loss and the acceptance of living under altered conditions. Not understood and not prepared for, grief is one of the most painful experiences we must endure. We must be prepared for the loneliness that comes after the loss (and therefore the severance) of a loved one and companion. Accordingly, if we are wise we shall prepare for the coming events ahead of time, now.

To do so, we must understand the scope of a final or fatal illness, when one is often bedridden, sometimes in a hospital. We must know how to be a helpful and intelligent patient, if that is our lot; and, we must know how to cope with a family member or companion in the sick bed. We must understand his or her mental framework as well as the futility of doubt that besets the mind, accompanied often by unbearable pain or fear of pain. If we are wise helpmates to those who rely upon our emotional support, and really feel that we have not rejected them in their hour of suffering, then we will enter bereavement with a clear conscience and a mind free of doubt. Overcoming grief may then be easier, although there are always some who find grief hard to bear. Let us now turn our attention to the period before death and go on to deal with the types of services we should negotiate and the understanding of the concerns and interests of the professional with whom we will be dealing.

3

The Travail of Dying

A correspondent wrote:

> I was with him when he died and will ever be impressed with the fragility of life. It is truly sobering to be confronted with the cessation of a life; alive and breathing (albeit with great difficulty) one moment and still, grey, and waxen the next.
>
> The nurses at Dad's hospital commented on the uniqueness of our involvement in his dying. They said it was unusual for a family to rally to a dying person's side. I think that is a very sad commentary on our times.
>
> Both Mom and Dad asked for cremation, and our graveside interment of the ashes was private. In Dad's case, just my three sisters and I took his ashes to the cemetery, and we enjoyed the personal involvement it gave us. We also celebrated a memorial service at our family home where family and friends were welcome. It was held outside with several of Dad's good friends participating in the service.
>
> Death comes inevitably to every living thing and is not to be denied by being ignored. It is as much a part of life as birth, and yet so few people know how to face it and deal with it. Of course, after what I have been through these past few months, I would be the last person to say it was easy. I struggle every day to accept the facts of my parents' death and to deal with my feelings as consistently as possible.*

"It is not so much death, as fear of dying that they fear," is a conclusion of Dr. Herman Feifel.[1] He likens it to the associations of extreme dependency, the sense of shame, the experience of pain and distress, and the long period of slowly disintegrating health. The process of dying is more dreaded than death itself, which as psychiatrists Dr. Kübler-Ross and Dr. John Hinton both point out, is a travail of suffering, often with indignity and anguish. Dr. Hinton suggests that when death is seen as involving violence, then the process of dying violently becomes too hideous to contemplate. As a psychiatrist he notes that death arouses fear only when it includes suffering. When he asked people how they wished to die, the almost universal response was "a swift, peaceful exit from life." In one group he notes 90 percent wished to die quickly and so avoid suffering. Another common wish is to pass quietly in one's sleep.[2]

We are led to an awareness that it is not death itself that people fear, but how they die; they seemingly dread the long, often prolonged, process of dying, and dying quickly is usually counted as a blessing.[3] Today, a number of reasons lead to a prolonged period of suffering and travail before "the light goes out." As I was driving Dr. Paul Dudley White, the noted cardiovascular expert, to a meeting, he once observed that heart attack, the number-one killer in America, is "a merciful epidemic," bringing "instant death" to many, whereas cancer, which is the second largest killer, is a slow, lingering, and often painful death.

In recent years, much study has been done on the nature of the dying process. Sociological data has shown that increasingly death occurs in institutions, whether on the terminal wards of a hospital, in custodial care homes for the chronically or terminally ill, or in rest homes for the aged.

Patients in such facilities share many similar situations, especially in the cycle through which the dying pass on their way from good health to the end of life. There is unhappiness from physical pain and the discomfort that must be faced; yet, in some way, there is a feeling that the pain will pass, based on their faith in the skill, knowledge, and medicine of their attending physician. Somehow, they trust, he will pull them through. Consequently, when intimations arise that this might be more serious than they had previously thought, the immediate reaction is, "It can't be true." They sorrow at the loss of life, they resent the realization that their life may be ebbing. How can such a thing happen to them?

For some, there is a period of denying the finality of their affliction: they refuse to succumb to weakness or other symptoms of bodily deterioration. In some cases, this period of *denial* will be of brief duration, as they face up to the realities of their situation. Others, however, undergo "a long and expensive ritual to support the denial" of approaching death.[4] They go from doctor to doctor, treatment to treatment, hoping to find the miracle cure that will work for them: the expert with the answers unknown to other physicians; the experimenter who dares try the new cure from which more cautious, timid doctors shy away. In the end they may be back in the same terminal ward, wearier, wiser, and weaker, drained financially as well as emotionally. Others just do not hear what is being said and lie there, waiting for the day of recovery when they shall go out. Some, of course, do not want to be told and are contented not to hear the expected outcome. Others, fearing the outcome, continue to plan for the future, pretending they will carry on as before. To some, denial is just a buffer after hearing the shocking news. It is desirable that patients discover their approaching death while in stronger health rather than poorer, Kübler-Ross believes.[5] Then they can take it better and discuss it easier, while it is not so imminent and there is still time to plan and make adjustments. Some take advantage of the opportunities afforded them to straighten out their financial, business, and legal matters, so they do not leave "a mess" behind them. Some use the time to make their own arrangements for their funerals. This is wholesome, but these steps cannot be taken until one accepts the fact of the approaching end. Thus, denial temporarily stops the ticking of the clock, and until they pass beyond it, little additional progress in readjustment can be made.

Some discover, or infer from their symptoms and the obvious developments taking place, that "this is it." To some, as Jung wrote, death is the fulfillment of life's goals, not merely a cessation of life, and they are ready for it. We are then reminded of the noble sentiment of William Cullen Bryant on those who, "go not, like the quarry-slave of night, scourged to his dungeon, but sustained and soothed by an unfaltering trust, approach thy grave like one who wraps the drapery of his couch about him, and lies down to pleasant dreams."[6] The road to be traveled, from the shock of hearing that one's time is fast approaching to acceptance of the fact of death, passes through denial (that this can happen to them) and the various other stages of anger, bargaining, and depression, with few shortcuts for most people.

We are all uplifted when we see those who die calmly and serenely. Perhaps they are like the caustic and tough-minded Thoreau who, asked by his aunt on his death bed if he had made his peace with God, replied, "We have never quarreled," and so is prepared to go forward without fear. Yet Thoreau had his resistance to what was happening. When questioned about his preparation for the next world, he is reported to have responded, "One world at a time!" This is reminiscent of that other iconoclastic American rebel, Ethan Allen who, when the chaplain told him that the guardian angel was waiting, responded: "Let him wait."[7] Perhaps Dylan Thomas best stated this strong tradition of resistance to the coming of the end:

> Do not go gentle into that good night,
> Old age should burn and rave at close of day;
> Rage, rage against the dying of the light.[8]

Some go fighting to the grave every step of the way. Edwin O'Conner, in his biographical novel *The Last Hurrah,* generally described as a thinly veiled life of a famous Boston politician, pictures the hero's death scene at the conclusion of the book. An inner circle of associates and family are gathered about the bed of the dying man, Extreme Unction has just been administered, and one person, seeking for the kindest words he could think of, suggested that if he could live his life over again he would probably have done so differently. The dying Skeffington pulled himself out of his coma and, with his dying rattle, raised his head and hissed, "Like Hell I would!" falling back in death.[9] There are those who justify and fight every inch of the way.

Some move from the position of denial to that of acceptance quite easily, but for most, once the idea has set in that they must face their approaching end, there then comes the period of *anger.* They are resentful that this is now occurring to them. "Why me? Why not others? Why should I be singled out? If there is any justice others should go before I do."

A well-known authority and psychiatrist has said that the distress of persons facing death grows out of the manner with which they faced life. Strong personalities will face it with resolution; weak persons—always blaming people, places, and things for life's adversities—will now blame everything else for their approaching demise; crybabies will cry their way to the grave; worrywarts will worry their way; and stoics will go resolutely and serenely to meet their destiny.

People who lived lives that lacked the fulfillments and joys of living to which they were entitled tend to face death bitterly. They will worry that people will not miss them once they are gone and are afraid that, being of little account in life, they will be quickly forgotten in death. Then there are those who blame the doctors, the hospital, the inattentiveness of their family and others for what is happening to them. Some are angry about dying alone; some, at the amount of pain they suffer; and some, at the lack of company and attention from family and friends.[10]

After working through their anger, some people will try *bargaining* for longer life. The traditional role of Faust selling his soul to the devil for more of life is an extreme case of what many would like to do. But, since Mephistopheles does not materialize before their eyes, they pray that death will not come yet, or they secretly promise God that if they are spared now, they will do his bidding all the remaining days of their lives, often becoming quite infantile in the promises they are prepared to make. Possibly they view their death as a matter of guilt and reparation, of logical consequences, of cause and effect. They may see moral issues wrapped up in what they did and behold their approaching death as the consequence required as retribution. But they are prepared to make amends, and by doing so they feel they should be able to have another choice.[11] As previously indicated, they might change doctors or hospitals, or try quack cures, all part of the bargaining process for deferring death. But this stage will pass.

Then comes *depression,* in which one yields to the inevitable. One knows he/she is going to die, and that no amount of anger or resentment or bargaining can alter the course of events: "The handwriting is on the wall." Along with recognizing that one is a terminally ill patient, one succumbs to the mental weakness that comes with physical frailty. The spirit is depressed; one is on the verge of giving up. One thinks of the loss of life and energy, of losing one's contact with family and loved ones. Loneliness remains much of the time. Having probably lost one's job if employed, one realizes that there is no hope of returning to work. One fears it will be impossible to straighten out the financial muddle even if one is able to go home from the hospital. A hundred small and vexing doubts clog the mind, and suddenly one is ready to be rid of them. One must be able to let go, and depression is the emotional or psychological instrument for relinquishing this anxiety-ridden hold on life. It enables one to come to accept that which has been fought against all this time. This is what Kübler-Ross calls "the preparatory grief that the terminally ill patient has to undergo in order to prepare himself for his final separation from this world."[12] She points out that a sympathetic person can help to unravel some of the unrealistic guilt borne by the terminally ill patient and free one from unnecessary mental pain or the shame one suffers. One should not be burdened by holding oneself accountable now for past failure.

It should be recognized, however, that part of depression is preparatory for future loss, and this is wholesome at the later stages of terminal illness. The patient should not be encouraged to look at the sunny side of things: this is both too superficial and shallow to do justice to the travail of one's suffering, and it cheapens the personal drama that has brought one to this point. One has a right to contemplate the approaching end, being in the process of losing everybody and everything loved. Depression has its own rights. If one can express — articulate — this sorrow, one will find peace and acceptance. Then the emotional and mental turmoil will end.

In resolving the conflict between self and the world, self and one's environment, one is prepared to surrender the external situation in order to meet the demands within. Depression is now beneficial because it prepares the patient for the next stage of acceptance and peace of mind. Through accepting the fact that the true state of affairs makes dying a reality, and by being aware, one can look death in the face. It takes time to arrive at this stage.[13]

Dr. Hinton asks, What allows a person to relinquish life while others cling to it so desperately? We suggest, as these studies indicate, that it is the ability to progressively pass from one stage to the other as one faces the shock and denial, the anger and outrage, the depression and isolation of facing this issue inwardly by oneself. If the patient works his/her way through these successive stages, he/she arrives at the point of *acceptance* and resignation, often with serenity.

The patient needs enough time to reach the state that is beyond depression and anger. Having expressed the feelings previously — envy for the living, anger at those spared while he or she is chosen—one will have already mourned the loss.[14] Before death, one will have gone through a period of mourning for oneself. These attitudes indicate the beginning of the end and signal to those in charge of the patient's condition that the line on the life chart is moving towards its terminal point. Many speak positively about consenting to life's end. Often they use the word *accept,* saying they had a good life. They seem to accept their own death according to their own philosophy of life.[15] Attaining acceptance, they may now recognize that while they would be happy to postpone death, they do not want to prolong the process and the agony of dying. They wish death to come comfortably, with dignity.

The majority of patients die in a stage of acceptance, without fear and without despair. "In the many terminally ill patients I have so far interviewed, I have not seen any irrational behavior or any unacceptable requests, and this includes two psychotic women,"[16] wrote Dr. Kübler-Ross. Given the opportunity to grow with pain, their agony, and their awareness of the finality of their situation, patients do not become irrational; only at the initial impact of the awareness of the situation are they emotional and disturbed. Given the opportunity to vent their feelings, their fears, their hopes, and to put their houses in order, these people walk serenely into that good night of which the poet spoke. Even the process of talking about their pain, discomfort, and anger, which gives them a chance to share their agony, provides a therapeutic ventilation essential to acceptance.[17]

When the patient has reached the point of accepting his/her death, however, the family needs to let go and allow him/her to articulate it, and plan for it. Family members should concentrate on the patient's needs, encouraging him/her that he/she has accepted the situation, to talk about it, but without belaboring the point and making it more difficult.

This stage leads to *hope:* hope for a relief from the lingering trauma of illness that is unrequited, hope for peace at last, and hope to end the ordeal they are putting others through. This is one of the experiences that comes with prolonged illness. In fact, throughout the various stages of coming to terms with death, "the coping mechanism," or defense mechanisms of the patients are fueled by hope. It is hope that holds them together, and keeps up morale at any level.[18] Patients deep within themselves feel that this agony which they are going through has some meaning and that it will eventually pay off.

Unfortunately, both hospital staff members and family members act at times as though there is no hope, and through the unconscious but significant gestures of body language convey this message to the sufferer. While there may be little hope, it is paramount not to regard one's case as terminal until the patient comes to complete acceptance.

Cardiovascular disease can cause either sudden death or an instant coma in which the mind ceases to function on a conscious level, snuffing out awareness without the experience of the terminally ill syndrome described above; but, for all other major killing diseases in which life lingers, such as cancer or respiratory disease, the stages of dying do apply.

Most observers agree with such writers as Kübler-Ross that the fear of death is universal.[19] The more we advance in science, technology, and institutional solutions, the more we seem to fear death because, as Hinton says,[20] there are many sources of anxiety over death.

Society is seemingly bent on denying or ignoring death. Until fairly recently, one major newspaper, *The Christian Science Monitor,* did not allow the word "death" to be used in its pages.[21] The entire coverage of the death of President John F. Kennedy—the national shock and trauma, the succession of Lyndon B. Johnson to the Presidency, the funeral of state, and the memorials in the Capitol Rotunda—was reported without ever using the word "death," a journalistic feat marveled at by newsmen. One way to escape coping with emotions in our society is to repress them: to refuse to admit the existence of a problem seemingly abolishes it. Hence, we are hard pressed to come to terms with death when confronting it head on. Often the question arises whether or not to discuss the true nature of an illness with the patient, but most of society shies away from the problem.

Kübler-Ross points out that part of the problem is that many doctors have not come to terms with the phenomena of death themselves: "The most important thing is our attitude and ability to face terminal illness and death. If this is a problem in our own life, and death is viewed as a frightening, horrible, taboo topic, we will never be able to face it calmly and helpfully with a patient . . . . If we cannot face death with equanimity, how can we be of assistance to our patients?" Many doctors have not faced up to their own mortality.[22]

Hinton notes that the entire thrust of medical ethics is to save (i.e., prolong) life, not to make death easier; hence, the Hippocratic oath has led doctors away from contemplating death and toward resisting it. They can easily change and admit that death—the enemy—can be a good, a blessing, a natural outcome.[23] The professional ethics and standards embodied in the Hippocratic oath, which requires them to preserve life and relieve suffering, "commits them to increasingly incompatible duties. This conflict of conscience is steadily magnified . . . . In consequence, the predominant forms of illness are now degenerative—the maladies of age and physical failure," and physicians are not prepared for facing the consequences.[24]

Another part of the problem is set forth by Professor Robert Fulton:

> I think it is regrettable, but I have had graduate medical students and graduate nurses in my Seminar on Death, Grief, and Bereavement *who have never seen*

a dead human body! Now you will say this is physically and professionally impossible. Not if you close your eyes! This girl is here and presumably practicing at this hospital. She will remain anonymous, of course, but you will appreciate the fact that she has gone through the nursing program and has never seen a dead body. This kind of experience is the lifetime experience of most of us in the privatization of death. The longevity of our citizens, the isolation of the elderly, the movement toward memorialization all contribute. We have no experience with death—and death is really the medical practitioner's problem.[25]

This situation is the same as Dr. Kübler-Ross found in Chicago and Dr. Hinton in England: doctors and nurses are not better prepared than the general public for coping with death.

Consequently, the almost universal attitude that it's up to the attending physician to determine when to tell the patient and how to do so often creates a social vacuum. In an interview on a Boston television station, the knowledgeable psychiatric Chief of Staff at Massachusetts General Hospital recently said that when a patient does ask him if he will die, he replies, "Of course; we all do; it's a question of when." Then, he felt it might be easier to flow into a discussion concerning the possibilities faced by the patient, once the issue had been addressed. Dr. Hinton observed that in practice probably the best and easiest way to approach the matter of dying with terminally ill patients is to allow them to speak of their suspicions or knowledge of the outcome. If necessary, they can be asked how they feel and shown that more than the polite, stereotyped answer is wanted. When patients mention that they feel upset, they can be encouraged to talk about it. Then the doctor may find there is little to "tell"; all that is required is to listen with sympathy. In these circumstances the dying person does not ask for courage. He or she may glance up for confirmation of mutual understanding.[26]

But what if this does not happen? Hinton notes that many doctors "use an oblique approach for letting the patient know he may be dying." Without deception, he allows an awareness of the outcome to develop by listening and letting the patient know that some of his/her surmises are true and some fears justified. "In this way, the dying patient should not feel too lonely, too uncertain, nor plunged into acute mental distress."[27]

Hinton also points out: "Although it is not an infallible guide to how much the dying patient should be told, his apparent wishes and questions do point the way. This means that the manner in which he puts his views should be closely attended to—the intonations and the exact wording may be very revealing. It also means that he must be given ample opportunity to express his ideas and ask his questions. If the questions are sincere, however, then why not give quiet, straight answers to the patient's questions about his illness and the outcome? It makes for beneficial trust."[28]

Some doctors avoid talking to the patient about the criticalness of his/her condition, but they might tell the family, thus making it their responsibility. This is not usually the best method. Hinton notes the irony of medical ethics involved because this policy reverses the usual convention of the doctor keeping confidential information concerning an adult. Usually he tells other people only if the patient agrees.

Hinton's experience is that patients, as their life course ebbs, are usually aware of what is transpiring. His records show that at the first interview one-half of those who will die in the hospital spoke freely and frankly of the possibility or certainty they will die. By the end, the majority are talking about it.

It is a mistake to make a pledge to keep patients in ignorance of the true state of affairs. They sense the dishonesty, and it can be extremely harmful and a source of guilt to survivors. Based on his many interviews with surviving members of families, Gorer discussed the morale problem raised in not telling the patient. The "conspiracy of deceit," as he called it, is particularly cruel and burdened the survivors as well as tormenting the dying, who frequently knew what was being kept from them. He quoted one widow as saying, "It was terrible having to lie to him, to be cruel really; I was abrupt with him, or I would have broken down." A forty-nine-year-old widow told how the doctor said neither he nor the hospital would tell her mate about his condition, so the spouse concluded if she told him he'd lose faith in the hospital. She said with remorse, "I told him awful lies." Another woman recalled the death of her parents, explaining that while her father was dying of cancer, her mother committed suicide because (as she stated in the note she left) she could not bear the burden of the secret she must keep from him. There is an ethical tragedy in requiring people who have been honest with each other all their lives to resort to deceit in the final phase.[29]

A therapeutic relief comes in talking about one's own death. Dr. Kübler-Ross emphatically stresses that when doctors talk freely and honestly, patients do not fear the consequences. "Such a patient will not fear isolation, deceit, rejection, but will continue to have confidence in the honesty of his physician. Such an approach is equally reassuring to the family who often feels terribly impotent in such moments."[30] Few patients fight to the end, she points out. The living sometimes fail to realize the dying reach a point where they no longer wish or need to struggle to live. Detaching themselves from life, from relationships, they cease the continuing, futile struggle, a defense to make dying easier.

But Kübler-Ross points out, the question is not "Do I tell my patient?" but "How do I share this knowledge with my patient?" Most, if not all, patients know or sense it anyway; but they need assurance that we are being honest with them, that their condition is not worse than it is. "I think it is the worst possible management of any patient, no matter how strong, to give him a concrete number of months or years," she says.[31]

Nor would she come right out and say, "You are going to die." She says, "No patient should be told that he is dying. I do not encourage people to force patients to face their own death when they are not ready for it.

Patients should be told that they are seriously ill. When they are ready to bring up the issue of death and dying, we should answer them, we should listen to them, and we should hear the questions, but you do not go around telling patients they are dying and deprive them of a glimpse of hope that they may need until they die."[32] Kübler-Ross points out that the heads of households must place their affairs in order, and Hinton notes that there are spiritual needs that might take precedence in a decision to acquaint the deceased with the possibility of death. If able, people need to place their legal affairs in order and, as both Kübler-Ross and Hinton have said, "to die with dignity."

Our discussion of the process of dying shows us that many families are prepared for grief long before death comes. They observe the stages by which the dying patient cuts his ties to the past, after his depression, anger, and hostility finally comes to acceptance. The survivors also have to go through the successive stages of grief, of accepting separation, and making necessary readjustments in living standards, life styles, and life expectations. Those who have an instant death have prepared neither themselves nor their survivors for the period of mourning.

The spiritual qualities of patients have much to do with how they can accept their approaching ends. Gorer has pointed out how Christian Scientists, with their absolute denial of death or the reality of the physical, die quietly and serenely. Spiritualists, with the strong sense of the continuity of life and the opportunities for earthly communication, accept death nobly. Orthodox Jews, with their precise definitions of mourning practices, are well prepared for their endings.[33]

Christians, with their concepts of an afterlife face death variously, often depending on their theological beliefs and the doctrine of their own church. For some, the fear of punishment creates terrors of what awaits them, making the acceptance of death difficult. Sometimes their own clergy, or available chaplains, can help them come to terms with life: confess or make amends, so that they depart with their minds at ease, knowing that they have made their peace with God.

A vast number of people throughout the world believe in reincarnation, and it is probably true that many nominal Christians do also, although it is not an official part of Christian doctrine. This concept gives a certain sense of altering life, nor the ending of life, and perhaps promises a great adventure. Death comes serenely to some who so believe. Many agree with Norman Cousins in *The Celebration of Life,* which stresses that the chain of life, of which we are all part, permits our life to continue through other life.[34] This naturalistic concept has many attractions for people who are basically humanistic, naturalistic, or scientifically inclined. Many of these later are able to hold a stoiclike attitude, drawing from the courage of Epictetus or the pagan wisdom of Socrates.

Kübler-Ross found that "religious patients differ little from those without religion," and she quotes Montaigne, "Death is just the moment when dying ends."[35]

We have seen how there are stages of acceptance through which dying persons, if conscious, will go. After their resistance, stubbornness, whining, and complaining, they will eventually arrive at acceptance. Now they can talk with confidence about placing their affairs in order, facing the future, and pass on those sage remarks and suggestions that are the quintessence of a life's distilled experience. (One's "final words," as it is often called.) One then garnishes the rewards of honesty in helping one face what cannot be denied, so that they do go serenely when the last breath is drawn. There is comfort here for the survivors, and fortunate are those who come to this point. Hard as the loss is, one is not as shattered as might have been the case if one were dishonest, nonsupportive, or uncooperative.

However, there are those who must accept a violent death, or sudden death for which there was no opportunity for preparation. Then what follows is all the more important, for unless there is a wisdom in planning for the memorial arrangements, one's stark reality of death may be heightened rather than lessened. It is our contention that memorial services should assist in the grieving process and not increase the sense of loss. Consequently, what follows is of the utmost importance.

We will now consider memorial and funereal procedures throughout history, and what their benefits, if any, have been and then deal specifically with the arrangements that each of us must be prepared to make for our loved ones. If we precede them to the grave, we can help lighten the load by preparations made ahead of time; if we are to bury or dispose of our family members, we will need the guidance that is to follow.

4

Funeral Practices from Prehistory to Today

A correspondent wrote:

The sight was amazing. There were more than 100,000 people massed at the end of the street, in the open square near the mosque where the King used to pray for Ramadan. The funeral service, if you can call it that, was extremely simple and quite moving. A plain white hospital ambulance brought the King's body to the mosque — in accordance with Moslem requirements. There was no coffin, no flowers; he was simply wrapped in a black shroud and carried on the Arab attendants' shoulders. The imam chanted a prayer, repeated at the other end of the square by another man. Then there was the prayer call that you may remember: "Allah el akbar" (Allah is the greatest) repeated about ten times or so, with deep silence in between each call, with the immense crowd (all men, by the way, and 99 percent in Arab dress) kneeling and bowing, foreheads on the ground, at each call. It was actually very moving in its extreme simplicity and faith. Then the King was put back into the ambulance and taken to his burial place, an unmarked grave probably in the grounds of his own palace. This also in accordance with the Moslem religion which stresses the equality and anonymity of all in death, whether King or street sweeper. The next day we saw on TV King Khaled and Prince Fahd receiving the people's condolences; everybody could walk in, shake the King's hand, kiss his right shoulder, or even his face. The milling of the crowd around him was unbelievable. The solders were pushing anybody who seemed to want to linger around — it must have been a security man's nightmare — we were horrified at the apparent lack of security, which may have been only apparent. One of the most moving moments of the King's funeral was at the end, when the camera showed the lone hearse driving away in the desert dust.[1]

Thus even in modern times are preserved ancient practices that show the ideals of their religions and the accommodation of civilization to ancient practices. Moslem principles are clarified in this account of the memorial service, or funeral, held for one of the world's last remaining absolute monarchs who returns to the anonymous status of a simple believer.

A larger perspective on death, dying, and grief is necessary than that which falls within our own experience. Such evidence is easily available to us because, since the dawn of history, humans have not only performed burial services or rites of passage for the dying, but the memorials and practices involved have been among the most enduring artifacts from ancient cultures. Indeed, much of what we have learned of certain primitive societies came from the burial mounds and tombs. These were built to endure, and often they contained the sacred and precious possessions of the times, including the unwritten indications of how they viewed life and what was of value.

Recalling the experience of the human race will help place in its proper perspective our own concerns and insights into the role of death, dying, and grief. Such understanding is both intensely personal and inclusive of human experience. After considering this broader perspective, we shall return to the specific arrangements with which all of us today should be conversant, as we strip away the mystique and deal with the practical matters that lighten the load at the time of travail and loss.

How one deals with death determines how one dealt with life: this sweeping generalization may intimate that death, throughout history and even into prehistory, has helped modern people understand early civilizations and the lives of their primitive forebears.

The reports of many discoveries deal with this subject. The anthropologist, Geoffrey Gorer, points out that in nearly all civilizations or societies, mourning practices are reported. He concludes therefore that mourning has elements that are universal to the human species and aren't, as Freud's studies might seemingly indicate, a sign of maladjusted behavior. It is such only when it becomes extreme or excessive.[2] The British statesman, William Gladstone, noted, "Show me the manner in which a nation or a community cares for its dead, and I will measure with mathematical exactness the character of the people, their respect for laws of the land, and their loyalty to high ideals."[3]

As far back as we can go in history or prehistory, we find a relationship between the concepts of life and death. René Dubos found it significant that at least one hundred thousand years ago, Neanderthal man buried his dead in a crouched position, oriented from east to west, in some cases in beds of wildflowers. He conjectures, or infers, "some form of ultimate concern may thus be coeval with mankind. The need to symbolize death and the afterlife may constitute one of the attributes that set man completely apart from the animal kingdom."[4] Later he notes the discoveries of Professor Ralph S. Solecki, the Columbia University anthropologist, in the Shanidar caves in Iraq. Here, in Shanidar, Solecki finds evidence that fifty thousand years ago Neanderthal men "buried their dead on beds of woody branches and flowers – a grape hyacinth, yellow groundsel, hollyhock and yarrow. Furthermore, one of the Neanderthal skeletons found in the Shanidar cave was that of an adult man who had been blind and whose arm had been amputated above the elbow early in life. This man had lived to the age of forty before a rock had killed him, and since he could hardly have foraged for himself, he must have been supported by his people for most of his lifetime. These discoveries suggest that *Homo neanderthalis* was truly human as far back as fifty thousand years ago."[5] Thus from the burial practices at the dawn of prehistory, we learn not only of the burial habits, but of the values, way of life, and compassion existing among these cave dwellers who already had developed a cooperative community of self-support and, obviously, a degree of reflective culture.

This becomes even more pronounced in the burial sites of the Middle East (known as the Near East in ancient history) where there are four striking examples that I have examined personally. Kathleen Kenyon,[6] the British archeologist, excavated the cave of the Jericho man. Here, approximately seven thousand years ago on the site of an Early Bronze–Middle Bronze Age (Middle Bronze I by Albright terminology), she had excavated over two hundred fifty tombs at the time I visited her site and discussed it with her (1962). Unlike the great tombs of multiple burials of early eras, she found individual tombs (or chambers) usually containing only one burial chamber together with several pottery vessels, daggers, and some jewelry.[7]

In Byblos, twenty-five miles north of Beirut on a sloping hill overlooking a fine seaport, the Giblites of the Bible had built an early city, frequently referred to as the oldest settled city. It was settled over seven thousand years ago.[8] The French School of Archeology explored and excavated the sites here, discovering numerous egg-shaped burial mounds with the body in fetal position. Thus, in symbolic manner the body is returned to the earth, mother of all, in fetal form. Notice my photographs taken on location of these ancient burial grounds that stem from the dawn of civilization in the Neolithic period, seven thousand years ago.[9]

Ancient Egypt, mother of civilization, is recorded and remembered primarily through its funereal practices. I visited the Valley of the Kings on the Upper Nile where, in the stone cliffs for the dynasties down through the nineteenth, the royal Pharaohs were buried. The intact tomb of Tutankhamen was in this valley (near modern Luxor) and excavated in this century. I investigated these tombs, and here in a vast underground labyrinth of halls, chambers, and passageways, the royal presence was prepared for its immortal journey, together with all necessary luxuries, produce, wares; representations of servants and pets, perfectly preserved; and the walls carved and painted in delicate fashion, so that his journey and wakening would occur in pleasing surroundings, with the hieroglyphics recounting his glories and record.

The ancient Egyptians believed in life after death. According to their mythology, whenever a person is born there is also simultaneously an invisible, corporeal "twin" known as "ka," a protecting guardian, whose most useful service follows death. The "ka" waits in the afterworld for the deceased; then, united, they live in happiness forever. There is apparently also the soul, a bird figure with the face of the deceased. It flies away at death and seeks for the deceased among tombs; hence, for the soul to recognize its person, the face of the departed must be visible. This is in part the motivation for the mummification and the elaborate coffins with the carved likenesses of the occupant. When the soul re-enters its counterpart, life is renewed, both within the tomb and the afterworld. Mummification, or embalming, is a process much like that used for drying fish. Briefly summarizing the funeral process, the body, during an elaborate seventy-day period of preparations and ritual, has all main organs removed (the brain drawn through the nostrils and destroyed; the liver, lungs, stomach, and intestines preserved separately in four Canopic jars). The hollow spaces of the body are packed with natron salts and the outer body swabbed with the same; after all the moisture is withdrawn (aided by the aridity of the desert air) the body cavities are packed with linen bunting; the body is anointed with coniferous resins and then wrapped in natron-soaked linen, creating the figure we all know.[10] This is then placed in the various nests of highly carved and ornamented coffins that we see in museums. Attached are photographs I took in the Cairo Museum. Some of the underground tombs in the Valley of the Kings extend over three hundred feet underground. There were both secret entrances and false entrances to discourage the vandals who systematically looted almost all of the tombs. Only that of Tutankhamen escaped this fate, and much of what we know is learned from this one marvelous discovery. See photos.

The earliest pre-Dynastic Egyptians were buried in sand in a crouched position, surrounded with water jars and food, and occasionally wrapped in reed matting and animal hide. Due to the dryness of the desert, many have remained. By 3000 B.C. stone tombs were being carved in the rocks to prevent vandalism and pilfering, furthering the evolution of the Egyptian funeral practices. From these developed the typical Egyptian tomb consisting of at least two parts: the burial chamber and the offering room. Most impressive were the pyramids (2800–2250 B.C.), which were colossal man-made stone tombs above the ground. Yet even the great pyramid of Cheops was plundered of the body of his wife before his own death, indicating that pyramids were also vulnerable.

Much of what we know of these ancient peoples is learned from the burial practices that show their faith, their way of life, and what they considered endurable and worthwhile. They lived in homogeneous cultures, bound together by some great ideal that, in making life meaningful, made death meaningful as well. The two—life and death—were the opposite sides of the same coin.

In cultures around the world, burial rites, funerary practices, and various disposal systems developed. Many seemed to be quite similar, even after making allowances for the fact that there are only so many ways of accomplishing a given end. Yet whether they were services of purification of the deceased, protection of the living, commemoration of the departed, survival of the community, appeasement of the gods, expression of the sorrow or loss, a pattern seemed to flow through various cultural customs widely separated by time and distance. To some, the sense of the totem that had taken on the spirit seemed important; to some, the sense of the separation and, hence, homelessness of the wandering spirit, freed from the body, predominated; for some the continuity of the family entity seemed powerful; for some, the need to purge the place of unclean spirits seemed important. Cultures widely separated, extending from the steppes of the Ural Mountains to the South Pacific, and from the Eastern Mediterranean Basin to the Mexican Highlands, carried out identifiable practices. This is recorded for us in the works of Durkheim, Malinowski, Sir James G. Frazer, C. W. Ceram, and Margaret Mead.

The ancient Hebrews disposed of their dead in tombs, such as that of Joseph of Arimathea in which Jesus was placed. "And Joseph took his body, and wrapped it in a clean linen shroud, and laid it in his own new tomb, which he had hewn in the rock, and he rolled a great stone to the door, and departed" (Matt. 28:59 RSV).

The rites of Osiris were celebrated for Egyptian dead and other converts of the mystery cults, not only throughout Egypt but in the cultures it had influenced before New Testament times. In the mystery cults, the form of the burial of the god Osiris was followed, and it was repeated for each member who died. During this period in far-off China, the head of the family conducted the rites for burial in the ground. Each new death added another to the honored dead who would from then on be honored with the ancestors. In India, great funeral pyres were the preferred means of disposal while Hindu prayers would honor the departed soul, now reincarnated into another life form.

Christians carried their customs into pagan Rome, and after Constantine, the Christian services honoring the dead who would be resurrected with

Christ became a prevalent pattern. The rudiments of the Eucharist had begun to evolve.

An important study in the evolution of funeral customs is found in the work of the French sociologist Philippe Aries, *Western Attitudes Toward Death: From the Middle Ages to the Present.*[11] He shows how the universal fact of death has evolved in the Western Christian tradition from the Middle Ages to the present, a period of over one thousand years. Philip Hewett, summarizing M. Aries' findings,[12] found that the person going to die in the earlier periods usually knew it and knew what should be done. Thus, in King Arthur's Round Table, Roland felt death approaching, "from his head it is moving toward his heart."

Hewett also recalled a passage in Alexander Solzhenitsyn's *Cancer Ward:*

> He remembered how the old folk used to die back home on the Kama . . . . They didn't puff themselves up or fight against it and brag that they weren't going to die—they took death calmly. They didn't stall squaring things away, they prepared themselves quietly and in good time, deciding who should have the mare, who the foal . . . . And they departed easily, as if they were just moving into a new house.[13]

It is obvious that in the Christian tradition, death has not always been the terrible, traumatic experience modern funeral practices make it out to be. However, Gorer notes that "people are today without guidelines as to how to treat death and bereavement and without social help in living through and coming to terms with the grief and mourning which are the inevitable responses in human beings to the death of someone they love."[14] He then comments, "The minority who are convinced adherents of religious creeds or sects have the assistance and comfort provided by the traditions and eschatology of their religious and (in some cases) by the social ritual which is interwoven with the religious practices."

Gorer, still speaking as the anthropologist, observes:

> Up to the beginning of this century, every society in the world, to the best of my knowledge, had explicit rules of behavior which every mourner was meant to follow. In the smaller societies, and in those which had a church or religion to which all citizens belonged by definition, there was most generally a single set of rules which applied to people of every social degree; in the complex heterogeneous industrial societies there were a number of accepted variants of the rules, dependent on creed, locality or financial or social status. These variants were socially determined; customs varying from the norm were followed because the mourner was a Quaker, or a Welshman, or an aristocrat; but, with quite insignificant exceptions, everybody knew how it would be appropriate for him or her to behave and dress when they suffered a bereavement and how to treat other mourners. People might feel that the accepted ritual was hypocritical,

because it forced them to display more grief than they felt, or heartless, because it placed a taboo on the mention of the dead person or any public signs of mourning. I know of no evidence to show that this resentment of the social rules resulted in aberrant individual practice.[15]

Remnants of such services are still carried on in what is called "the traditional American funeral" or by a modern memorial service. Funeral and memorial arrangements serve two purposes: the proper, sanitary, civilized disposal of the remains with dignity and decency; and second, the facing of the fact of severance and finality. *They* are gone, but *we* remain. Around this single fact, life must now be reoriented. Does the developing tradition of the American style of funeral, so characteristic of many elements in our culture, do this properly? What role is there in our society for death, grief, and mourning?

Dr. John Hinton, the English psychiatrist, deals at some length with the value of the mourning rituals as they help relieve the sense of loss and suffering, which seems to have been compounded as society has advanced. Perhaps it is because we are so fractured in our own lives, more insecure, that death may have become a traumatic experience as we become isolated in the lonely crowd. Hinton noted that mourning is "shaped by convention and the immediate duties which have to be carried out after death. If mourning proceeds normally the emotions and activities of the bereaved will gradually move toward a stable adjustment for the altered future." He goes on to say,

There is usually sufficient harmony between the feelings of the bereaved and social practice for people to find the custom of mourning helpful. In the usual circumstances of our society the open expression of strong emotions is largely inhibited. During times of mourning, however, an outward display of grief is regarded sympathetically. Friends may even encourage and join in the shedding of tears. A few of the bereaved, however, would rather that the contagion of others' sorrow and repeated references to the death were not there to increase their own distress. During mourning the instinctive withdrawal from conviviality is fostered, with an expectation that social engagements will be limited. If not dressed in the black of deep mourning, the bereaved are expected to choose somber garments which reflect their mood. Gay [i.e., brightly colored] clothes which enhance the appearance would seem disrespectful or adjudged so symptomatic of human vanity as to be callous or near to wickedness. The Jewish mourner maintains the tradition of wearing a rent garment. It parallels the more vigorous damage to self or garments frequently seen in other cultures.

In Western civilization, religious observances for the dead appear to be diminishing. Jung has said that in our more sophisticated society the need to do something for the dead has been almost rationalized out of existence. In Britain the panoply of death has been reduced over the last few decades. There is no longer the extensive Victorian ceremonial of black-edged invitation cards, full mourning, velvet-palled coffin, garlanded horses, with a sumptuous repast after the interment. The monuments are not so huge or pretentious; nowadays we are not necessarily filled with respect at the sight of some of the ponderous marble carvings in Westminster Abbey. The taste of ceremonial is less, except when a public figure is mourned.[16]

The ceremonials and rituals found in some religious mourning customs, the Reformed Jewish, the Orthodox Jewish, and the Roman Catholic, will be found in Appendix A. The detail and involvement of these centuries-old practices greatly assist in the working out of grief, as has been pointed out by Dr. Hinton and Sarah Morris,[17] despite the reduced influence of organized religion on our society's members.

Our concern must inevitably be larger than religious and ethnic considerations and go beyond the consideration of religious rituals. Because religious services are notoriously slow in altering with changing conditions, they often have failed to serve, for the modern person, the same helpful role they obviously served in more primitive or simpler societies. Our basic concern with death and grief is the continuing effort to develop constructive roles that aid in the control of grief. The sooner the mourner is able to resume his or her place in society as a whole personality, no longer emotionally wounded, the better off that person will be; the society in which he or she lives and moves will benefit as well.

The process of dying in America has changed radically in the past few decades.

Social changes such as the trend to smaller homes and families, increased mobility, and the removal of the elderly from the community of one's active life to a retirement community have made death in an institutional setting commonplace. Usually this means impersonal surroundings where, in spite of the best efforts of thoughtful nurses and caring medical personnel, the environment is strange, insular, and isolated: this is the nature of institutional life. No amount of special effort, training, and programs aimed at creating compatible controls succeeds in making our mammoth hospitals and institutions for the ill, infirm, and aged into adequate substitutes for the home. Lacking is the warmth of familiar surroundings and personal family concern and care; too often, many spend their final days almost in an animated suspension from life.

Death in institutions away from the center of the family probably increases the remorse and shock felt by the survivors, since they are not as involved in the process of the day-by-day relinquishment of life.

Through the breakdown in styles of mourning in the current century, we face the loss of a unified cultural orientation in an age that lacks a vision of spiritual reality. Our pluralistic society, with its fragmentation of practices, customs, ideas, and ideals; different religious heritages; ethnic and cultural traditions; and economic and class distinctions hastens the breakdown of uniformity in the American funeral pattern.

Funeral practices are universal and found among all peoples. The presence of grief and social conventions for dealing with mourning follow a wide variety of practices: not only in the United States, but around the world and in all cultures throughout history, there has been some type of observance and some system for easing grief. Let us look at how we do so in modern America, and who and what are our resources. We begin with the professionals.

5

Physicians and Funeral Directors

Our correspondents wrote:

> I'll be particularly interested in the outcome of this survey. As an
> anthropologist I have been very interested in the ways different cul-
> tures handle death, especially in relationship to their belief systems.
> (In addition to my own purely personal interest.)
>
> As an additional comment, I feel there is some emotional conflict
> existing in myself (and perhaps others?) as to whether a service should
> be more appropriate to the beliefs and wishes of the deceased, or those
> of the survivors. Sometimes, I've noticed, this can be quite a wide
> difference.
>
> Good luck on this survey—it is a good one, I think, and important.*

> My situation is somewhat unique in that the funeral director who per-
> formed the professional duties for my mother's funeral is a close per-
> sonal friend. In fact, I worked for him and his family most of my teen
> and college years as a babysitter, receptionist, and at times managed
> the business while he was away.
>
> Much against my own personal convictions and those, I might add,
> of the funeral director, the family decided on the full, socially accept-
> able for the community, barbaric display. In any study of death and
> grief the role of the community must be considered. To add to your
> work I'll say that my mother, the wife of a professional man (engi-
> neer), was "laid to rest" in a community of three thousand. Her service
> was the standard Protestant form. Anything other than that which
> was done at that time and in that place would have been considered

disrespectful. From what I've seen in recent visits, there has been no change in the community attitudes or customs.

I'm sure you know G.H.S., Jack's grandmother. The service read for her was so entirely appropriate to her enjoyment of life that the family was indeed comforted.

Another facet of a study of death could be "appropriateness." At ninety-three Mrs. S. had begun to lose her will to live. She had been ill for so long and unable to lead an active life. My mother, by contrast, was forty-four. The reconciliation of a family to an early death is more difficult.

All of this has occurred to you, I'm sure. Please call on me if I can be of any help. *

We are people close to sixty years old. About twelve years ago we joined the Church of the Larger Fellowship while living in Salina, Kansas, where my husband was briefly stationed while in the Air Force. Due to many moves and events that have transpired during the years, I am ashamed to say we gradually lost contact.

We just buried a precious sister, who especially requested that a Unitarian Universalist Minister be the guiding hand, with cremation and interment in her late husband's grave, and no services be held, as she had a horror of viewings. The director said he tried but couldn't obtain the services of a Unitarian Universalist Minister as he was away, so he hired one of another denomination. She was cremated and interred as requested. However, they talked the son into holding two viewings and a service, "as the services are for the living, not the dead": quote. Unknown to them, this meant embalming, which my sister particularly did not want, and which is not needed when cremated, but is needed for "showing." Altogether the children now find themselves over $2,000 in debt. This was exactly what their mother was striving to prevent. She would have preferred that the money spent on banks of florals be donated to help the living. We're not blaming the Director because they are friends of the son of the deceased who was the executor, and her wishes were in the form of a personal letter to her son. It's hard to be practical, especially when one of your best friends happens to be the son of the chosen undertaker, as was the case in this instance.

This incident has shaken us deeply and made us realize the waste and greed involved. I used to have your addresses of Memorial Societies but due to so many moves, lots of personal things were lost. Can I obtain another copy? In my papers I found one burial contract. Will an undertaker, in the light of today's inflation, honor such requests with any dignity?

After being so negligent I hesitate to ask for help, but will you send us the nearest Minister's address, telephone, and church location? We are still sort of in the backwoods country. *

All people are familiar with death in the abstract, in the sense that all know that death occurs, that it occurs to one's loved ones, and that in time it will occur to each person. Some naturalists have suggested that perhaps one of the distinguishing features between humankind and the rest of the animal world is that *Homo sapiens* alone seemingly contemplates and is aware of mortality.

The dimension of death, therefore, rapidly narrows down to the personal aspects of loved ones, comrades, and self. It hardly seems necessary to document a universal observation. Perhaps two examples are in order.

Elizabeth Kübler-Ross, noted psychiatric expert of the dying process, recalled how it was in her youth in these recollections of a childhood reminiscence. Recalling a deathbed scene, she wrote,

> He asked simply to die at home, a wish that was granted without questioning. He called his daughters into the bedroom and spoke with each one of them alone for a few minutes. He arranged his affairs quietly, though he was in great pain, and distributed his belongings and his land, none of which was to be split until his wife should follow him in death. He also asked each of his children to share in the work, duties, and tasks that he had carried on until the time of the accident. He asked his friends to visit him once more, to bid good-bye to them. Although I was a small child at the time, he did not exclude me or my siblings. We were allowed to share in the preparations of the family just as we were permitted to grieve with them until he died. When he did die, he was left at home, in his own beloved home which he had built, and among his friends and neighbors who went to take a last look at him where he lay in the midst of flowers in the place he had lived in and loved so much. In that country today there is still no make-believe slumber room, no embalming, no false makeup to pretend sleep. Only the signs of very disfiguring illness are covered up with bandages and only infectious cases are removed from the home prior to the burial.
>
> Why do I describe such "old-fashioned" customs? I think they are an indication of our acceptance of a fatal outcome and they help the dying patient as well as his family to accept the loss of a loved one.
>
> This is in great contrast to a society in which death is viewed as taboo.[1]

Following the death would come the burial, and this account is given by another psychologist, recalling what the old-fashioned funeral really was like in the early years of the century. Bonaro Overstreet recalled:

> It may seem odd to say so, but in my childhood nothing gave me a stronger sense of neighborhood than did the events surrounding death. In time of

sorrow, all petty quarrels were forgotten. Folks drew together. . . . Watching all this, and helping out when there were errands to run, I had a chance to assimilate as best I could both the meaning of communal experience and the mystery of life. . . . Many years later . . . I knew . . . I and my neighbors had experienced . . . catharsis of the emotions through pity and fear. . . . But every so often, as a community group—a handful of humans standing close together under the sky—we lived drama, and were purified by mystery, and felt very near one another.[2]

Old-fashioned ways, such as these two women recall from their youths, are changing in urban society. The English anthropologist, Geoffrey Gorer, discovered in his study of death in England that "precisely half the deaths in the major sample had taken place in hospitals; of the remainder, 44 percent had died at home and the rest had died elsewhere. It would seem therefore that to die in one's own bed is becoming slightly exceptional.

"It looks as if the pattern of dying is changing. The younger the bereaved respondent, the more likely he or she is to report the death in hospital; . . . by a relatively small figure more parents are reported dying at home than spouses or siblings."[3]

This would seemingly indicate that the older generations preferred home for a terminal illness, but that younger, more urbanized, or modern generations turn to the hospitals. Since Gorer's study took place in England over a decade ago, it might be presumed that a more rapid breakdown of the family homestead is underway in America today; and, as shall be seen, others indicate this is so.

Dr. Kübler-Ross wrote about "the scientifically trained younger physicians who cannot deal with death or are uncomfortable in facing it."[4] She noted the hostility of the vast majority of the younger physicians in the terminal wards of the hospital. "Approximately nine out of ten physicians reacted with discomfort or annoyance, or overt or covert hostility when approached for permission to talk to one of their patients. While some of them used the patient's poor physical or emotional health as a reason for their reluctance, others flatly denied having terminally ill patients under their care. Some expressed anger when their patients asked to talk to us, as if it reflected on their inability to cope with them."[5]

She noted a distinction between the clinically trained younger physicians and the older generation of doctors " . . . who—we presume this only—grew up a generation ago in an environment which used fewer defense mechanisms and fewer euphemisms, faced death more as a reality, and trained doctors more in the care of the terminally ill. They were trained in the old school humanitarianism and are successful now as physicians in a more scientific world of medicine. They are the doctors who tell the patients about the seriousness of their illness without taking away their hope."[6]

In part the problem is, according to Dr. John Hinton, that "doctors and laymen usually have different problems in evaluating" the situation.[7] However, doctors are human and tend to bring their own social, spiritual, emotional, and psychological weaknesses to the bedside with them. Thus, in a day in which dying increasingly takes place outside the family, no one is readily available to supply the answers and support the surviving family members' needs.

Kübler-Ross related an experience when the patient had died, and the wife sat with the corpse briefly before she was lead away by her son. Then the staff followed "the normal care of the body after death" procedure. "The body is wrapped in a sheet and taken to the morgue which is a small clothes closet where an emergency stretcher is kept. The wife comes back . . . and wants to see the body once more. Permission is refused because of the state of the deceased." Kübler-Ross is asked what should have been done, and answered,

> I think it is important to allow the family enough time to stay with their deceased relative. When the family is then ready to leave, you can ask if they plan on coming back again in a short time. Explain to them what is going to happen and give them the option of staying a little longer or, in case they change their minds, coming back a second time. They will know that the body has been packed and if it is very necessary, you may ask an orderly to unpack the body once more in order to help the family to come to grips with it. If you have a good relationship with the funeral director, you can ask him to talk to the family and invite them to come to the funeral home later on after the necessary procedures have been done there.[8]

In similar vein, she is asked by a nurse how to handle the situation with the widow who feels intense guilt because her husband died in an argument with her. Her doctor simply tells her to "snap out of it." The nurse feels a loyalty to the physician's professional judgment, but the widow turns to her for help. Kübler-Ross answered,

> I don't understand why nurses or neighbors, for that matter, have to undersell themselves. I have seen more dying patients helped by nurses than by a physician or anybody else. If it had not been for the nurses and the clergy I don't know what would have happened to my hundreds of patients. A nurse who empathizes, who obviously has some feeling for this woman, can help this woman probably better than the physician who tells her to "snap out of it" which is a silly request. If she has such unresolved guilt that she cannot just simply snap out of it, she may need professional counseling to help her out of her guilt feeling that she "killed her husband." In the meantime, you are the one who can stand by and let her ventilate and talk. You will help her much more than somebody who wants to simply "brush it under the carpet."[9]

Another question she was asked was, "Why is it so hard for many physicians to deal with death . . . ?" She answered, "One of the biggest problems is that we train our physicians during four years of medical school to cure, to treat, to prolong life. The only instruction they receive that has anything to do with death and dying is how to ask for an autopsy. It is very understandable, therefore, that 'patients who die on them' are often seen as failures as the physician gets no training on how to be a good physician to patients who are not going to recover."[10]

As to what should be done about the inability of physicians to cope with death, she answered,

> The first thing we have to do is to include courses in medical schools in the art of medicine, so that more physicians become better equipped and more comfortable in dealing with terminally ill patients. The second thing we can do is to have a "screaming room" in the out-patient clinic where people who come in regularly and need to ventilate their feelings or their fears can sit with a member of a helping profession or a trained volunteer and share some of their needs. The third possibility is that every out-patient clinic can start group therapy for patients who come in regularly and also for parents of leukemic children. This has been found to be extremely therapeutic for all participants.[11]

One account of failure is given as follows.

> We were called at three o'clock in the morning and told that the physician thought it best that we come down to see our father. My brothers, mother and I dressed and went to the hospital, suspecting that a crisis had occurred. We were asked to sit in a dark waiting room with only one dim floor lamp bulb illuminating the room. The hospital at that hour was unusually quiet. Nobody seemed to be stirring except the receptionist at the desk in the lobby. After forty minutes a young physician in a white coat walked to the door, looked at us, cleared his throat, shut the door, which let in a shaft of light behind him, cleared his throat, placed a hand to his forehead as though in pain and announced: "Mr. N. has passed away. You may collect his belongings on the floor. We need the name of the funeral director as bodies must be removed within twelve hours." He turned and left the room. We were stunned. We thought we had been called down because of a crisis, or a desire on his part to talk to us for a last time, or simply for a last visit or look. Helplessly, after our mother had sobbed for a few minutes, we made our way to the room where he had been. His body was on a stretcher-bed in the hallway, covered with a sheet. We never saw that young doctor before or since, and only were able to talk to the attending physician over the telephone.[12]

In such contrived and strained confrontations, situations are made far worse than they otherwise would be. Kübler-Ross's proposals that students be taught how to deal with death and emotionally assisted to come to terms with the idea of death seem like a good alternative. Hinton observed that death is counter to all the training received by a physician whose major training is to save life, to prolong life, not to make death easier. "The Hippocratic Oath has led doctors away from contemplating death and to resisting it. They cannot easily change and admit death, the enemy, . . . to be a natural outcome."[13]

Hence, it is seldom that the physician is able to offer the solace and comfort the grief-stricken family needs at the moment of death.

The possibility that funeral directors are the best trained and most available persons to help the survivor thus becomes a dominant factor at the time of death. The family, it appears, is not usually prepared; the physicians increasingly are not; the clergy are often not prepared; and so, with relief, the family turns to the man whose business is dealing with death.

The funeral director, therefore, usually becomes the central figure and major advisor of the stunned and bereaved next of kin to whom the legal responsibility falls. The morticians are creatures of their own calling and experience and, perhaps, have never thought that there might be a better way. The next of kin are ill prepared and grateful to find a knowing, eager, willing counselor at their side. The grief-stricken person says oftentimes, "You know what to do; you handle the arrangements and do what's best, and tell me what to do. I am so confused." Only the few who have planned ahead do not get caught in this predicament.

Funeral directors have a vested interest in funeral arrangements, and there is bound to be a conflict when they advise a family regarding them. They may manipulate and guide the mind of the bereaved, who is too stunned and filled with grief, remorse, and shock to raise such indelicate matters as costs, alternatives, simplicity, etc. Often, the funeral director is somebody they see for the first time, whom they do not know, whose values and judgments they have not seen in action, and who does not know their family or understand what to them would be correct. All he can do is generalize and offer what he considers the typical funeral arrangements, which include costly cosmetic details. He therefore is not to blame oftentimes for assuming the family would wish all these added touches to the funeral to properly impress the well-wishers who attend. If they do, perhaps he may be excused for assuming that money is no object.

The laws governing the disposal of the dead are found in sanitary codes and public health statutes. These laws are not sacred or mysteriously mystical requirements above examination, although many people who approach a funeral establishment go away with the sense that there is some sacred code or legal requirement that is beyond questioning. Apparently, funeral directors sometimes discuss social customs as the "expected thing" in such a way that the bereaved think they mean legal requirement. They describe the requirements of a service, meaning the conventions often followed, and people presume they mean laws, when in point of fact they merely mean the extras one must have: i.e., if you agree to an open coffin, then obviously you must have the body embalmed and cosmetically arranged. Thus funeral directors appear at times to have misrepresented the requirements when they perhaps quite honestly did not. Obviously one solution is the pre-arranging of funeral details *before* there is stress or emotional duress. Ahead of time, the family can calmly and quietly discuss the details, knowing they are working out a business contract with ifs, and, and buts, and subject to negotiation as well as bargaining over costs.

Because of the difficulties and confusions that arise out of the conflict of interest, there has been much discussion of the role and value of the funeral director. Out of this discussion have come certain negative attitudes regarding the mortuary profession.

The Federal Trade Commission funeral practices rule of August, 1975, if it becomes effective in its present form, will bring consumer protection to bear in these areas and help eliminate the confusions that we have just noted.

LeRoy Bowman, in his study of the American funeral, sought to evaluate and bring together material on this subject. He reported that the National Opinion Research Center (University of Chicago) conducted a poll some years ago in which funeral directors rated lower than any of the other professional workers. The results follow:

SCORE:

PROFESSIONAL WORKERS		BUSINESS OCCUPATIONS	
Supreme Court Justices	96	Banker	88
Physicians	93	Small Factory Owner	82
Ministers	87	Print Shop Operator	74
Lawyers	86	Funeral Director	72
Priests	86	Chain Store Manager	69
Sociologists	82	Operator of Lunch Stand	62
Biologists	81		
Public School Teachers	78		
Welfare Workers	73		
Funeral Directors	72		

Among laborers, the funeral director rated between a trained machinist, 73; a bookkeeper, 68; and a carpenter, 65. Thus, while funeral directors insist they are a profession, the public-at-large places them in the business category or laboring force.[14] Considering the few months of training required, with a brief apprenticeship for licensing, this seem to be a proper appraisal. For instance, in the Commonwealth of Massachusetts, whose regulations are in most situations considered equal or superior to most other states, registration requirements for funeral directors, according to the General Laws of the Commonwealth of Massachusetts, state in Section 83:

> Each applicant for registration as a funeral director, who shall furnish the Board (of Registration in Embalming and Funeral Directing) with satisfactory proof that he is a citizen of the United States of moral character, and that he is twenty-one years of age or over, that he possesses the educational qualifications required for graduation from a high school, or has attained a practical equivalent to a high school education, that he has been graduated from a funeral directing school approved by the board which gives a course of instruction of not less than nine months, and that he has served a term of apprenticeship of not less than two years with a registered funeral director, shall, upon payment of ten dollars be entitled to . . . be registered by the board as qualified to be licensed under section forty-nine of chapter one hundred and fourteen as a funeral director.[15]

These qualifications when compared with other professions — medical, dental, legal, clergy, or educational — are academically inadequate when measured in terms of classroom hours or formal training before the apprenticeship or internship requirements.

The National Funeral Directors Association in its own poll found that 38 percent of its respondents checked it as a profession on the same level as a physician or lawyer; 33 percent stated it is a profession of a slightly lower status than a lawyer or physician; and 29 percent checked the statement that he is a businessman.[16]

A bulletin of the Association of Better Business Bureaus, Inc., stated:[17]

> All states now require that embalmers be licensed. Funeral Directors are licensed in forty states, while four states issue combination licenses covering embalming and funeral directing. Among the requirements for licensing are attendance at a recognized college of embalming for at least nine months and completion of a one to three year apprenticeship. Applicants must pass examinations given by State Boards which issue licenses that may be revoked for cause.
>
> There are twenty-four accredited colleges that teach one- and two-year courses to aspiring funeral directors and embalmers. The training features studies of the specialized technical aspects of the profession. For example, over twenty medical subjects are taught in a mortuary science college.

The bulletin also stated:

> Only a few problems involving the services of funeral directors, cemeteries and monument makers are brought to the attention of Better Business Bureaus according to a recent survey by the Association of Better Business Bureaus. Paradoxically, the same survey and other studies have disclosed the existence

of a noticeable degree of public suspicion and criticism of funeral directors and allied groups. There are two explanations for this unusual situation:

1) Widespread public ignorance and misunderstanding of the services performed by these groups; and

2) Questionable advertising, high pressure sales tactics and serious malpractices by a small minority such as exists on the fringe of any business or profession. They victimize bereaved families and create public distrust out of all proportion to their numbers.

Providing elementary facts which every family should know because death is a visitor whom every family must anticipate, this bulletin will assist you to plan intelligently in advance. It will also help you to protect yourself against the plausible pretenses of "fringe" operators.

The Better Business Bureaus noted the existence of a fringe group that is unethical in its practices:

Better Business Bureaus have record of many schemes and "promotions" designed to prey on recently bereaved people. "Hearse Chasers" seek to victimize survivors by collecting for merchandise which is falsely represented as having been ordered by the deceased. Sometimes they render bills when nothing is owed. Sometimes they claim part payment has been made by the deceased and endeavor to collect the alleged balance.

Some promoters make a living by mailing unordered merchandise such as religious items and plastic-sealed replicas of death notices. You do not have to pay for unordered merchandise unless you actually use it. You are under no obligation to return anything so received and you can make a reasonable charge for storing it. Survivors who accept the offer to include the deceased in a biographical book may subsequently discover that they have contracted to pay high prices for engravings, reprints or other extras.

Money management is often a serious problem for survivors who suddenly find themselves with more funds than they have ever had before at one time. Before succumbing to the temptation to invest a legacy in any propositions which promise large returns, but which actually may be risky or fraudulent, follow these two invariable rules of the Better Business Bureaus: READ BEFORE YOU SIGN – BEFORE YOU INVEST – INVESTIGATE.[18]

Many persons become funeral directors through family success in it, through inheritance from father to son, husband to wife, or by marriage. However, steps are taken to recruit members, particularly by the schools. Bowman reported these findings:

Recruiting appeals, which indicate the incentives that probably lead to the choice of vocation, stress economic security and independence. The large associations and the mortuary schools in their recruitment pamphlets warn that expectancy of great financial returns is liable to lead to frustration. The drawbacks are seldom minimized in these appeals.

There is no one type of person who enjoys and succeeds in undertaking, to be sure; but there is fairly general agreement among practitioners, leaders in the associations and directors of mortuary schools on the question of personal characteristics that best fit individuals for the work. First is desire and ability to work with people; second is conformity to the norms of respectability in the community. It is often labeled "good habits" and strength of character, although the latter also means ability to stick out the periods of difficulty. Willingness to give services, especially to join organizations, is prominently mentioned and also ability to work hard and continuously. There are women practitioners and successful ones, sometimes widows of funeral directors. Men predominate, however.[19]

The human qualities of the funeral director are indicated in these recruitment appeals. One sees here a listing of commendable qualifications. He should be one who desires independence without expectation of great wealth, one who likes to work for and with people, and one who conforms to prevalent community standards of decorum and morality. Thus we see a standard of persons who will try to help in time of need, and who are somewhat conservative in human and community values.

One minister described the kinds of services funeral directors helpfully perform. "A skilled and sensitive funeral director can be of great help. . . . The making of many other arrangements: the phrasing and placing of newspaper notices, the securing of needed transportation, and in the checking of details, the funeral director can be of considerable assistance. It is a help to know in advance of emergency, the funeral director or undertaker to be called."[20]

The funeral director is important in the assessment of the nature of funeral practices, and the sensitive and helpful funeral director takes into account family values and wishes in conducting the arrangements. Such services are very helpful and valuable.

Contemporary families, facing the changing style of funeral practices in the contemporary context, seek outside help. The modern physician is no longer the family counselor, as in the days of "the family doctor," and the funeral director stands waiting to serve. Yet they violate one of the basic rules of public service, namely, self-interest. Can they serve impartially, considering that their livelihood is dependent upon the services they can sell to the grieving family?

But there remains another resource: the church and the minister. How well can they serve the family in facing the grief that engulfs it?

6

The Church and the Clergy

Our correspondents wrote:

> The ministers could be more innovative and plan the service more to
> my wishes rather than to what the people expected. This is especially
> true if one has a Unitarian minister.
>
> Another point I didn't see covered is that I wish to remember my
> loved ones as I last saw them and was with them, not as a made-up corpse
> in a coffin, with family members and friends remarking on his looks.
>
> Basically, I do not believe in funerals of any sort. They are just a
> chore which the stricken widow or daughter or whoever has to go
> through with no matter how efficient and understanding the funeral
> director and the minister are.
>
> It is really through our prayers and our actions after the death
> which show our appreciation of all the deceased has meant to us. And
> it is through our church affiliation that we can get help in re-adjusting
> to our new life. The actual expression of sympathy, understanding
> and help by our family and friends is invaluable. It can be shown by
> telephoning, visiting, invitations, letters, etc. And it should continue
> long after the funeral, not for a few days, but for months. *

> In response to your request for feedback about funerals:
> I grew up Christian, and left the church fifteen years ago as I real-
> ized even a liberal church like Disciples of Christ caused too much
> emotional conflict to serve my needs. I discovered the Unitarian Uni-
> versalist Church twelve years ago in San Diego. I've been an active
> Unitarian since then.

My dad died suddenly Christmas week. I flew home to Idaho to help my mother and participate in his funeral. She planned a traditional funeral—lots of scriptures, a casket closed until the end of the funeral, a soloist singing his favorite song "I Shall Not Pass Again This Way." A radical departure, for her, was a violin solo "Going Home," at his request. I was glad he waited until now to die. A few years ago, the experience of the awful soloist accompanied by a Hammond organ, the fat, dumb preacher mouthing much meaningless, irrelevant scripture etc., would have caused a much more violent reaction for me. Now, I can be pretty detached from it.

I needed something for myself to read at the service, so I got a copy of The Prophet[1] *from the library, in the town where I grew up. I read from the first part, starting "How shall I go in peace and without sorrow?" The reading ended—"And ever has it been that love knows not its own depth until the hour of separation." While rehearsing I was able to do some good crying. Many people, accustomed to traditional Christian funerals, commented favorably about my reading. I had copies made for my children's scrapbooks and for my brothers.* *

I have filled out the questionnaire and am enclosing it, although your follow-up letter is right in assuming that I can't make my own experience fit the questionnaire very well. In the first place, I have no recent experience of bereavement in the family. My parents died in 1958 and '59 at the ages of eighty-eight and ninety, under circumstances causing no agonizing grief— rather relief that they and we were spared a long interval of unconscious half-life in a hospital.

In the second place, the only funerals/memorial services I have attended for the last twenty-five years have been—with the two exceptions of my parents—were conducted by Steve,[2] who is able to make an otherwise ghastly, open-casket, Forest Lawn set-up, which he detests as do I, a life-affirming and strengthening experience. Most of his services for church members and friends are memorial services in the one hundred-seat small meeting room of the church, usually one or two weeks after the death— with beautiful piano music beautifully played by our organist; a single bouquet of flowers (floral "offerings" a no-no); often participation by friends, with brief statements, readings, and a tribute by Steve; and a quiet social gathering afterward. The service itself takes usually half an hour.

I go into this detail because this format has, by frequent testimony of bereaved families and friends, been marvelously satisfying and comforting. Without any Christian Science nonsense about There Is No Death, Steve makes the service the celebration of a life, as well as the frank facing of loss, and—as you might guess—instead of mentioning heavenly rewards, lays on his hearers the obligation to be the better for the experience, and the more loving. There is a total lack of sentimental mush, of course.

Steve asks for and uses biographical material and recollections of the spouse, children, friends. In other words, his services are almost an antithesis of the Episcopal impersonality and ritual rigidity, without being as formless as a Friends' funeral, or as tear-drenched and hyperbolic as most Protestant ones.

When requested, he goes to Forest Lawn and other mortuaries, and single-handedly overcomes the surroundings by what he says and how he says it. (He just did it again last week.) The organist at Forest Lawn knows just what music not to play, and loves him. They both prefer Bach.

What I seem to have been doing here is to respond to your invitation for an interview enlarging on the questionnaire. I apologize for the one-sided nature of the "interview." Blame geography and airline fares!*

I would like to add that I am a Union Official and during the course of a year I attend ten to twelve funerals. I have attended two Memorial Services and the rest have been the regular services. I find the regular service too long and drawn-out. Most of these services are also very costly, whereas a Memorial Service is not. Most Priests and Ministers are sympathetic and kind but do not know the answers, and I believe the bereaved next-of-kin go away bewildered and confused.*

Few people seemingly write or speak negatively of the clergy, but in the approach to their role in death, there tends to be a great silence; and this is odd, considering that death and religion are usually coupled together. In fact, the funeral service is one of the traditional rites of the Christian church, and other faiths have rituals or prescribed patterns of conduct and service to follow.

Hinton noted, "In Western civilization religious observance for the dead appears to be diminishing." He also noted a "decline in modern society of funeral practices."[3] One must wonder if these two go hand in hand.

Gorer noted in his summary that people are without adequate guidance in how to treat death and how to come to terms with their grief. "The minority who are convinced adherents of religious creeds or sects have the assistance and comfort provided by the traditions and eschatology of their religions and (in some cases) by the social ritual which is interwoven with the religious practices." Gorer continued,

It has been demonstrated that only a minority of the British are active in the practice of their religion—less than a third attend a religious service once a month, and less than half say daily prayers; consequently, the fact that the only social techniques available for coming to terms with death and dealing

with grief are phrased exclusively in religious terms means that the majority . . .
have in effect neither help nor guidance in the crises of misery and loneliness
which are likely to occur in every person's life. I think my material illustrates
the hypothesis that this lack of accepted ritual and guidance is accompanied by
a very considerable amount of maladaptive behavior . . . .

To the best of my knowledge there is no analogue from either the records of
past societies or the description of present societies outside the Judeo-
Christian tradition to this situation.[4]

This being so, it should appear quite obvious that the church and its ministry can serve a useful purpose for its believers at the time of death. When
we speak of the church we are ignoring the distinctions and variations between creeds, practices, rites, and forms.

Ernest Morgan, who prepared the *Manual of Death Education and Simple
Burial* for the Continental Association of Funeral and Memorial Societies,
described the role of the minister in relation to death when he wrote, "The
most important role of the minister in relation to death occurs well in advance of death. In fact, it is when death is not even in prospect that families
can be encouraged to think through their wishes and make their plans."[5]
However, there is another, perhaps more important, role of the minister,
and that is his role as the religious leader, the spiritual counselor, the resi-
dent philosopher of his congregation. His preparation of his congregation
to face the great issues of life, the question of the meaning of life, the
awareness that life is temporary and transient, but that our hopes and aspi-
rations are eternal, should all be part of the pattern of proper preparation.

A clear statement of the relationship of the church and minister to the
death situation is presented by The Reverend Frank O. Holmes in his
helpful booklet:

One of the primary responsibilities of every religion is to provide its followers
with a dignified and meaningful way of dealing with death. A church is concerned for the whole range of its members' experiences; it assists them to enter
instruction, and also by offering the inspiration of the marriage service and —
at the birth of a child — the baptismal, christening, or dedicatory service. So, in
reference to death, the church holds before its members, week after week, a vision of life as so significant in quality and opportunity that death is seen, not
as final and tragic, but rather as the necessary ending of a particular phase of a
process which is, in its larger dimension, enduring and eternal.

When death comes, a church helps its members to recall this vision of the
larger, enduring significance of life, by providing the survivors with a dignified
procedure to follow, and a religious service in which to share.

It is quite true that a funeral or memorial service is not necessary when a
person dies, any more than is the holding of a religious ceremony in connection with the beginning of a marriage. There have actually been times when it
has been, briefly, the custom even of church people to omit religious services

in connection with both marriage and death — as was the case among the early Puritan communities in New England. However, most young people entering into marriage prefer to have their largest hopes articulated in the religious language and symbolism of the marriage service. So, too, it is part of the aesthetic strength of the human spirit that it has been able to develop ceremonies which relate death meaningfully to the larger religious vision.

To persons who have had little to do with them, or whose experience has been of such services conducted insensitively, the funeral or memorial service may seem of very questionable worth. They may even be regarded as barbaric rites inherited from an outmoded, primitive past; an additional ordeal for the bereaved; at best, a social convention to be reluctantly tolerated. Honesty requires the admission that such services are sometimes so arranged and carried through that they violate rather than strengthen the better feelings of those who attend. It should be emphasized, however, that this need not be the case. Sometimes, the person who makes this kind of charge is one who has never himself been present at a well-conducted funeral or memorial service. It is by no means unusual for a minister to receive this kind of appreciative expression:

"I have always felt that funerals were only a survival of tribal rites, but like many of the adolescent opinions we discard with experience, it is gone . . . . Your beautiful service was a great consolation to me."

In those moments of deep and solemn feeling to which the experience of death impels one, a religious service which makes wise use of the rich resources of art, language and thought, available to us through the culture built up by the generations before us, can help us to see and celebrate with some adequacy the nobility of a life in terms of its own worth and achievement, and also as sharing in the promise of the mysterious Divine Creativity in which we continually live and move and have our being.[6]

Jackson, in his discussion of *The Christian Funeral,* began by noting: "By meeting death wisely and well, we mean not to be stampeded into foolishness or extravagant activity on the one hand, or retreating into denials and deprivations on the other. Rather with a full recognition of the needs of the body, mind and spirit we would employ with wisdom the full resources of the Christian community in order to emerge, strengthened and sustained by 'an unfaltering trust' that there is more to life than death as a goal and more to grief than blind and meaningless suffering. From these affirmative hopes grow a body of practices and attitudes . . . ."[7]

In a study of "Anxiety About Death," Professors Blackwell and Talarzyk discovered that "slightly less than 50 percent of Americans state that they are not afraid to die; nearly 17 percent state that they are very afraid to die; about 20 percent say they are nervous when people talk about death; almost two-thirds think about how short life is."[8] Such concerns over death seemingly indicate an area in which the church and its ministry have responsibilities and opportunities. Traditionally, the concern over death and ultimate ends have been considered religious. When people have such thoughts they frequently turn to the church or consult ministers. It would be of interest to know whether the 37 percent who indicated extreme anxiety or nervousness over the subject were or were not church affiliated.

These two researchers found helpful data pertaining to religious attitudes that are set forth in their Table on "Views of Life After Death," as follows:

WHICH OF THE FOLLOWING COMES CLOSEST TO YOUR VIEW OF LIFE AFTER DEATH?

Response	Percentage
I don't believe that there is life after death.	6.3
I am unsure whether or not there is life after death.	10.8
I believe that there must be something beyond death, but I have no idea what it may be like.	30.7
There is life after death, but no punishment.	3.6
There is life after death, with rewards for some people and punishment for others.	40.8
The notion of reincarnation expresses my view of what happens to people when they die.	4.5
None of the above.	3.3
	100.0

IF A CLOSE FRIEND OR RELATIVE WERE TO DIE, HOW IMPORTANT WOULD EACH OF THE FOLLOWING BE IN HELPING TO GIVE YOU PEACE OF MIND ABOUT THE PERSON'S DEATH?

	Very Important	Important	Don't know	Unimportant	Very Unimportant	Percentage Total
Talking to someone about the death	27.5	36.4	18.4	12.3	5.4	100
The religious convictions of the deceased	34.0	30.2	13.7	14.4	7.7	100
Your own religious convictions	39.2	32.7	9.5	11.5	7.1	100
Reflecting on way the deceased lived	26.1	43.3	12.5	13.7	4.4	100
Expression of concern and care by friends	22.7	51.8	13.2	9.5	2.8	100
The accomplishments of the deceased	12.7	35.8	15.9	27.9	7.7	100
The funeral and visitation of friends	11.8	40.5	15.8	22.1	9.8	100
Religious services or ritual	21.6	38.7	12.8	17.5	9.4	100
Knowing that survivors have financial security	29.5	51.9	7.9	6.5	4.2	100

Only 40.8 percent believed in the traditional Christian concept of a life after death with rewards and punishments. The non-Christian concept of reincarnation was held by 4.5 percent. The classical Universalist position of life after death without punishment was held by 3.6 percent. Non-Christian, liberal secularist, and scientific viewpoints are reflected in 30.7 percent who believe in "something beyond death" of an unknown nature; 10.8 percent unsure; and 6.3 percent who reject belief in immortality. Only 3.3 percent did not fit into any of these categories.

Another revealing study pertaining to "obtaining peace of mind" concerning death was presented in Blackwell and Talarzyk's Table, "Means of Obtaining Peace of Mind about a Person's Death." Religious convictions are second in importance in this table, coming after financial security for the survivors, which is most important for peace of mind. In view of the emphasis on funerals, the respondents rated the funeral and visitation of friends lowest in importance.

Gorer pointed out that "people today are without guidance as to how to treat death and bereavement and without social help in living through and coming to terms with the grief and mourning." It would seem that the church has an opportunity to be of greater assistance to persons in this situation. It apparently is difficult for people to talk about death, and Gorer noted that "at present death and mourning are treated with the same prudery as sexual impulses were a century ago."[9] This Victorian "conspiracy of silence" where death is concerned has been noted by a number of writers,[10] but it would seem the church should speak out. It was Emerson who noted that an institution is but the lengthened shadow of one man,[11] and to some extent this is so at any given period of a local church's history. Much of the church's ability to communicate, to offer solace, to blend its special gifts of arts, theology, philosophy, common concern, and human worth is channeled through the personality of its minister.

In my questionnaire a variety of points of view concerning the clergy emerged. Clergy themselves often demonstrated their own attitudes toward death. It reminds one of the experience of others in the field.

The role of the minister is set forward in comments of respondents, particularly those conscious of what may be called the spiritual side of death as recorded in the opening letters of this chapter. The church as a caring community is here suggested.

There is of necessity a question for the clergy similar to that asked of funeral directors: "How well do they perform?" Are they sympathetic to the needs of the family, and can they follow through with their healing ministry to the mind and spirit of their members, not only in the way they officiate, but in their ministry to the bereaved? Whereas funeral directors know in advance that their daily task will be dealing with death and with grieving families, ministers, like doctors, have many other responsibilities to consider, and death and its ministrations are but an almost peripheral aspect of a many faceted career. Preliminary study and correspondence as the survey project was set up made one conscious of this fact, so that before the survey was completed, one was prepared for some negative reactions. Initial correspondence indicated that clergymen bring their own human frailties to the subject and to their careers.

Indeed, it seems wise to point out that just as Dr. Hinton and Dr. Kübler-Ross both found that medical people—doctors and nurses—have hang-ups about death,[12] and approach the problem with their own personal, emotional reactions, so do clergymen. Kübler-Ross noted that there were many chaplains or clergy who only asked the mechanical questions concerning types of services, arrangements, religious persuasions, etc., instead of discussing the deeply felt needs concerning one's destiny and doubts and expectations, leading her to conclude that the clergy were often ineffectual.

"What amazed me, however, was the number of clergy who felt quite comfortable using a prayer book or a chapter out of the Bible as the sole communication between them and the patients, thus avoiding listening to their needs and being exposed to questions they might be unable or unwilling to answer. . . . They were very occupied with funeral procedures and their role during and after the funeral but had great difficulties in actually dealing with the dying person himself."[13]

There are many clergy who fail to come to grips with death in an open and freely discussable manner. In response to the request for names for the study, one minister wrote:

> I cannot send names—somehow it doesn't "sit right." It is not like asking for names of people who subscribe to a particular magazine or express certain views. My relationship with parishioners who have experienced the death of someone close enough to make "funeral" decisions is "special."
>
> I would be glad to be of assistance in other ways. I have just had the experience of being called to a home where a twelve-year-old boy had hung himself, and I spent intensive weeks and months with the family . . . .
>
> But it just doesn't seem appropriate to send names. Maybe you will get other responses that differ from mine. I'd be interested knowing.

The negative nature of his sensitivity to opening avenues of communication concerning death was not shared by many clergy. Indeed, many responses from individuals who volunteered from the brief published notices, as well as from those whose names were submitted by clergy, showed a strong social, almost spiritual, desire to be of help to others in similar situations. Perhaps to write out one's thoughts and to put before others one's reactions serve as a form of therapy.

Another clergyman who also rejected participation wrote, "After giving the matter some careful thought I would just as soon not have members of our congregation surveyed. I appreciate your desire to seek the consumers' viewpoint, but I feel your need for this information must be weighed against the already tender feelings of those who would be targeted for your survey."

Another one wrote of being favorably impressed by the policies of a local undertaker:

> He even has people dress the deceased — especially if it's a child and they feel they can. He feels we should overrule having the committal inside . . . that there should be the committal at the grave — and even sometimes has shovels so that people can add earth to the grave . . . .
>
> I feel that many of our liberal principles are being challenged — this is just one area.

The imagery that arises to mind is out of Ibsen's *Peer Gynt,* or the witches' scene in Shakespeare's *Macbeth,* so powerful are the negative ideas suggested here. Normally, ministers would be expected to be more protective of the already tender emotions of their shocked parishioners.

While the negative approaches of some clergy have been pointed out, it should be stated that these were only in a minority of situations, and that many, indeed most, clergymen had highly positive reactions to their role in the death situation. Some felt that they handled death situations particularly well, and that this was a constructive and meaningful part of their ministry. Some found that, due to the prevalent conventions or attitudes of their community, they usually were asked for only a funeral service, as indicated in one opening letter to this chapter.

Others were in churches that had a deep-seated preference for memorial services, which so identify the church and minister as memorial-oriented that they are asked to conduct such services for many outside of their churches. "I went over the funerals I have done here and they have all been memorial services. They seem to like them, and, in fact, I guess I have a reputation by now, because lots of people not in the church call upon me at the time of death to do a simple memorial-type service."

Some wanted to make clear that while they favored memorial services, they nevertheless felt the body should be viewed by the bereaved. "Personally I feel that the family should see the person dead at some point, although not necessarily at the service, and preferably without the cosmetic job. I feel it establishes the fact that the person is dead and it is easy to fantasize without that established fact."

It seems clear that the clergy is basically the best source of personal help available to the grieving family, in spite of those similar to the ones who were the dismay of Kübler-Ross,[14] or the British clergy who failed Gorer's respondents.[15]

To summarize, Holmes, with the wide experience of a very personal ministry behind him, could make sense for us when he wrote,

> What a minister can do, or will be called upon to do, when death comes, will depend in considerable measure upon the tradition of his church, the intimacy of his relationship with the person who has died, and the preferences of the family.
>
> A minister can be of far greater help if he is notified at once when death occurs. If he can do so, he will wish to call immediately, to express his pastoral and personal concern, and to be of assistance in any ways that he can be. Sometimes it is possible for him at this first visit to help by making suggestions in regard to the time, place, and character of the religious service to be held. Often, however — and especially if the death has come unexpectedly — he will seek, first, to give what comfort he can, and will postpone consideration of those practical decisions which the members of a family are not yet ready to make. It will then be advisable for him to have a second conference with the family, either at their home or at his study. At this second conference, the family will be encouraged to talk easily about the person who has died, and to make the necessary arrangements for the service. Even if a minister has been well acquainted with the deceased, such a conversation is of great help to him as he completes his preparations for the service; it also is a help to the family to have an opportunity to express their feelings to one who is concerned for the religious meaning of life. It may or may not be considered appropriate for the minister to include in the religious service a direct eulogy of the person. In any case, the clearer and closer the minister's acquaintance with the feeling of the survivors, the more surely that feeling will find its expression in the service he conducts, in the selection of readings, and in the phrasing of prayers.
>
> All arrangements regarding a funeral or memorial service, including details of place, hour, music, and flowers, should be decided upon in consultation with the minister. He should be accorded every opportunity to conduct the service on a high and sensitive level.[16]

Suggested here is the flexibility that many modern clergy may bring to the grieving situation from their vantage point on the frontier of the changing mores and values in our transitorial society. They are counselors without a vested interest of a pecuniary nature in the type or style of service.

They can help us move from "the dead forms of the past" to meaningful fulfillment through the trauma of death. Some of us have experienced such modern adaptations and can speak of the value, hope, and meaning found in them. Such explorations into new meanings through death and grief can enhance one's total response and make one proud of noble actions.

But, some say, such are without warmth or comfort. The answer may be in personal experiences.

A modern and altruistic approach to death need not be cold nor lacking in emotional warmth. The author's experience is common to that of many others in the frenzied and accident-prone society in which we live. One quiet evening the telephone rang, and a police sergeant in a distant town said, "We are sorry to tell you that your mother was seriously injured in an accident in New Jersey on an approach to the turnpike. She is in the hospital in Montclair and has not recovered consciousness according to the report in front of me."

She never did. Several days later death claimed her. We were thankful for membership in a memorial society and, through a local contact, made arrangements at the local crematorium. With my brothers there, a simple service was conducted, and a memorial letter sent to all known friends. We used the addresses we found in her "little black book" as well as her Christmas card list. That letter served to notify and involve in the circle of sharing and caring her many friends, few of whom could have attended a memorial service in New Jersey.[17]

When we asked about procedures for donating her eyes, the doctors immediately made arrangements, and they also told us about the ear disc bank operating out of that hospital. We agreed. She was a musician, with great sensitivity to sound, and that her ear discs would help others hear and enjoy the rapture of music was a most pleasing thought.

The Eye-Bank for Sight Restoration in New York City wrote us:

> May I take this opportunity to express our sincere appreciation for the donation made by your late mother, Margaret Marshall, in leaving her eyes to the Eye-Bank for Sight Restoration, Inc.
> Through this generous act two people today (who were among the many thousands of men, women and children dependent upon the Eye-Bank) will in a short time be restored to normal active lives in their own communities.
> We should also like to express our sympathy in your loss and we hope that you will find some consolation in the thought that through such a generous gift the spirit of your mother will live on in the sight of others.

The Ear Bank also wrote that through her donations one person had hearing restored and the other disc was used for research purposes. To my brothers and me, this was immortality of the most meaningful kind. It pleased us immeasurably to know this was done.

Scattered families and friends sometimes make difficult a gathering for a meaningful public service. Hence small, private services are increasingly used, followed by a memorial letter. An early example of such letters was that sent by the family to friends of the poet, Marshall Schacht.[18] Shorter letters and other types of tribute have been used by others.

Still another constructive memorial is through the donation of the human remains to a medical school for the advancement of medical knowledge and the teaching of a new generation of doctors. These schools must eventually dispose of the remains, and this is usually done through cremation, unless the family requests burial. The schools make arrangements to do so with dignity and beauty. One such example was related by a widow, living in the greater Boston community, who described the experience. Her husband's remains had been donated to the Harvard Medical School and that school, with others in the area, maintains a cemetery at Pine Hills for the burial of the cremated remains of the cadavers used in their institutions. She sent a copy of a report written by her minister and published in a suburban paper. He wrote:

> It was an uncommonly beautiful spot.
> And I was there on an uncommonly beautiful fall day—one when summer seemed to send lingering memories of warmth to bless the rich blend of golden red maples and changeless deep green pines.
> The simple sign on the entrance post told me it was a cemetery; but, once inside, there was nothing visible to make me aware of the fact. Indeed, it was an uncommon cemetery. There were no work crews surreptitiously lurking about, prettying the grounds for commercial traffic. There were no protrusions of granite or marble, marking the garish competition of lingering materialism, difficult for us to subdue even in the presence of the great democracy of the dead. There were no bouquets of wilted flowers or blossoms of eternal plastic to serve as ironic mementos.
> It was, in truth, an uncommon burial place.
> But for a reason that reaches far deeper than the absence of the superficial marks of identification which we have grown so accustomed to.
> For here were gathered in final rest those who shared one very special gift in common. Here were gathered to the final keeping of the great mother earth those whose bodies had been donated, at the time of their death, to the medical schools for study and research. Beyond any immortality (or lack of it) which we may draw from the deep springs of our faith, here I knew I stood in the presence of certain immortality. Here I knew that the gifts of these lives after death represented lasting evidence in memorial to the continuing advances of medical research.
> It was an awesome experience. I could not help thinking of the poet who said, "You give but little when you give of your possessions; it is when you give of yourself that you truly give." It was as if I were standing on ground more holy and in a quiet spot more sacred than any place on earth I have ever been.
> I found my mind wondering "how manay human beings all over the earth are alive and well today because of the research made possible by those in whose presence I stand?"
> A thousand? Perhaps a million?
> I felt a sudden sense of gratitude that I had known just one who rested here.
> I felt a strange sense of humility that I was still alive . . . that so many of us are still alive . . . and unable to find the time or the desire to give a portion of ourselves. Yet, here in death, so many have become truly givers of life. And I suspected that they were those who also sought to give of themselves while they yet had lived.[19]

Other medical schools use the ashes in gardens, return them to the families, or make otherwise respectful arrangements for the disposal of the final remains after science and humanity have been served. Upon request of the family, arrangements will usually be made to bury the remains in consecrated ground, and with the choice of a clergyman of the family's choice. It is advisable to contact church and clergy for assistance in such arrangements.

7

The Service: How Traditional?

Our correspondents wrote:

Arrangements were left to me when my brother, son, mother and father passed on, and in each case cremation followed with a memorial service at the convenience of the family, which in the case of my brother was many weeks later.

My husband was in favor of the memorial service for our son but had traditional funerals for his mother and father as the rest of his family expected.

The visiting hours were tiring, but the older generation didn't seem to mind. The open casket was repulsive to me. As far as I was concerned, it could have been any human body being displayed, not the loving, warm person I remembered and loved, whose spirit, I felt, had departed that body for another life.

Flowers in staid wreathes and set pieces that looked unnatural were placed on the graves. What a waste of beauty and money! How much more we appreciated the gifts sent to charities where the money can give aid to others.

At the memorial service in a relaxed attitude I find my thoughts reflecting on the life of the deceased, whereas at funerals I find myself "uptight," not wanting to gaze at the casket, or join the parade past the casket, or participate in the graveside service that follows.

Perhaps more people in this generation will find comfort in the memorial service. *

My father died in 1967 and my husband died in 1968. My father's death was sudden and unexpected. My husband died after an illness of eleven years. There was similarity between the two men in that both of them were men of great stature in their professions and internationally known.

My father's funeral service, traditional in every respect, was a hideous experience for us all. I am sure that it influenced me in trying to do something different and meaningful by way of a service for my husband.

I have enclosed the memorial program and a recording of that service.

As you will see, the memorial service was treated as a piece of theatre. It followed a very specific format to serve very specific needs of family and friends. This format has been used since very success- fully in a number of diverse funeral services here in the community. A friend of mine, Father James, is also using this format in the Catholic funeral services of his Padre Redemptoristes Order in Paraguay, South America.

Frankly, I think this format, or variations of it, does the job well, because it is not primarily serving the interests of the mortuary or the sponsoring religious institution but is serving the needs of the family and friends of the person who died.

The key to this whole approach is to treat the funeral service as theatre. Now, if the word "theatre" connotes to you hypocrisy, sham, undue emotionalism, etc., then we have nothing further to discuss.

However, if you can be persuaded of the notion that good theatre can give insight, lend strength, and help to heal, truly heal, then per- haps we have something additional to talk about together. *

I would like to remark that since I have experienced both types of funeral arrangements I find that my memories of my husband who was cremated are—shall I say—less morbid—and healthier than my memories of the traditional burial.

This attitude on my part developed after once feeling that I couldn't stand the thought of cremation of a loved one, but now I know it is far better for all concerned—and I am convinced that one day it will be mandatory by law. *

I am sorry this is so late, and it may be of no help to you. My mother's funeral was neither traditional nor memorial. She was a Bap- tist all her life, and when she died I did not feel I could have a strictly Unitarian service. The Unitarian minister did an outstanding job in combining mother's beliefs and mine together, and his wife sang spirituals accompanied by guitar. The funeral home wrote me a letter after the funeral saying it was one of the most inspiring services they had seen (considering how many there are around, I felt this said a lot). My mother's family was not too impressed by the funeral—there was none of the usual "ashes to ashes, and dust to dust" tradition that tears your heart out — but I felt that it was a great comfort to both my mother and me. If you can use it, I have a copy of this service, and I would be glad to help in any way possible. Since I was an only child, mother's death was very hard for me, and I feel that I have worked through a lot of feelings about grief and dying.

I am pleased to see the church interested in people's reactions to various services. Please let me know if I can be of further help. *

So death approaches on silent feet. What action do we take? What decisions do we make? To whom do we turn? The doctor has already given his condolences and counsel. We must now turn to the funeral director and the clergy or, if we have planned ahead, to the Memorial Society. Whether we have planned ahead or not, we now face the question of "How traditional of a service do we want?" For religiously motivated people the question is easily answered. For others, including the vast number of persons who rarely enter a church, the desire to avoid hypocrisy is important.

A service should not do violence to life values. It should carry its own integrity and put the signature to a life now completed. To do so in a manner not in keeping with its scope is an incongruous and meaningless formality.

We want to properly and reverently acknowledge the life and the value to us of the life now completed. Do we do so with a personally developed service in keeping with the person departed, or do we simply have "a traditional service," similar to so many others? There are conformists among the dead for whom such a service would be valuable, because that was the nature of their lives. We love and honor them for their homey virtues and commonplace assurances, and such a traditional service is what they would want and what their friends expect. We will follow their wishes. But there are others who stood out from the herd and walked independently through life, and we will honor them by a fitting remembrance. Others may be appropriately honored by either type of service, for there are elements of both the traditional and the adventurous in their life.

Accordingly, let us review the possibilities open to us.

A few years ago *Reader's Digest*[1] carried an article about funerals entitled, "Death on Parade," and to some extent this public display takes place with a funeral. This, in spite of the fact that many of the writers quoted referred to "the conspiracy of silence" concerning death, and Gorer stated that "death and mourning are treated with the same prudery as sexual impulses were a century ago."[2] Yet it is also true, as Dr. John Brantner stated in the medical school symposium, that death is not experienced first-hand by large numbers of people in our day. The value of a funeral may be that it introduces many to death and leads to a confrontation with it.

The prevalent American funeral, regardless of religious heritage, touches certain basic concepts and insights that seem to be common to all.

Human culture in various ways has offered some method of ritual awareness to help in what are called the *rites de passage*. The journey from life to death, perchance from this world to another world, gives an opportunity for a service of celebration, an opportunity to "grieve one's grief out," an occasion to share sorrow and accept the sympathy of the larger family of the community or congregation. Fulton has dealt with the social meaning of attitudes toward death in American culture and found three purposes: first, to properly dispose of the body; secondly, to aid the bereaved to reorient themselves from the shock of death; and finally, to publicly acknowledge and commemorate a death while asserting the viability of the group.[3]

Jackson noted three aspects to the Christian funeral: (1) a time to face death and hence the meaning of life; (2) Christian message and resurrection; and (3) the mystery of death made meaningful in the funeral service.[4] He stated that the funeral "can be the most significant activity at the time of death."[5] Finally, he suggested that there is a breakdown in conventional beliefs about immortality, or life after death, and that because of this many may seek compensation in more elaborate services than heretofore.

This was presented by Patchell and Woodward in *Facts of Death:* "With fewer people believing in an afterlife than ever before, death is even harder to bear: without belief in an afterlife we are left with the cold, barren facts of death as a last event. Perhaps the increasing elaborate ritualization of death is compensation for lost belief in an afterlife."[6]

Exactly what is involved in a traditional funeral? There are several parts that appear, regardless of the church or minister in charge. These are:

The opening sentence is a direct statement by the minister, in his own words or drawn from scripture or liturgy, which, in effect, announces why the people have gathered together.

Readings are chosen that unite, or relate, the deceased, the gathered throng, and all humanity together. Ancient readings from scripture (such as Psalms 121 or 90) connect today's mourners historically with those who have gone before. Other readings — perhaps modern — may relate, or suggest, universals. All somehow should convey a sense of the quality of human experience.

A *eulogy* speaks directly of the one in whose memory the group has gathered. If known personally by the speaker, then some trait or characteristic that endeared the deceased is focused upon. If not personally known, then something general that reminds the survivors and friends of the strivings and victories of the human spirit in which the deceased shared. A eulogy may be omitted and replaced by a reading relating to the hobbies, profession, or major characteristics of the deceased.

A *prayer* is offered in which all are drawn nearer to one another through common hopes and shared mysteries.

The *benediction* in which the deceased is blessed concludes the service. It will suggest the confidence that there is a meaning beyond that which can now be seen or expressed.

The funeral service is followed by a committal service, usually held at the grave, the crematorium, or following the funeral service itself. In inclement weather, it is usually held directly following the service with a sentence-announcement that it will now take place. The committal is usually described as a brief prayer at the graveside. It has three parts:

Opening sentences, which remind one that "No man liveth alone . . . " or "No man is an island entire of himself . . . ," as well as of the transitoriness of human life, and the fact we are all part of a natural process of earthly components ("dust to dust");

Prayer, which expresses respect for the one who lived among us;

Benediction, which states man's hopes and returns us to our daily living.

In connection with these words there are usually a few words that commit the body to the earth and the spirit unto the universal sources of life, normally simply called God.

A funeral is a service in which the body is present. The funeral is a time to offer a respectful farewell to the body, to provide opportunity for appreciation of the life of the person who has died, and to celebrate that life. Following the local custom of the church and community, the coffin is brought beforehand into the church, funeral home, or other place where the service will be held. If it is the church, it will usually be placed below the chancel steps or pulpit, or at the head of center aisle. The immediate family, a few minutes before the service is to begin, is ushered into reserved seats or pews, perhaps from an inconspicuous side entrance, so that they are not in procession at this time of heartbreak. The minister enters immediately before the service begins (or leads the procession if it is a service in which such is held); he conducts the service from the pulpit or lectern, or, more commonly, on the floor of the church at the head of the casket. At the conclusion of the service, the minister leaves the same way he entered; the members of the family return to the room from which they came; the congregation leaves; and the coffin is carred from the church to the hearse. In some churches it is the custom that the casket be carried from the church in a recessional, preceded by the minister and followed by the congregation or family.

Custom varies regarding the use of pallbearers, active or honorary. When such are chosen, they are friends of the family invited to carry or follow the casket. Sometimes when there is to be no immediate graveside service, the coffin or casket is left there to be removed later.

Opportunity to view the body after the death may give comfort to the bereaved members of the family, mitigating in some measure the shock or loss, and giving more time to accept the physical separation that is so often overwhelming in its suddenness. Its meaning rarely goes beyond the immediate family and few close friends intimately associated with the deceased. Usually, arrangements are made so that the general public may view the body ahead of time, at the home or at a place provided by the funeral director. Information to this effect is included in the newspaper notices. Most churches no longer encourage opening the coffin at the time of service, although it may be opened afterward for those unable to view the body ahead of time, such as relatives who have come from a distance.[7]

However, viewing the body may be an expensive luxury if there are no other compelling reasons for embalming and cosmetic preparation. State laws do not require embalming except under unusual circumstances, and an immediate burial may take place without it. Usually, when there is a funeral instead of a memorial service, it is presumed that the decision has been made to embalm, however, and hence the showing is quite in order, at least prior to the service. The sense of calm and acceptance elicited by the comforting words of the minister are usually considered the final benediction on the life now closed. Ministers often consider the reopening of the coffin and displaying the body after the service to be tantamount to opening an old wound, and they frown upon this practice.

Embalming, as practiced in the United States and Canada, is a procedure that grew out of practices initiated during the Civil War and widely used to ship Union soldiers home to the North for burial. Most books and treatises on the subject[8] usually date the American practice to the Civil War. For instance, Edward C. Johnson, a faculty member at the Worsham College of Mortuary Science, Chicago, wrote:

> Modern embalming, the process which is applied to the majority of all dead in the United States and Canada, had its impetus in the care afforded to the American Civil War (1861–65) dead by such men as Thomas Holmes . . . . The modern embalming operation comprises the injection of several gallons of embalming solution into an artery . . . . The solution permeates even the most remote tissue cells and clears the body of blood which is drained from a vein opened at the place of injection. . . . By 1900 production of formaldehyde became cheap enough to permit the inclusion of formalin as an integral component of the embalming fluids and all state laws require the incorporation of a fluid definite percent of formaldehyde in the embalming fluid.[9]

Embalming affords the funeral director his best opportunity to display his artistry and the skill of his profession, and he is reluctant to forego this opportunity. It is at this point that persistence on the part of the purchaser of what is, after all, a consumer service is called for. There are financial and economic factors extremely important in funeral planning, and the services once rendered cannot be returned or exchanged. Too many families have come close to bankruptcy due to extravagant commitments (or permissions granted) at the time of intense grief when funeral arrangements are consummated. Thus, a word of caution in completing arrangements is in order.

The question is often asked, "Is the funeral for the living or the dead?" "Do we express our views, or theirs, in the service and the way it is handled?" Some of our respondents found genuine satisfaction in following the wishes of the older generation in doing the services their way. If the deceased and their colleagues or neighbors maintain belief patterns that require a public display of the body, then it is probably in order, if affordable.

Sometimes, however, in spite of our best efforts the services become an ordeal, representing outgrown ideas of the survivors, who do what must be done and go through a service with which they can no longer identify.

Can one avoid unfortunate, incongruous experiences? The answer found by many is the modern memorial service. Increasingly, such services are being held in churches of many denominations, college chapels, and public or semipublic gatherings, as well as at intimate family gatherings. More and more distinguished public figures are honored by a memorial service rather than a public funeral.

Simply stated, the differences between the memorial and funeral services are that in funerals the body of the deceased or casket is usually present. The funeral deals with the issues and meanings of death, cast primarily in religious terms, and draws upon the heritage of traditional religious concepts and sacred writings. In the memorial service the body of the deceased is not present; the service is held at a time and place convenient for the family and is in keeping with the person commemorated. The words are about life, and the entire spirit of the service is to share in glad recollection of the goodness, usefulness, richness, challenge, and uniqueness of the deceased's life. He or she may be represented as a good companion or an associate or family member who had human qualities, good and bad, frustrated or fulfilling, which made the person a personality that touched other lives in some significant manner. Hence one notes, perhaps mourns, his or her passing. Life has ended for this person, and that fact is marked with comforting words and pleasant memories, if such there are, in a spirit of reverence without morbidity. The company notes the rich variety of life that ends for all, and the survivors are reminded to accept gratefully these limited days given to each who walks this earthly path.

A memorial service may be preferred because it is separated from the farewell to the body. It affords time for consideration, and for planning the social occasion after the arrangements are made for the disposition of the body. It separates the two activities from each other, so each can be handled separately.

Usually a service is held within a few days or weeks of death, but it can be held even later, sometimes running months later. One notable example occurred a few years ago when the Pulitzer playwright Elmer Rice was stricken aboard ship crossing the Atlantic and died in a hospital in Liverpool, England. Later, after returning to the United States, his widow arranged a memorial service at the theater in New York City that he once owned, where many of his plays and those of his associates had been produced. Several members of the theatrical community participated, including fellow playwrights, actors, dramatic and literary critics, in what the *New York Times* described as a fitting occasion. An Ethical Culture leader represented the religious community in this memorial service. This type of flexibility in scheduling is possible with a memorial service that is not tied to the rigid time schedule for the disposal of the body.

For many people, the last farewell, and the one they remember most, occurs when they last visited their loved one before death, or while they sat silently beside the body after the last breath and perhaps held a still warm hand. This private moment, perhaps alone with the beloved remains of the one they loved, has meaning that no public service can ever displace or replace. Then, the body is taken from the home or hospital for its preparation for final disposal. Later viewings of the body, after attempts to re-create a living likeness, can never surpass the remembrance of the person as in real life. A correspondent to our project summed up the view expressed by many: "I wish to remember my loved ones as I last saw them and was with them, not as a made-up corpse in a coffin, with family members and friends remarking on his looks."

Following the personal farewell just before or after the drawing of the last breath, the arrangements for the memorial service can be made in consultation with other family members and associates without the pressure of time, date, and complete arrangements.

The service may be held in the home, church, university chapel, club, or in the out-of-doors, at a grove, glen, beach, or some place that seems natural and correct for the person whose life is to be commemorated. There is increased flexibility as to place of service as well as to scheduling.

A memorial service aims to be a celebration of the life, rather than a confrontation with death. The service is designed to help the family, friends, and associates recall the deceased's life. Many who have experienced such a service feel it puts the emphasis on the spiritual rather than the material, stressing that the body is but the vehicle of a spiritual life that is glorified, not the physical body. Proponents of the memorial service have stated that the undertaker's art unwittingly puts the emphasis on the material rather than the spiritual qualities of life.[10]

One value of the memorial service is that it may be tailored to each individual's set of circumstances.

There is no rule of thumb for funeral or memorial practices. For some, cremation is the easiest and best way, and where there are no family objections, it is to be preferred. It is the most sanitary and the least expensive, provided cremation is handled without embalming and without the foolish purchase of an expensive casket to burn.

One of the dangers of traditional funeral practices is the wastefulness often practiced and usually recommended. The burying in the ground of great treasure, or the burning of it, often deprives the family that is living of needed funds for support. For the most part, the high cost of funerals can be avoided. Death is not a unique experience; it comes to all men, and it should not call, therefore, for extra-ordinary expenditures. In these various forms for funerals, it is advisable to bear in mind what debts are being incurred: memorial services minimize costs.

The second factor to be kept in mind, if immediate cremation is not followed, is that immediate burial of the body, without embalming (which is unnecessary and preserves the body only briefly) can take place with a memorial service in the home, the church, or other suitable place. If desired, a simple committal over the closed grave may be held. This can be the most beautiful and satisfying type of service for the family preferring a burial. Families should understand that all that goes into the ground in a brief period returns to the dust, and that it is needless to spend large sums of money with a false sense of preserving that which no longer can be preserved. The dead person is not in the casket. The person departed with the spirit of life. All that we can hope to do is to dispose of the remains with dignity and respect. The assurance that is felt comes equally, and with more satisfaction, when it is in a less ornate, less expensive, and a less formalized type of service.

In both of these services there is but one parting: when the life has left the body, which is all that should be asked of any family. In both of these services there will be a memorial service without the presence of the body and, if desired, a simple committal at a closed grave.

The third option is to have a closed coffin at the service, with the committal at the service rather than the grave. If it is desired to have the committal at the grave, then there should be a lapse of time so that the coffin may be buried. Families are often swayed by funeral directors who say, "The community expects to see the body"; or "The people will think something is wrong with the body if they don't see it." These are the same undertakers who say to the minister, "It may be better for your faith or the family to have a closed coffin, but it's better for my business to have an open one."

For the most part, people do not expect to see the body. Many of the largest and best-established churches require closed caskets at services. A mourning family does not have to prove anything to friends and is not on the defensive to expose the body to public inspection.

Such services are frequently held in a church. There are both a logic and certain advantages that favor utilizing churches for this purpose.

A funeral or memorial service may be held wherever it is most convenient for the family and friends to gather: in the family home, in a funeral or crematory chapel, or in a church or church chapel. There are times when it is convenient and proper to hold a complete service at the grave.

Increasingly, services are being held in churches or church chapels. There are many advantages in this custom. Since the church building, unlike the funeral chapel, is assocated not with death alone but with the whole religious life, it carries with it larger, affirmative associations. In the church, better musical facilities are usually available, and all arrangements, including those for music and flowers, can be made under the direction of the minister and church staff. If the deceased was an active member of a church, it is certainly fitting that the service shall be held in the building which served as his spiritual home.[11]

The only possible solution, short of personally experiencing a service, is the testimony of those who have. The correspondence attendant upon the author's research project produced many collaborating statements that offer witness to the value of the experience, the varying nature of the memorial occasions and the response of those who mourned the deceased.

Many accept death serenely. One widower described his sense of satisfaction about the memorial service for his wife.

When my wife died at the age of seventy-two this was not a terribly traumatic experience. She had lived a considerable period of productive and rewarding years. We had had a wonderful marriage of forty-six years. I wanted a memorial service to celebrate those years. We gathered at the church on a Sunday afternoon. The organist played some of Ruth's favorite selections. We continued the service by singing one of Ruth's cherished hymns. I then spoke briefly of our years together and of how much each had meant to the other. Following that — there were in the Asheville church several people who had known and worked intimately with Ruth during all our years in Detroit — and I asked them to reminisce a bit. I had prevailed on Ruth's sister — the two of them had always been very close — to recall early memories — and she did in a very moving and effective way. After that, a reading or two and closing with another of Ruth's favorite hymns.

Some of the people who have participated in memorial services describe genuine satisfaction and contrast their experience by indicating that much of the duress and heartache of a traditional funeral was absent. They held services of sharing memories.

Not all memorial services, however, proved able to meet the needs of the bereaved.

There are specific times when a memorial service is almost a necessity rather than a matter of choice, exemplified by deaths where there is no body, as in cases of death at sea, accidents, fires, or natural calamities. Under these circumstances services may tend to follow a more traditional funeral style, even though the body is not present. On the other hand, they lend themselves to the memorial service naturally and gracefully, so that a meaningful expression may be made for those who died under unusual circumstances.

One such service was reported by a correspondent in the survey who sent newspaper accounts of her husband's death. The newspaper reported on March 12, 1973:

> Memorial services will be held for Roland Alan Lincoln, 40, of Santa Ynex, who died in an explosion at the General Electric Re-Entry Development Center in Lompoc last Sunday at 11:00 A.M.

Wednesday, March 14, 1973, the account of a reporter who attended the memorial service was printed locally. It began:

> I went to a funeral yesterday morning at East Beach. It was a gathering of one hundred friends and fellows in support of a family plunged to the depths of stunning sorrow and sadness. Our task was to bring them back to light and happiness.
>
> Alan Lincoln, friend and fellow, lost his life Sunday but did not die. And strangely, in spite of the absence of his earthly remains, he was there. He was the grass beneath our feet where some of us sat and others stood. He was the scent of the boughs over our heads and the lyrical winds that morning which stirred those branches.
>
> A seaman and a sailor, this outdoor man, it was his day; weather lashing the surf into spumes and outboard winds the way he loved them. The kind of day he might have been out in his daily sailer,[12] bow deep in gray-green rollers, finding a good blow to test the reef in his rigging.
>
> In the midst of our one hundred sat his widow, Anya, with Alan's fifteen-year-old Dalmatian quietly at her side. One-eyed and aging, Spot is a part of the family and seemed so very right being there; as much as Kenneth, a son, and Leslie, a daughter; parents on one side and a brother not far away — all in that circle of one hundred.
>
> Jim Dace, a Unitarian minister, came more than a thousand miles to speak for ten minutes. At his feet the folk singer, Sherry, made soft music as he talked.[13]

This was a friend's sentimental account of the spirit and nature of a memorial service. It illustrated elements not possible in a traditional funeral.

The absence of a body is also occasioned when the body is donated to the medical school or teaching hospital. When limbs, organs, tissue, etc., are donated, or radical autopsy is performed, burial or cremation immediately afterward is usually called for, and under such circumstances a memorial service is often preferred. Certainly the body is disposed of without embalming or public showing. It frequently happens that people who have willed, or directed, such a donation in the cause of science or humanity have a natural tendency for a memorial service rather than traditional services.

Writing about her service for her husband, a widow who lived in Illinois told about arrangements with the Demonstrators Association of Illinois. Their material stated, "The Demonstrators Association, which is the official representative of all the medical institutions in the state in need of bodies, will receive and prepare the remains for medical education and research."[14] Her letter showed how simple and easy it is to carry out such arrangements, once they have been made in advance.

> My husband died at the age of seventy-five on May 13, 1974. Some years before, he had arranged with the Demonstrators Association in Illinois to give his body to Northwestern University for medical purposes.
>
> Upon his death I phoned the Demonstrators in Chicago and they instructed me to contact a funeral home in Springfield, which I did. The funeral director took charge of taking the body from the hospital and to Chicago. The funeral director was very nice to me and my son-in-law and in no way made us feel we should have a funeral at their funeral home.
>
> We did wish to have a memorial service and, since our daughter was in the hospital at the time of her father's death, we decided to postpone the service for two weeks.
>
> I must admit that before my husband's death I had qualms about going against the custom of the community and not having the traditional funeral and "visitation," which my husband disliked. In fact, two neighbors came in and questioned me on the matter. But I felt I should follow my husband's wishes.

There are those who simply prefer to choose cremation as a method of disposal and hold, accordingly, a memorial service. Such a service offers them an opportunity to be informal and to create a fellowship of sharing. A minister wrote of this experience:

> The daughter of a member of the church died. Her father asked me if I would come out to their home some evening for a memorial service. I, of course, agreed, and on the designated evening arrived at the home to find a group of about twenty friends, relatives, members of the family sitting informally about the living room. We formed the semblance of a half-circle before the fireplace. I had been asked to begin with a few relevant readings, which I did. There followed then an hour during which members of the circle simply reminisced, recalling incidents and qualities in the life of the one we were honoring. It was a very moving and meaningful occasion and, I know, deeply satisfying to those who took part. I had been requested at the end to close with another reading or two and a final period of meditation.

A wife, who originally did not approve of her husband's expressed desire for cremation, acquiesced and made this comparison of his memorial service with a more traditional family funeral she recently attended: "I find that my memories of my husband who was cremated were, shall I say, less morbid and healthier than my memories of the traditional burial."

Memorial services are a private and individual matter, usually chosen for personal reasons by either the deceased or the surviving next of kin. The memorial service justification lies in the nature of the service itself and the needs the family seeks to meet. However, because the memorial service is, in many quarters, still looked upon as innovative and contrary to traditional practices, those who believe in it frequently have banded together for mutual support, educational purposes, and in order to find funeral directors who will be cooperative. As a result memorial societies, as voluntary organizations, have come into being. It is not necessary to be a member of a memorial society to hold a memorial service, but it often helps.

Memorial societies have been formed by persons in various communities who believe memorial services to be socially useful and desirable. Persons desiring simplified modern memorial services need guidance and guidelines. Many clergy in most denominations are cooperative and helpful in planning services but, without the experience and prepared materials of the memorial society, they might be at a loss concerning how to proceed in the preparation of a memorial service without benefit of funeral direction. Likewise, when the minister feels a simple modern service will fit needs better than a traditional service, helpful educational materials are useful, and these are readily available for the people in question.

You will recall that a memorial service is often preferred when there is no body to bury or cremate. This can occur following violent disasters, wars, drownings, accidents, and disappearances. It also happens by pre-arrangement, when the body is donated to a medical school or otherwise to science, research, and humanity. One moving account of such a pre-arrangement was printed some years ago in a magazine. Participating in the author's survey of death patterns was Ms. Elizabeth T. Harris, the writer of an article, "On Giving Oneself Away," published in *Harper's Magazine.*[15]

She explored the legal, practical, and conventional issues that must be resolved before donating one's body. In a marginal note she stated that her name could be used and her article quoted. A marked copy, which she enclosed, is applicable at this point of the study. Harris described how she moved slowly from the idea of donating eyes for corneal transplants, but she remained haunted by the out-of-character, lavish, expensive, and pretentious funeral given her grandmother. It seemed to deny the remarkable accomplishments and severe values by which she lived. Then Harris read an article entitled, "Let the Dead Teach the Living," in *Reader's Digest,*[16] and this started her thinking about the need that can be met by donating the cadaver to a medical school. She discussed the various pros and cons, the arguments she had with herself and, for practical reasons, decided that such a donation was the sensible course. She made no pretense of being a Saint Joan of Arc, making a great sacrifice of her body, for it would no longer serve her needs. But in life she would not want to be treated by a doctor who did not have experience on a human body. She wrote to the Columbia University College of Physicians and Surgeons and to the Cornell University Medical College. The latter was receptive to her offer.

She learned that arrangements must be made for the transportation of the body by a licensed undertaker in New York state. She had to have three relatives including the next of kin sign the authorization, since at that time in New York "the next of kin owned the body." The transportation problem led her into dialogue with funeral directors over arrangements that revealed their attitudes and demonstrated that a strong will is sometimes required to overcome their protests. She reported one funeral director's comments:

"Mrs. Harris, a basic principle of the American way of life is involved here. How can you ever consider giving your body to a medical school instead of having a dignified, traditional funeral? . . . What would people say? And have you considered the feelings of your loved ones? How can you inflict such distress on them?"

Nevertheless, she persisted and worked out adequate, tentative arrangements, learning other matters concerning death and the law that are helpful information, and she had the additional satisfaction that "my grandmother would have approved!"[17]

Memorial services serve a variety of useful functions due to the flexibility permissible, the options open to one, the quality of service made possible by simple and less ostentatious planning, and the spiritual quality of a service that stresses the individuality of the life commemorated, rather than being preoccupied with the problem of death. To many people this seems a desirable alternative to the traditional funeral.

To recapitulate, in this service the body is not present and, therefore, there should not be the expensive arrangements for preparation of the body or for an ornate and elaborate casket to be placed on display. Likewise, the abundance of floral pieces are not desired and usually are omitted by request.

The service may be held almost any appropriate place. The service takes almost any form, from a structured set of readings and comments to an informal discussion replete with recollections by friends and family.

In the memorial service, since the body has been disposed of by burial, cremation, or donation to medical science and humanity, there are no concerns of its disposition to intrude on the memorial service.

Usually, it is helpful if the service is pre-arranged by the deceased or his family in more healthful times, when there is no emotional duress to interfere with rational decisions. Those holding such a service, and the participants, often feel there is a gracefulness and personal quality that is memorable.

At the time of death there are tender feelings exposed, and there is a heightened sense of the need to be correct in what one does. The public observance creates a situation in which it is frequently said that one is "on display." The memorial society gives assurance and support at such a time that one is not alone in the pattern followed. Its existence serves as a demonstration that these ideas are not all that unique, and this family is not the first, nor the only one, to veer from the traditional pattern of mourning. In answering questions of the curious, in overcoming the criticism of the accusing, and in the interpretation of the reasoning to friends and family, the memorial society material is of great assistance.

The memorial society serves as a liaison with funeral directors, many of whom cannot understand why their full line of services are seemingly rejected in favor of an austere, almost Spartan approach to public display and the ornate ceremonial approach of the industry. Memorial society material and leaders are able to explain and interpret what is to be done, how simple a service is desired, and why simplicity is the chosen method.[18]

8

Children and Death

A Sequence of Family Letters

First letter from the Mother:

> *In a way, we have a special problem with which we are dealing as a family. Two and a half years ago our sixteen-year-old son, Robert, died while away at a summer enrichment program in physics at the state university. He was an especially gifted human being—not only intellectually but in the area of music. Most of all he was a truly loving and gentle human being. We miss him.*
>
> *A liberal, kind, Lutheran minister came to help us during these painful early days of grief. We went to his church for a time, also having family gatherings with CLF material when we could here at home.*
>
> *Now, Sarah is searching—this is well and good. She has had such a hard time dealing with the loss of a dear brother. Seven years ago she lost a six-weeks-old brother to Sudden Infant Death Syndrome. At that time we were in Massachusetts and called on a Unitarian minister in Bedford for help. I regret we did not then make an effort to attend his services as a family. Perhaps we couldn't—that loss of a healthy baby was hard. It was not used as a learning experience for Robert, Sarah, and Johnny. From my readings since, we would now handle things in a less protective manner.*
>
> *I have the resource material here and will look for some books which might be especially helpful to Sarah. She has not learned to talk of her loss but is receptive to reading material.*
>
> *Perhaps if you know of any especially good books on dealing with*

81

the never-ending process of grief, you could let us know. I have read Talking About Death *and* Up From Grief — *a very fine book.*

Letter from Sarah:

You'll have to excuse me for not answering sooner, but I've been so busy lately that it completely slipped my mind.

Thanks for your letter — I really appreciated it. I'd like to continue to correspond with you, if you have the spare time.

Sometimes I miss my brother so much I pretend it's not true — especially around graduation time. It's hard for me to watch the seniors graduating and receiving their diplomas. I know it's not right, but lately I tell any new friends I might have made that I have an older brother in college, even though I know it's not true. I just hate listening to them talk of their older brothers and sisters. For a while I kept telling myself it was true, that I really did have a big brother that was alive, but no matter how hard I tried, I couldn't make myself believe it. I was getting pretty depressed, so I took on another job to keep me busy. It has, believe me. It's a conservation job in conjunction with the U.S. Forestry Service. It's fun, but hard work. I work nights at Arthur Treacher's Fish 'n Chips. In spare time I paint watercolors; I want to be an artist. Next year I'll be graduating and I'll probably enter college in the fall of 1980.

Letter from the minister to Sarah (extracts):

First of all, let me thank you for sharing your thoughts with me. When I wrote to you I did not know but that you would think it was an intrusion, even though, in a technical sense, I am your minister. I do know, however, that no one knows the pain that another feels and that it takes a lot of courage to tell someone else of your feelings, as you have done. I hope that it has been helpful just to express those feelings.

It is very natural to pretend that someone has not died. Those who have done much more with the study of death and grief tell me that this happens very much. With the death of a loved one the load of grief is so great that it is too big to accept all at one time. Then we pretend that the person has just gone away, hoping to remove the sting. But eventually, as you know yourself, the truth must be faced and accepted. A close friend of mine who has written a book on the subject, Rabbi Earl Grollman, suggests that one say it out loud — "My brother has died." You have to hear it to feel it. He points out, "Good mental health is not the denial of tragedy, but learning to live with it."

It takes a lot of time to face the truth, and I am interested in knowing how you have been handling this since you last wrote.

I see that you have been working hard to overcome your grief and that can be healthy, but any good medicine taken in excess becomes poison. Allow a little time to yourself. You can't run away from pain. You have to face it and confront it.

Second letter from the Mother:

Please accept my appreciation for your expression of care to my daughter, Sarah, in your remarkable, helpful letter of July 11. As you correctly sensed, her coping has been made even more difficult by an inability to squarely face the grim fact that her brother, Robert, is dead and no longer a tangible, daily presence in her life. It is so strange how difficult it is to accept death, which is as perfectly natural as life, and surely occurs as often. Robert was a beautiful human being, and for a while the pain from his death was my best hold-on contact with reality—for that reason I see pain as a very useful phenomenon. The pain told me I was still "here." *I think your thoughts will be a big help to Sarah. Thank you so much.*

Second letter from Sarah:

This is probably going to be a rather strange letter. You'll see what I mean. Lately, thoughts of Robert haven't bothered me too much. I still think of him and I miss him, but in more of a positive way. The real test was in one of my classes when somehow the subject was brought up, and I was able to talk without crying or feeling a great deal of self-pity. I surprised myself. I regret he is not here with me now—I could really use a big brother. I get jealous when someone mentions their big brother because I know mine is the best, but he's not here. I wish I could talk to him now, because I am so scared about graduating from high school. I have built up some good relationships with my teachers, and I know I have to move on, but I'm really going to miss them and a lot of my friends. I will probably have a wonderful time in college—it's just the idea of leaving is scary to me. You know, I have found a great release thru writing poetry. I have made two books (approximately two hundred lines each) for creative writing projects. *

Letters from Others Also Touched upon the Death of Children

On December 7 our fifteen-year-old daughter and one of her classmates were killed in an auto accident. We attended the boy's Catholic funeral and came away totally convinced we had done the right thing for our daughter with a simple observance of silence at our church and at the school. Her body was donated for tissue research. Each decision we have made was easy and still seems like the correct one. Friends agree that our attitude and apparent peace of mind couldn't be better. We'd be happy to share it with you.

A few of our friends are still struggling to accept her death, so I'd say your project is certainly worthwhile. *

Two months ago, our thirteen-year-old daughter, Julie, was struck by an out-of-control car while riding her bicycle. She died four days later, without ever regaining consciousness.

And that was when my wife and I found how much we needed the Church. As liberal humanists we had always concentrated on life; we celebrated it and tried to make the most of each moment. Faced with the awful meaninglessness of Julie's death we felt frightened, we felt despair, we felt we had nothing to help us. Somehow, however, inside me something said not to give up—something directed me to turn to the Unitarians.

Help came in the form of the Rev. Bruce Findlow, Principal of Manchester College, in neighboring Oxford. When we first went to see him, the day after Julie died, I told him that I thought that we Unitarians were pretty good about handling life, but expressed doubt about our dealing with death.

But Bruce and Unitarianism did help us. They said nothing about eternal life, they said nothing about God's will, all of which would have troubled us more. Bruce said simply that there was no meaning in her death, but that death was simply part of life. He comforted us intelligently, but with great feeling, and, joined by many others, led us away and accepting with love. He led us to see Julie's immortality in the lives that were touched by her and in the love and joy she brought us during her brief life.

This road away from the grief of a child's untimely death is a long one, but the Unitarians have helped us along that road. Starting with the fundamentals we arrived at long ago, kept nourished by the CLF, and given a God-sent help in Bruce Findlow, and, finally, reinforced several weeks ago at a memorial service at our old home, the Unitarian Society in Plainfield, New Jersey, Unitarianism has shown us how to find our way. For this we will always be grateful.

Rev. Marshall, somehow I had to thank the church. I convey these thanks through you.

Julie was a faithful member of the Junior Fellowship. Please let them know. *

We had five children—one with cerebral palsy. Last August our John, age sixteen, drowned. He was a good swimmer; affected with C.P., he had participated in Special Olympics. Apparently he had a seizure while swimming alone. John's palsy was severe. His "shakes," as he called them, made everything he tried to do so difficult! He was men- tally retarded, too—more so than most people thought. His death was such a shock to us and we miss him terribly. One of the very first peo- ple to respond that day was a Lutheran minister who lives in the next block and knew John personally. He also volunteered his services "in any way," and he would up using material from the CLF booklet on services, etc., which we picked out. The funeral was in the Lutheran Church—a mentally retarded friend of John's played a flute solo. John's uncle wrote some words about John, and a wonderful young psychology major who was John's teacher's aide in his classroom read the uncle's words and wrote some beautiful words of his own which he read, too. I'm sending you copies of those words. *

From a Teacher's Remembrance

As assistant to John's teacher during the last school year, I grew to know John very well. And in looking back on the many times we shared the joys of simple achievements or wrestled-through frustra- tions, the very least that I can say is that I shall dearly miss John as a student. But I will miss him even more as one of my finest teachers. For all the while I was teaching John fundamentals, like arithmetic or read- ing or even some macramé, he was teaching me much greater things.

He was teaching me how to be patient when I thought all patience was gone. He was teaching me to understand without pitying. He was teaching me how to accept people instead of merely tolerating them. He taught me to be thankful for my life and good health, and he taught me these things in a vibrant, incessant way so that I might never forget. And he taught these things, I am sure, not only to his teachers, but to his family and friends, and any who grew to know him.

John lived with many barriers to his potential. But now the walls have all come down, and his spirit is free from the trembling that tor- mented him so; and he knows, perhaps better than any of us could ever know, the beauty of being still.

But we must not be still and forget the things he showed us. His greatest memorial would be that we continue in the awareness to which he brought us: that we keep in touch with those things he brought out in us—the patience, understanding, and acceptance that made us feel so good about ourselves—and use them to the service of all the other special people still waiting for that benefit.

John was a good student. He was a great teacher. And I thank God for both.

An Uncle Remembers

The world has lost a good friend in John. He was a kind, warm, affectionate person, and a true inspiration to all those who knew and understood him.

What John lacked in mental and physical capacity, he more than made up for in spirit. It was his spirit that enabled him to accomplish many things in his brief life—things that would be considered routine for most people.

John could have lived a much more sheltered life than he did. But through his untiring efforts, and through understanding and allowances given to him by his family, John was able to live up to and beyond his capabilities.

John had become increasingly aware of his limitations, and increasingly frustrated as a result of those limitations. But he never gave up, never quit trying. He was not satisfied with all he had accomplished. He wanted to accomplish more. It is certain he would have.

John deeply appreciated the love, patience, and understanding of his family. He deeply appreciated the fact that they allowed him to live as happy and normal a life as possible. He wouldn't have wanted it any other way. He also deeply appreciated the kind thoughts, words, patience, and understanding showed him by friends and acquaintances who took time to care. To all those people, John would say thank you.

John touched many lives in a special way. He was deeply loved and will be sadly missed.

There are two aspects to the death of children. One is how parents deal and cope with the death of a child. Considerable amounts of writing have been done by parents who have experienced and survived periods of intense grief. The other aspect is how to share with children the knowledge of the death of a loved one: how to help them understand what has happened and express their sorrow and grief, and how to assist them in making the adjustment back to normal living without a sense of insecurity or fear.

It is difficult, to say the least, to accept the death of a child or young person whose life had not been fulfilled. Few aches can equal that of the loss of a youngster. Pathos, trauma, and tragedy touch us at such a time. There is an emptiness to life, an inner void that seems never to be filled, and we are apt to recall over the years what might have been "had only he/she lived."

Parents and relatives who suffer this experience might learn from the writing of others who have shared their loss. The volume by the noted foreign reporter, John Gunther, on the death of his son — a teen-age youth of great promise, struck down by cancer — is a touching journal of the lingering death, the great spirit of the boy, and the close communion of two divorced parents who are united together in a common and impending sorrow through the approaching death.[1]

Bereaved parents have sometimes banded together for mutual support and comfort through the sharing of experiences. One such example is the Society of Compassionate Friends. This society of parents united in offering consolation in the loss of a child began in England in 1970 and now has various regional chapters in metropolitan areas throughout the United States. Again, this is evidence that persons who belong to "the fellowship of those who bear the mark of pain" have much to contribute to one another. So often it seems that those who have walked the same path have a special empathy and comprehension of the anguish and inner turmoil that touches life. This is not always so, for no two experiences are exactly the same, each being unique; indeed, the whole proposition of professionalism rests upon the foundation that help can be given by those properly taught and clinically trained. Yet, when the well-meaning friend or professional says, "I know exactly how you feel," the plaintive heart cries out, "How can you? Have you ever borne a baby, stayed awake nights with its suffering, recognized its every motion, squirm, and sound as though it was from your own heart, and then seen it lie lifeless and dead before you?" This protest is justified to some extent. But help does come from others, from their words and from the compassionate care and concern that others bring, just as surely as it comes from the inner resources of the soul and heart, and, eventually, from the peace we make with life and our comprehension of death.

Lois E. Flanagan wrote of the loss of two sons. About the oldest, Sean, diagnosed as having acute lymphocytic leukemia, she wrote:

> I felt as though I had been thrown into a pitch-black cavern and then was told to find my way out. Everything I had ever known was forgotten; every emotion used to face the normal complexities of life was totally useless to me. He was eight years old at the time of the diagnosis, and I did not see how he could possibly face what must surely lie ahead. During the first months, I had to fight continuously against an all-consuming fear — an urge to panic and go crashing against the concrete wall that had become my life. When he was diagnosed, I was faced with a stranger who was entirely unknown to me. This stranger was grief in its rawest, most painful form — that of a mother for her child. My son was desperately ill, and there was nothing I could do but allow the painful treatments that would prolong his life.
>
> Sean lived two years and ten months. This period of time was a roller-coaster

ride of hope and despair, of remission and relapse, of fear and then thanksgiving that yet another crisis had been met.

Sean learned of the seriousness of his illness soon after the diagnosis and
accepted it. His acceptance helped me to live it with him openly and honestly
and encouraged me to learn all I could about death and dying so that I could
help him. At the outset, we tried to live this tragic ordeal with faith, and faith
sustained both of us. We often talked of his dying, but only when he wanted
to. He'd let me know that he was bothered, and we'd talk it out. If any one
thing helped, it was never shying away from the one subject people almost
never can talk about—death. The fact that Sean had faced the unknown world
of dying was to help me when he was gone. His courage lived on, and I could
never forget how beautifully he lived his illness.[2]

Mrs. Flanagan found that the one thing that helped was talking openly
and completely about his problem with Sean so that he was fully prepared
for death. She never shied away from that subject, and this, later on, was
her greatest comfort.

Contrast this with the bitter experience of Mrs. Keyser, who wrote of the
tragic death of her son, Kenny. For the six months during which he was
dying, she carried on as usual, pretending that nothing was happening. This
included going through the Christmas season, turning aside his questions,
and avoiding his pleading eyes. Finally, the day came when he lay dead in
the hospital, and, "We left with Kenny's suitcase, concrete evidence of our
bereavement . . . . Instead of being comforted by relatives and friends who
stayed close by, I was impatient and annoyed. I needed to start assimilating
the facts at a deeper level. It could be done only in the solitude which I craved
desperately."[3] She began a process of writing out her thoughts and remembrances, summing them up with this revelation:

Since there has been much pain in the fact that we never knew Kenny's inner-
most feelings about his illness there has been compulsion to dwell in this area
of regret. The wonder of Kenny's choice to maintain a strong image no matter
what received much attention too. I reviewed qualities which seemed to have
added up to this—sensitivity to others, dignity, courage and above all the innate
hope of youth, that jewel-like trust that the bad will be overcome somehow.
Our decision to withhold truth imposed on him the game of pretend—pretend
that death from the disease was not inevitable. This was always the real cul-
prit. Would we ever become reconciled to the only way we had been able to
function—now that there was limitless time to review the restrictive hurt of it?
In time I found peace over one point. During the illness Kenny sometimes
needed to deny to himself. Because the truth had not been inflicted there was
leeway for this temporary escape. What if such small relief had been closed to
him? And yet when he felt up to it he could face what he must have known in
his heart to be true. While Kenny was alive and for a long time afterwards I
couldn't tolerate the idea that he understood what was happening to him.

> I was angered when people intimated, carrying an unreasonable suspicion that they were pushing something on me which I was unready to face.[4]

Part of the reason for their failure to tell Kenny was the obstinacy with which they failed to accept the reality of dying. "A cure will be discovered in time," they thought; "I used to argue with myself, 'It won't happen to us that way. Kenny's case will be different.'" Warmth and comfort come from sharing anything, even grief, and she found relief in finally expressing her pent-up feelings.

The slow balm wrought by time did its work, and recently she picked up the notes she had written at the time, and she now could report:

> Brushing by these pages several years later I am startled. Was all this mine? The pain stands out so raw and naked. The years that have elapsed have also made it possible for me to look now at the wrongness of keeping truth from Kenny and to see what I couldn't bear to see before. Nature protected me from deeper understanding before I was ready for it. And I shudder over that terrible decision even while I am unsure we could do differently if faced with the same dilemma again. One thing remains unchanged as time goes on, the desire to "do" something about the disease that took Kenny's life. It is not possible to remain with quiet acceptance while such a killer is still on the loose. The search for a niche where I can contribute still goes on.[5]

Thus, from the experience of bereaved parents we learn the value of sharing and discussing the true situation with terminally ill young people, letting them know the situation as it really is, not pretending and not shying away from honesty. This is the same as it is so often with adults. Again, however, we are reminded of the sound advice of Kübler-Ross given earlier, that one should not give answers that take away hope, but leave the door open, recognizing, as both she and Hinton pointed out, that generally the terminally ill come to the point where they are ready to talk and pretense is false.

The terminal patient usually finds strength in talking to others, and the survivors find strength in the recognition that time is the great healer. But, time must be allowed to move at its own slow, measured tread; we cannot advance time, nor can we undo it. It will simply come at its own pace.

Also, we see the therapy of writing, or writing out one's thoughts, remorse, and recollections. Perhaps this is one reason why, at any age, the letter of condolence, and the writing to others about the experience, help one face the reality. Therapy has long known that the expression of ideas, the articulating of what we have experienced and hidden within, is helpful. Through articulation we give expression and expose what is within the mind and subconscious depths of the mourner. We bring ideas, tears, guilt feelings, and emotional reactions out into the open. This is helpful.

Our respondents have already shared their experiences at the unexpected, sudden, tragic deaths of children in accidents. To then accept and do what seems in keeping with one's values gives the greatest comfort, and the funeral or memorial service often proves helpful.

One correspondent wrote, "We came away convinced we had done the right thing for our daughter." When each decision was "the correct one," so that each decision made "was easy," it is much easier to live with the experience than to do "what others expect." Remorse is built up when integrity is lacking.

Finally, we should note that dealing with grief over the death of minors is little different from grief in general. The lessons learned in the chapters on death, grief, and dying at the beginning of this book apply here. Youngsters are surprisingly rational and perceptive, and in many instances they can assess and understand their own situations. However, just as one must take into account the uniqueness of the situation, the individual's ability to accept and withstand, as well as endure, a bitter truth when dealing with adults, so must one do likewise with children and adolescents. We have given accounts of two different experiences, but undoubtedly other parents could offer contrasting experiences that seemed to bring forth responses similar to those of Mrs. Flanagan and Mrs. Keyser. The real message of both is: Don't try to protect older children as though they were not prepared for facing reality.

Parents need the assurance that what they did was done for the best, that they did all that they could, and that their emotion-laden sense of guilt at having failed must be laid aside. Until that time they will mourn. All that parents are able to do is use their human wisdom; there are no mandatory requirements to qualify for parenthood: no diploma from school, no psychological degree, and no character training that assures them of being panic-proof in adversity. As human beings they face the trauma and tragedy of life as best they can.

When we must tell healthy children of the death of a friend, relative, or adult, we seem to face a different set of concerns. How are we to break the news to them? Are young children able to conceptualize and understand what death is? Are their emotional natures developed enough to accept the loss of a dearly beloved person without breaking under the emotional shock? How to tell them about Grandpa or Grandma, about baby sister or big brother, about Mr. Wilson who lives next door, and about Mother? These questions bother adults. These are realistic situations parents and guardians must be prepared to handle.

As a parent and a pastor the author has seen and worked with many family situations, and intimately known many children: known their thought processes, their yearnings, their comprehensions, and their worlds of minor tragedies. A sympathetic adult can understand even when he cannot identify, and there are certain conclusions that become obvious. One is that children are not as ignorant of death as we imagine. It always seemed difficult for me to understand that the young Prince Gautama could grow into adulthood without once seeing the sickness, poverty, crime, or death that led him to reject the life of royalty and seek the contemplative life of a monk in order to find the essence of meaning. Even a royal decree, it would seem, could not prevent an experience with loss, privation, suffering, and inner distress.

Every young child knows of the death of small animals, of pets, of flowers and other growing things. Little, materialistic creatures that they are, they know the loss that comes through the breaking, wearing out, and loss of cherished toys. They cry real tears and know deep sorrow at the loss of that which they dearly love. All of this is preparation for the greater losses of life. The words of J. S. Bach's "Meine Seufzer" are useful here: "My sighs, my tears, cannot be measured. Daily melancholy, lamentation! This pain prepares for us the way of death." It does seem that out of the tears and heartache of life, out of the losses and endings with their melancholia and sense of separation, comes the comprehension "that good things end"; and yet, experience leads to the discovery that "life goes on and on." Every little youngster from three or four years onward has some comprehension of such matters. They have been prepared by life's little, terrible, traumatic ordeals in the nursery and home for the endings, losses, privations, and separations of life. With favorite toys, objects, plants, and pets, they come to understand that there is a terrible sense of pain when cherished objects are gone, that tears give vent to their emotions, and that time brings a sense of peace. They do go on, replacing the old with new discoveries and new joys and new attachments. "This pain prepares for us the way of death."

Consequently, children can understand that death has occurred and that it is a loss that will dim in time, and that new meanings will fill the void that has been left. Children should cry over death, just as they cried over many earlier losses in their lives. We should talk with children and, in honesty, try to lead them to comprehend what it means. We should admit that we do not know where or why or how or to what end such things as death relate. But resignedly and philosophically we must accept the fact of life, which is also the fact of death, and communicate our own sense of mature acceptance as well as sorrow. What is not expressed, but seen and found in us, will give them the greater comfort needed. But actions alone are insufficient; there is a need for expressing feelings about death, for attempting to put such emotions into words, and for listening to the child's questions and to his or her formulations of what death might mean.

Children do not have blank minds; they constantly absorb, question, and answer. Through imagination and the association of ideas, children fill their minds with conceptions that would often amaze their more prosaic elders. Lacking experience, they often create a world of "what if." This mental exercise, they have often learned, is one that their parents and other adults refuse to play, so children withdraw and stop asking the "what if" questions of elders. They internalize their own conceptions.

When death of a loved one occurs, children should be encouraged to question and explore their "what ifs." Even the most childish ideas, if they offer hope or "make sense" to the youthful mind, should not be summarily dismissed. Youngsters may pick up the traditional concepts of a Christian heaven and hell, of reward and punishment in the neighborhood from more orthodox friends. These ideas should be expanded and discussed, not dismissed. Denial is easy but insufficient. Alternative ideas may be injected by a thoughtful parent: "Have you thought of this idea . . . ?" The parent may then expand on Socrates' conceptions of death either, as a visit to a place where all the dead abide, where one can meet old friends; or, as a long night's sleep without dreams, wherein nothing appears better than such a restful night's sleep. A parent might recount that in the East many people believe that the dead are born again and live many lives, one after another. Then, there is always the idea of the religious liberal who tells us that the dead live on in us: in our memory, in how they influenced our lives, and in what they have given to us and contributed to life. Such concepts can indeed be helpful and lead our youngsters to a broader kind of acceptance.

Our children do not grow up in an intellectual and social vacuum. They have playmates, classmates, and neighbors, and some of these will have undergone intense religious training, so that they know the answers of an adult church and can repeat like jibberish: "The dead go to heaven and live there with the angels," a friend might say. "There they will play harps of gold . . . ." or they might hear, "If they are good, they go to heaven, but the bad go to hell." The wise parents and guardians must watch for the repetition of such monstrous statements, which may never have been expressed in a religious liberal household, but which have been picked up in the yard, at the street corner, or the classroom or nursery. Because we do not want such thoughts to be secretly harbored by our children, some talk is necessary to encourage children to express ideas about death which they accumulated from outside the home.

Sometimes, of course, the ideas have come within the walls of the home by unmonitored listening to radio or viewing of television. Here one is exposed to all types of ideas, both meritorious and menacing. Certainly, the visual recording of violence and death has been presented to most children at early ages, and it is hard to imagine that some conceptualization about the meaning of such "bang, bang" deaths has not already taken place.

The prevalence of violence and death in the media may cause children to question other aspects of death. Perhaps they fear death, fear their *own* death. "Now I lay me down to sleep, I pray the Lord my soul to keep; if I should die before I wake, I pray the Lord my soul to take." What a terrible idea! Some youngsters dwell upon this fear: they might *not* wake up; "the

Lord" might take their soul! This means their lives. And, it might *hurt* to die! Who wants to go through that?

It is one thing to be confronted by the thought that Aunt Hattie has simply taken a long, dreamless sleep from which she will not awaken, but it is quite a different thing—when you are six or seven, or ten—to think you might not wake up. Waking up should be a certainty in a child's life; just like the coming of night or of Christmas, it will come.

The great African explorer David Livingstone related how he was captured by a lion and in the moment when he was caught in its jaws, he was saved by a companion's perfect shot, which instantly killed the beast. Livingstone could not get over the sense of great calm that had settled over him the moment he felt the hot breath of the lion upon his thighs. Later, he recollected how the small animals captured by the carnivorous beasts in the jungle fight or flee up to a point of hopelessness, and then succumb in complete calm. Many have observed this in the game played by the cat with a mouse; finally, the mouse, realizing it is doomed, becomes completely at ease, is released from its panic, and often sits there quietly, sometimes washing its face with its paws while awaiting the inevitable end. Livingstone theorized, based on his observations of animal death along with his own close brush with death, that nature has provided for our dying with a mechanism that shuts off pain in the final moments, so that we can enter death painlessly. Death itself is painless. Some children can understand this concept, and it may help make their fear of death less of a concern.

Children, as we have said, know the loss of things, know about brokenness and lostness and endings. Upon these concepts we build a broader foundation for death. When we discussed grief, we recognized that grief occurs not only at death, but at many losses: transferring from school, moving from city to city, losing friends, familiar haunts, and old, reliable relationships, facing divorce as well as death. In all such experiences a child's awareness of the grieving process will help explain the dying process.

Our study has indicated that the death of those upon whom one is dependent is the most difficult death to accept, and so it will be with our children. The death of a parent, or a closely allied adult, will be the most traumatic and will require considerable guidance and consolation over a longer period of time. Family patterns are apt to change with the death of a father or mother, so that the security of schedules and routine is lost, bringing new difficulties. Hence we see that one insecurity leads to additional and subsequent insecurities as changes progressively unroll, extending the period of grieving. Just as some relief seems to come, another development often takes place, plunging one back into grief. For example, in many instances the death of a mother necessitates taking the child to a day-care center during the father's working hours; when the father has to travel, the child must be placed in an overnight home; later, a move to a new location may mean giving up the home associated with mommy. Each stage increases the feeling of impermanency of life to the youngster. This must be counter-balanced by other permanent and secure relationships that undergird the child's sense of well-being.

The loss of siblings is secondary to this loss of the person on whom the child depends, according to the Survey on Death and Grief conducted by the author. It may be said that the loss of one's closest contemporaries, beginning with siblings and expanding to classmates and close associates, causes the most pain, following the loss of those upon whom one depends. We need to remember this when a child loses a playmate, sibling, or class-mate. It may seem a remote loss to a parent when it is a classmate or friend, but it can be nearly as meaningful and terrible a loss to a child as would be the loss of a parent. Thus, we should take all such losses seriously and help our youngsters do their mourning and participate in the experience of say-ing goodbye for the final time.

Whatever the occasion, we should not neglect the childish concerns, but must stop and listen to them. We should not brush them aside with a nega-tive "no, no." Rather, help them open the door a crack so that, as their per-ception grows, their comprehension of death will also grow into a mature recollection.

Gautama, the prince who became the Buddha, the Compassionate, dealt with the issue of death and the problem of grieving as a major cornerstone of the religious philosophy that grew up around him, including accounts of his personal relationship to suffering. We have already alluded to his "four sights." As a youth, who had been protected in the castle or palace, he finally came out on a hunting trip with Chanda, his faithful bodyguard. On his way he saw a man wracked in pain, all skin and bone, and the prince asked his servant, "What is wrong with this man?" and received the answer, "This man is ill and in great pain, my Prince." This made Gautama very sad.

The next day he went out from the palace again, and saw an aged man, his back curved, his head bowed, his hands trembling, and he walked with difficulty using two canes. "What's wrong with this man? Is he also ill?" asked the Prince. "Oh no, he is an old man, and that is the way of old age," he was told.

The next day he went out again, and this time he saw a funeral proces-sion. "What is this?" he asked, and Chanda responded, "Death is the way of every man; whether he be king or pauper, death in the end claims all," and again Gautama went back to the palace to ponder what he had seen.

Still later he went out into the marketplace, and amid the clatter and confusion of the merchants with their wares and the purchasers haggling over prices, he saw the serene countenance of a monk, undisturbed by the confusion around him. That was the most compelling and startling sight of all. It led the Prince to flee the palace, put on the yellow robe of a monk, and in time become a seer, one who had found answers that made him the most compassionate of men.[6]

So it is with our children: we may try to shield and protect them from the knowledge and the experience of suffering, but we cannot do so forever. Just as the royal, materialistic, joy-laden life of the Prince was so destroyed by the discovery that "bad things do happen" in life that he rejected the false façade of the life of ease, so does the shielded child react.

We must share with them the realities of life. Suffering is universal and all must share in it. This point is made later when the young Prince had matured into the religious leader known as the Buddha, the Compassionate. A grieving mother came to him saying, "Can you, O Master, relieve my suffering for my son?" The Buddha looked at her compassionately and said, "If you bring me some mustard seed from a house in which neither parent, child, relative, nor servant ever died, I shall bring your child back to life again." The woman went away in search of the mustard seed from such a house. Months later she returned to the Buddha, and to his query she responded, "No, I have not found such a household. Wherever I went I learned that death had gone before me. The dead are many and the living are few." Then the Master, now that her mind was open, taught her the truth that suffering is universal, and a bond that binds all together. Through understanding (contemplation), one finds the way to peace again.

The lesson is simple, and in one way or another, it is told and known in every culture and every land. We, too, are bound by the common experience of mankind.

Some find relief in the knowledge that death is a universal experience, shared by all, and there is basically nothing unique in it for us, only the timing, and the loss of that personal and precious relationship that leaves a void where once there was warmth and love and laughter and consecration.

Some find relief in the processes that we have already discovered are worked out in grief: shock, suffering, and recovery. These take a period of many months before the mourning is completed and the vessel has been refilled with the new wine of new relationships, insights, purposes, and dedication. Then we can go forward. We must help our children to do likewise. They too must find new activity, new security, and new fulfilling relationships. As they are growing, reaching outward, expanding, this should not be so difficult for them as it often is for sedentary adults. Hence, the morose and morbid, unhealthy attitudes of some adults toward death should not be allowed to pervert the more natural instincts of the young.

Some parents revert to traditional modes of thinking and try to give explanations of immortality that imply that one has not really died but "gone to live in another place," usually described as "in heaven" or "with

God." These concepts are perhaps more confusing than the straight fact that a life has ceased as we knew it, but that the spirit and memories we have live on in us and in our love. If questioned further, it is entirely proper to indicate that life may live on in different forms that we do not understand, because we cannot see it.

In all probability, fanciful stories, such as that of the mother living on as a star seen at night, are not helpful. Any such fantasy is confusing and implies an unscientific, or unnatural, explanation of the universe that soon will have to be unlearned by the young child. Myths and fantasies perhaps comfort the adults more than children, because adults thus avoid facing the problem of reality.

Adults tend to have a Santa syndrome by which they tell fanciful myths to children rather than delve into the most difficult task of explaining the realities of life. "Santa stories," false stories about our mortality, or simplified accounts of the very complex Christian doctrines of immortality are really distortions of adult understandings that confuse and debase the child's quest for comprehension. Children have the right, and usually the fortitude, to know.

The further question that must be faced is "what to do" with children and young people at the time of death and of the funeral or memorial service. Children should not be shut out of the big events of life nor shunted aside when they raise questions that arise out of natural curiosity. They strongly identify with the family, the adults about them, those they love, and with the social units to which they belong; and they will react as human beings. They will feel remorse, suffer or mourn, and cry. It is helpful for them to know they belong to "the fellowship of those who bear the mark of pain."[7] To have suffered as well as thrilled to life's pleasures assures them that they will have developed their entire emotional apparatus in its full range. Often adults wish to spare children pain, and often they wish they could absorb the anguish felt by the youngster; but we all know that cannot be. But as they share grief, they can know that they share a common sorrow, each understanding how the other feels, and in that sorrow all can be drawn close to one another. This sharing is solace for each during the long months of mourning, when one can aid the other.

Children should never be shut out of the family circle at the moment of crisis, for then the more terrible feeling of rejection may set in, and in the withdrawal that develops, more dangerous psychic damage is done to youngsters.

Should they be included in the funeral or memorial service? The answer here probably depends upon three factors: their age and ability to comprehend what is involved; their experience at adult functions and ability to respond or behave properly; and their interest in attending without a sense of coercion. Many youngsters are highly dramatic and would like to be a part of such traumatic experiences. The research project undertaken as preparatory to this study indicated that, particularly in memorial services, children fit in easily and often gain a great deal from the content as well as from the sense of fellowship of sorrow and appreciation shared together.

Hence, aware that children know how to accept loss and have much experience in doing so, we can assume they can, in Huxley's terms, "grieve their grief out," and then go about the process of living as healthier individuals. Knowing also that children have thought about death and perhaps discussed it with others having a different frame of reference and quite different values, they need the support of their family's values and explanations. Otherwise, they are turned loose into a weird world of monstrous imaginations and fantasies far worse than any reality can be. We will have done much to share our value system with them and to have put to rest the awful imaginings of unanswered and unspoken questions locked in the recesses of the mind.

Confidently, hand in hand, the wise adult leads the child into a growing appreciation of the wonders of life that includes its unknown destiny in death.

9

Modern Issues concerning Death

A correspondent wrote:

I wondered how I would react when I would have to go through seeing the death of a loved one. Would I resort back to my fundamentalist teaching of a God who sees suffering, knows about it, but has reasons for allowing it? For three years I watched my mother suffer a horrible, lingering death. Her peace of mind was with this personal, caring God of hers. She would call me on the phone and say she was so weak and couldn't speak at times and suffered a loss of memory. Eventually she didn't know anyone, couldn't speak, and we were forced to put her in a nursing home. She looked like a skeleton. For eight days she lay without food or water, and I literally saw her rot before my eyes. Her God did not even care enough to give her knowledge of him.

I'm grateful for Unitarianism because I didn't feel this ugly, bitterness I felt when I was taught a loving God knows my hurts and needs. As I watched during the last hours—her eyes were staring and her mouth was opened and gulping away—I thought of the people who believe in mercy killing and how right they are. Until then, I didn't think there was any harm in any religion. However, when I see the guilt that one encounters when one cannot "buy" the fundamentalist point of view and the unnecessary suffering because of their viewpoint against "mercy killing," I realize the need for spreading "the word of Unitarianism."

This right to die does not need qualifying. Our right to live is modified by life and laws from the moment of our conception—abortion laws, hospital rules, parental influence, school rules, traffic

98

laws, job rules. And it is not necessary to qualify this right in our Constitution. It should be so with the right to die.

If you have ANY doubts about the need for this constitutional right, I beg of you go spend two or three hours with my eighty-six-year-old father in the Missoula General Hospital. You may not realize it at first (for it is sometimes impossible, and ALWAYS extremely difficult for him to speak, and it is nearly impossible for him to see and to hear, and it is now impossible for him to even stand—it has been difficult for him to walk for the past three years, and he has fallen scores of times before now—and it is impossible for him to move to TRY to get comfortable in bed without help—which, due to his handicaps, is most often impossible), but his mind is still working well most of the time so he is very much aware of his miseries. I have not mentioned all his physical troubles. Not one of them is temporary. The only relief for this sensitive and compassionate man can come with death. Yet this GOOD, decent law-abiding man is sentenced to punishment worse than that meted out to hardened criminals, for he has no constitutional right to death!

If you still doubt the need for this right, visit a rest home for a day. Now try to imagine yourself or your mother or father or other loved one in the place of my father or some of these most hopeless and help-less condemned innocents.

The right to a dignified death should be a constitutional right!

If that right had been available to my father, how different his final time (weeks, months, years?) could have been. When the X-rays showed the broken hip, he could have asked for and received a medication to ease him into a final sleep, and he would have been spared all the mis-ery he will now endure. And those of us who love him could have remem-bered him living his last years in some measure of peace and comfort, instead of suffering with him through a prolonged and entirely useless degradation of hopelessness, frustration, and pain.

Who would have been hurt had my father been granted the right to death when he was ready? And he was surely ready. He has been ready for the last three years of increasing disability and increasing loss of ability to communicate.

One cannot, with honesty, say that to allow him to die with medi-cated ease is tampering any more with life than to medicate people and operate on them to allow them to LIVE! It is only the other side of the same coin.[1]

In a sense, there are no modern issues in death, only modern pressures raised by the advances in technology and the complexity of our civilization, compounded by the pluralistic nature of the ethico-social confusion of the times.

An informed, or sensible, view of death raises major issues, including euthanasia, suicide, eugenics, tissue/bone/organ transplants, and ecology. The advanced technological developments that touch these and other related fields may lead into further ramifications that create ethical, humane, economic, and moral dilemmas for the sensitive person in the modern world. They also result in legal and medical problems with which the individual is ill prepared to deal. Indeed, neither the legal nor medical profession can solve these issues, nor is there a heritage of laws and precedents that take into account the changing status that modern technology has forced upon us. Yet life is a living, breathing, emotional experience with which individuals must cope, from day to day and issue to issue. The trauma of anxiety created by the confusion and indecisiveness of modern collective consciousness forces the individual into a tenuous dilemma. The question of what is humane and ethically desirable creates additional problems for the survivor or terminal patient.

Most noticeable among such questions is that of euthanasia, in which the question of mercy death is raised. Since the most primitive of times, the question of whether a person should be allowed to die quietly and peaceably, or be forced to live a prolonged life of suffering has created a dilemma. Today it is complicated by the so-called heroic measures, by which machines (with no will and no heroism) take over the perfunctory task of operating the organs of the human body that no longer can function voluntarily.

Today machines may be set in motion that will perform bodily functions such as compressing the diaphragm to induce breathing; stimulating the heartbeat so that circulation is maintained; providing intravenous feeding so that nourishment is supplied; and then draining the bladder and bowels so that the elimination processes take place. No will is required, no heroic fighting to live on by the patient is necessary, no conscious sense of joy or pain manifests a sense of life, and the human body is turned into a machine as fully as the technological apparatus that has taken over the life functions. Once this process is set in motion, a horrible dilemma is created—who now dares to unplug the machines?

In the 1975 case of Karen Ann Quinlan the New Jersey Court ruled that the decision was not that of the family or relatives, but belonged to the medical doctors under Court supervision; however, the state's Supreme Court upheld the right of the parents to change doctors and hospitals. Once the responsibility is shifted from the family, where compassion, love, and a sense of human values exist, to the medical profession, subject to determination of laws, precedents, and the ever-imminent malpractice suit for dereliction of duties or faulty decisions, decisive action is effectively immobilized. As both

BYBLUS, long regarded as man's earliest settled town, shows 7,000 year old fetal burials. Note egg shaped remains. See page 94. Pictures taken on location by the author, 1963.

7,000 year old funerary remains

EGYPT - Mummy cases in likeness of deceased royalty to attract the "ka." These have been removed from Tutankhamon's tomb in the Valley of the Kings to the National Museum, Cairo. Three of the four Canopic Jars also bear likeness for proper "ka" (the fourth was on tour.) Photos by the author. See pp. 94 - 97.

Extravagance of Funerary Arrangements will be Noted

JERICHO MAN - cave burial and reconstructed skull, Kathleen Kenyon, photos taken on location by author, 1963, Jericho and Amman, Jordan, see page 94.

7,000 year old funerary remains

EGYPT - Valley of the King walls in tombs were beautifully decorated with depictions of life during the reign of the Pharaoh. Photos by the author. See pp. 95 ff.

The Hieroglyphics are 3300 years old

EGYPT, in Valley of the Kings, the Pharaohs were buried prior to 1100 B.C. (Nineteenth Dynasty). Tutankhamon's tomb was discovered in the twentieth century, A.D. Photos taken on location by the author. See pp. 95 ff.

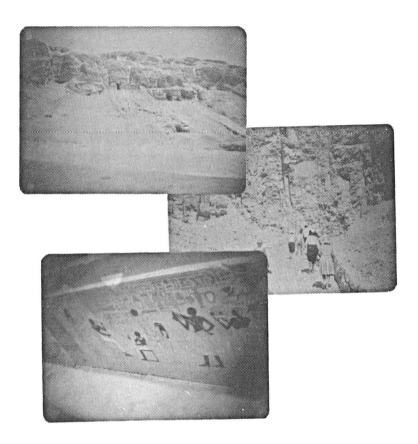

Tombs cut out of stone 3400 - 1100 B.C. After 1100 stone tombs (pyramids) were built above ground.

Dr. Hinton and Dr. Gorer pointed out in other examples, doctors, conditioned by long training to the pursuit of life-saving procedures, are ill prepared to surrender life. By long training, they are conditioned to see this as an admission of professional failure. Hence, they fall back on the canard that "Where there's life, there's hope," even after the brain is dead and the heart is no longer capable of initiating a heartbeat. In addition, the Hippocratic oath requires doctors to persevere for the preservation of life, and a strict or narrow construction of its words seemingly forbids assisting the ending of life.

Of course there is value in not rushing too hurriedly into any human endeavor, including death. Death is too final. How many times have persons died just before a medical breakthrough occurred that would have saved their lives! People often have hovered at the brink of death and made a total and complete recovery to radiant health, including active old age for a series of active years.

Consequently, one should not rule out the possibility that new medication, new techniques, new insights may be brought to bear that assist the patient to turn the corner. Norman Cousins related how in 1960, acutely ill in the hospital, one doctor wrote on his chart, "I'm afraid we are going to lose Mr. Cousins." He could have given up, but did not. He was determined to live, and to pull himself through, and that story is the basis of his latest book, *The Anatomy of an Illness.*

In addition, persons are cautioned to be sure within their own minds that they prefer euthanasia before a too hasty consent. One of the fears that has long delayed the public approval of euthanasia has been the possibility of persons proposing it to relatives or friends for selfish or vindictive reasons. This matter has not been helped by the fact that in two of the early cases in which the court approved the removal of heroic methods (as in the Karen Ann Quinlan case), death did not result but the body, without a conscious operating mind, continued to live without extra-life support systems. She continues to live in her quiescent state five years later. If hasty or faulty miscalculations occur in instances where the action is taken out of love, there remains need for careful monitoring of the decision-making process involved. It may be unfortunate that two prominent, media-disclosed cases seem in retrospect to be premature, because it will support the arguments of those who say all euthanasia cases are suspect. Many suffering persons know this is not so, and that there is suffering beyond endurance that should be terminated.

For these true sufferers, it may be fortunate indeed that there are many doctors who act as does Robert Ray McGee, M.D., of Clarksdale, Mississippi, but few are courageous enough to publicly admit it, as he did.

> I've pulled the plug on quite a few respirators without waiting for approval from the gentlemen of the bar. I simply told the patient's family: "She (or he)

is dead. The respirator is keeping some body functions going, but I think we should turn it off and let nature take its course." No family has ever disagreed. They haven't worried about whether I was breaking some law, and I haven't worried either.

Am I playing God? Certainly not, I'm just giving God the opportunity to play god. If he wants, he has the power to work miracles, and he can do so after I've pulled the plug. So far it hasn't happened — meaning, I figure, that he has agreed with my action.[2]

Some would question whether or not Dr. McGee is right. We have elsewhere reported on the situation concerning the Pritchards in upstate New York. Mrs. Pritchard, looking at the body of her husband kept artificially alive by such mechanical means for two weeks while in a coma, exclaimed, "We wouldn't do this to a dog." The issue is should we do it to a human? Why cannot any doctor, like this honest man, "pull the plug" when he sees that life no longer really exists, even though certain bodily functions are maintained mechanically? This is what is called passive euthanasia, the acceptance of the fact of death, and ceasing the mechanical (falsely called heroic) measures to maintain certain bodily functions.

One is sometimes constrained to wonder whether such meaningless prolongations of animated death are maintained for economic benefit to the hospital, medical support personnel, and apparatus companies. A usual hospital response is, "It does not cost the family anything; we have arranged for the bills to be paid by the government." Is this a case of "milking the government?" This question is rarely asked, because it seems too delicate a matter to raise publicly; yet, it is often thought in private. Honesty in this matter is required because, medically, theologically, and socially, there is no useful purpose achieved by animated death — we cannot say animated life for it is not a living entity at such a time, nor is it apt to become such again.

Since many now see the need to resist the prolonged use of medical support systems, it is hoped that legal progress can be made to allow the "pulling of the plug," as it has come to be called. If so, it would be considered a legal victory by the proponents of euthanasia. The Living Will of the Euthanasia Society is considered by many to be far-sighted and courageous in merely stating this is one's wish. This Living Will reads:

TO MY FAMILY, MY PHYSICIAN, MY CLERGYMAN, MY LAWYER —
If the time comes when I can no longer take part in decisions for my own future, let this statement stand as the testament of my wishes:

If there is no reasonable expectation of my recovery from physical or mental or spiritual disability, I, _____ request that I be allowed to die and not be kept alive by artificial means or heroic measures. Death is as much a reality as birth, growth, maturity and old age — it is one certainty. I do not fear death as much as I fear the indignity of deterioration, dependence and hopeless pain. I ask that drugs be mercifully administered to me for terminal suffering even if they hasten the moment of death.

This request is made while I am in good health and spirits. Although this document is not legally binding, you who care for me will, I hope, feel morally bound to follow its mandates. I recognize that it places a heavy burden of responsibility upon you, and it is with the intention of sharing that responsibility and of mitigating any feelings of guilt that this statement is made.[3]

The more basic question of active euthanasia is considered in this "living will." Active euthanasia involves the opportunity of mercy death, or mercy killing, rather than merely the withholding of artificial life support. This is as different as a bath in lukewarm water is in contrast to a dip in an icy lake: a chilling, challenging, dashing confrontation with the question of undesirable life or preferable death, of death with dignity or life with suffering. How to decide? When to decide? Why decide? Who should decide? Who will administer the lethal drug?

A courageous, one woman's fight has been waged by one of my correspondents in Montana for many years to secure a "Death with Dignity Amendment" to various state constitutions; some of her thoughts are presented in the opening letter to this chapter.[4]

A wire service news story was carried in many newspapers across the country in 1972 concerning her "One Woman's Crusade"—long before the increased public discussion of euthanasia, the right to die in dignity, and the "pull the plug" controversy had propelled the issue into national consciousness. That article from Helena, Montana, reads:

Poignantly tracing the lingering death of her eighty-six-year-old father, a housewife pleaded with a committee to provide in a new state constitution the right to die.

"I maintain that to give to people facing certain death . . . the right to die quickly, easily and in peace when they want to do so, is being compassionate, intelligent and humane," Joyce M. Franks of Alberton told a hushed audience Thursday in the Senate chambers. "And I affirm that it is an act that God, who gave us all life, would approve of."

Mrs. Franks, the mother of two children, described her father's suffering to the Bill of Rights Committee at the Montana Constitutional Convention.

After her father broke a hip, his doctor described the necessary operation. "Dad asked me if the doctor would please give him something to put him to sleep right then," said Mrs. Franks, but she did not ask the doctor to do so.

As his health deteriorated, she related, her father made the request again.

"My father had been a farmer, and he had given merciful death to animals who had been pets and companions," Mrs. Franks said, sobbing. "He could not stand to see them suffer prolonged and agonizing death when they were severely mutilated or dying of illness.

"He was compassionate and merciful. He asked for the same mercy for himself.

"For eight weeks he died, little-by-little, minute-by-minute, day-by-day," Mrs. Franks said.

"He was just denied a release from the suffering and torture which he knew, and we knew, and the doctor knew he faced.

"He died in December.

"Have you wiped the eyes that will not close and that look as though they had never closed in over eighty-five years since they opened on the world?" Mrs. Franks asked.

"Have you struggled with your own breathing, trying unconsciously to help his labored gasps which came nearly as fast as your own pulse beats?

"Have you wiped the thick, choking mucus out of the mouth that filled again nearly as fast as you cleansed it?

"And have you, then, rebelled at a system where this barbaric suffering was called necessary because unfeeling and unimaginative men declare that God willed it?"

Mrs. Franks said it was inconsistent to call it merciful to kill mortally wounded animals but not humans.

"Do you call veterinarians murderers?" she asked.

Mrs. Franks proposed constitutional language saying, that "every citizen be allowed to choose the manner in which he dies."

"The legislature would have to outline specific detail, if the proposal were adopted," Mrs. Franks said.

She advocated a proposal that would guarantee an individual's right to determine the manner of his death, barring accidents. "Moreover, it should be legal for a person to receive a quick, medicated death if he desired," she said.

Mrs. Franks said a constitutional proposal introduced by Robert L. Kelleher (D-Billings) does not go far enough. It says: "The incurably ill have the right not to be kept alive by extraordinary means." This stopped short of the active euthanasia she proposed.

One committee member asked if enacting such a provision would not put the patient's family and doctor into a position of "playing God."

"I would have been glad to play God for my father," she said.

Mrs. Franks has written letters to delegates and editors of Montana newspapers, polled doctors, and spearheaded a move for the right to die with dignity.

The committee took no action but stated it would consider her suggestions later.

Three years later, she was still active in her effort, appearing before many state legislatures, a circuit rider reminiscent of Dorothea Dix's crusade for better treatment of the mentally ill a century ago. She confided in a letter to this author that the bill was being sponsored again in the Montana legislature, but she wrote,

> Unfortunately, one of the Senators on the health committee is a neurologist with whom I talked two years ago. He wants the right for doctors to "pull the plug," but he is vehemently opposed to giving me the right to escape unwanted and unnecessary suffering (if I choose) by a medicated death. But, at least it will get the proposals taken out and looked at again, and that is something.
>
> I had hoped to have some concrete provisions written by the insurance industry, but haven't been working hard enough. Still have hopes, but it might be too late for this legislature session coming up. However, on good authority, the insurance industry does not see that legislation for either positive or passive euthanasia will have much influence on the industry. So, that is helpful.
>
> I wrote to all the medical schools. Many of them answered and many of those said they have started new programs to deal with ethical questions like euthanasia. And, quite obviously, there is a lot of programming on TV, articles in the newspapers and magazines. So, people are thinking at least.

So she marks the continuing struggle for the right to die in dignity. In February 1975 she wrote again.

> Thought you'd be interested in the fate of my bill to let people decide for themselves how they wanted to die when the time came. It got four favorable votes, four abstentions and eight against. Much better than two years ago . . . I'm going to try and get some church support before next session! Too much Right-to-Life and Catholic opposition . . .

So the struggle runs on. There is church support. The Good Death Fellowship was started by the First Unitarian Church of Denver in January 1974, spurred on by the Reverend Richard Henry, minister. As reported on page one of the *Unitarian Universalist World,* its scope was explained thus:

> Passive euthanasia is now used by some doctors although it is illegal, as a merciful means of easing patients into death when the doctor sees nothing ahead for them but continued pain and misery.
>
> Much of the impetus for the Good Death Fellowship and its program resulted from the efforts of Mrs. Elsie Garman, an eighty-six-year-old Denver widow.
>
> Noting the progress with birth control, Mrs. Garman called for "another pill," which would give pain-ridden old people "a good death." Unlike many advocates of euthanasia, Mrs. Garman prefers to administer the lethal dose herself, to spare the family and the doctor the guilt for terminating a human life.
>
> Good Death Fellowship is a non-profit educational organization with dues of $4 per year. The address is 853 Ogden Street, #5, Denver, Colo., 80218."

It is not just Unitarian Universalists that are concerned. Other church people speak out also, although they are largely ignored by the media that seemingly prefer to give news coverage primarily to the opposition to progressive measures. The large, middle of the road, United Church of Christ debated a significant and far-reaching "Right to Die" resolution at its Ninth General Synod in St. Louis, Missouri, June 22–26, 1973. This resolution said in part:

"We believe there comes a time in the course of an irreversible terminal illness when, in the interest of love, mercy and compassion, those who are caring for the patient should say 'Enough'; we do not believe the continuance of mere human existence is either morally defensible or socially desirable or is God's will.

"Christian teaching does not require that mere physical existence in itself be preserved in all instances. We are unable to reach a conclusion about the issue of actively intervening to end a life in these circumstances but realize it is none the less a real and pressing dilemma for those faced with this decision."

The resolution also states clearly that "nothing in Jewish or Christian traditions presumes that a physician has a mandate to impose his or her wishes and skills upon patients for the sake of prolonging the length of their dying . . . ."

This forthright resolution ends with the following "Challenge" that all will do well to heed inasmuch as new conditions face all of us:

"The progress of medical technology has developed new possibilities and new problems in the care and perpetuation of human bodies. New conditions inevitably raise new ethical and religious questions. They call for fresh deliberations and possibly new answers.

"We call upon the members in the United Church of Christ to recognize the new problems, consider the principles set forth above, and to seek to determine, with tolerance and prayer, the Will of God in today's world. We encourage the Church, pastors and lay persons, to stand with those who face these decisions."

A prominent Episcopal theological professor and cleric who has written much on the medical ethical dilemmas of our day discusses the ethical issues in his foreword to the Beacon Press book, *Death of a Man*. Dr. Joseph Fletcher said:

> Modern medicine has succeeded so well at resuscitating patients whose lives a decade or two ago would have been over and finished, and at artificially supported human functions like breathing and heartbeat long after they have come to an end spontaneously, that we now find ourselves crossing the line from prolonging their living to actually prolonging their dying. When do we stop the intravenous fluids and remove the nasal and tracheal tubes and turn off the respirators? It's a fallacy, an irrational hang-up, to feel that an increase

or stubborn lengthening of life in and of itself is a good thing—just increasing the quantity of life regardless of its quality.

The popular notion is that elective death is morally all right if you elect to stop fighting it off but morally wrong if you elect to facilitate it. This shifts the focus from a positive reasonable decision to terminate hopeless suffering to a negative or passive acceptance of death that comes on its own terms, without further struggle.

Indiscriminate "life saving" by the staff of intensive care units can be cruel and inhuman. But to dampen down the compulsive undiscriminating life saver only meets a part of the whole problem. It is nothing more than indirect euthanasia, of the living will variety. In fact, it is at most a sort of grudging or half-baked sympathy for the dying—what the Victorian poet Arthur Clough expressed:

> "Though shalt not kill, yet need not strive
> Officiously to keep alive."

A recent Harris poll found that 62 percent of the public believed that a terminal patient ought to be allowed to die, and only 28 percent would say it is wrong to stop treatment. On the other hand, although 53 percent opposed direct euthanasia, 37 percent favored it—an impressively large, and enlarged, number.[5]

With the imposing support from religious quarters, one is tempted to ask, "Then, why the opposition?" The answer often lies in religious beliefs. The opening letters of this chapter give such an explanation popularly held by many.

Euthanasia may now be seen in the dual light of either passive or active: permitting a person to die without "heroic," i.e., mechanical means of sustaining life, which is the passive method, or permitting mercy killing, which is the active method. Should doctors help such patients as those who, in giving up hope for a life with dignity, request help from the physician in speeding their end? Should people with only the barest life spark, the feeblest energy, the immobility of paralyses, the meaningless, purposeless, unbearable pain and suffering be allowed to end it all or have others end it for them?

Many do elect to end it all when the time comes, and in moments of good health, sobriety, and rationality, make such a decision. One clear explanation of the thinking in this regard was given in a letter to the Editor in the *New York Times* issue of April 26, 1976, in which "X. Y. Z." responded to a news account with this letter:

Your April 18 issue carried a news story on "Gramp," an old man who died incontinent and hopelessly senile; yet his family insists that he "died with dignity" because he "died on his terms." I completely disagree. No one who is senile dies on his own terms. Death during senility is not death with dignity.

My wife and I, some years ago and while we were both sound in mind and body, decided that we would not live to be a burden to ourselves and to those who loved us but would commit suicide when we could no longer live a life useful to others. I naturally expected to have to take action first, because I was six years older and women live on an average of about five years longer than men.

But she got cancer, which spread to an inoperable part. I told her. Despite pain, she dictated during the last months of her life for a friend who was interested in oral history her life story as the daughter of poor immigrants who made an importantly useful life. When that was done, she committed suicide by taking pills with my full consent and cooperation. (Our children were her heirs, not me.)

I was proud of her in death as well as in life. She left her eyes to the eye bank and her body for medical research. I have provided for the same disposition of my body.

Everything I have seen in old-folks' homes, or learned from friends who have a senile parent, convinces me that what she did, and what I intend to do when I can no longer live usefully without being a burden to myself and others, was right. Death by suicide, provided it is not a sudden decision based on pain or disappointment but is carrying out a decision arrived at before the stress of pain or uselessness, is death with dignity. Death after sliding into senility is not.

These folks made a rational decision not to become a burden on others, and she administered death by her own hand, as he plans to in time. Sometimes it is not handled with such serenity or ease, and there are lingering problems of guilt, culpability, or possible participation that would be interpreted by the law as being an accessory to the taking of life.

Many cases are reported each year of older couples who make "suicide pacts," when the one, unable to see the continued suffering of the other, administers a merciful death and then commits suicide rather than face the ordeal of a trial. They know they persuasively cannot articulate in court the reasons that in their heart they know to be right. They have little chance to justify themselves legally the way present laws are constructed, but they feel they are morally justified, and they therefore inflict a penalty of death upon themselves.

Should laws be changed, and if so, how? Can the mutual support and guidance of voluntary societies such as the Euthanasia Education Fund in the United States, the Euthanasia Society in Great Britain, and local groups such as Denver's Good Death Fellowship help those persons facing the dilemma of mercy killing?

Another issue sometimes closely related to euthanasia is that of suicide. As indicated, many desire to take their own lives rather than endure the meaningless suffering and slow endurance of deteriorating death. Some, knowing the end is merely slowed in its approach, take their own lives rather than ask family or physician to do so. "Despondency over poor health," the reports generally indicate.

In like manner others come to feel, for a variety of reasons all leading to despondency, that life is not worth living and decide to end their existence.

There are a number of studies of suicide that are helpful in exploring this field. Many feel isolated from the mainstreams of life; some live with a strong sense of loneliness; some know a purposeless and meaningless existence; some have guilt feelings that hound them to the grave; some have strong resentments and wish to make others suffer; some are driven to death by the unkindness and cruelty inflicted on them by others.

Traditional Christian practices have denied the rites of the church to suicides and, hence, the blessings of religion to them and the comfort of religion to their survivors. Religious liberals look upon this as a further indignity and accept death by suicide as they would any other. All Unitarian Universalist ministers and any such church or fellowship would be available to provide the solace and understanding that can come through religious ministrations available in all such circumstances.

Another issue somewhat allied to euthanasia in certain circumstances is eugenics. In discussing euthanasia we did not deal with the question of prolonging the life of the birth-deformed and birth-defective infant who never can become a functioning, rational, viable human being. Should extreme steps be taken to save such defective babies? There are many instances in which parents, whose first thought was to not save the deformed child, subsequently come to love the child and find a genuine sense of purpose and meaning in caring for the helpless human. Often value comes through serving a dependent, loving creature; yet in spite of these instances, eugenics raises the question of the quality of life, that a person be physically, mentally, and morally able to cope and function at a meaningful, pragmatic level of existence. Certainly, as more and more deformed, retarded, and physically incapacitated infants are preserved, society has an increasing burden of caring and managing institutions to care for such persons. With the world population growth, the obvious need for the redistribution of the earth's produce and products so that both the developed and developing nations have fair shares, there is an increasing pressure for greater efficiency in managing the world's food, space, and energy.

Since it is often charged that eugenics tends to be heartless – just as many make this charge regarding mercy killings – many feel that eugenics should not be advanced. Fearful of all intellectual solutions, and suspicious of all academically inspired programs, their absolute standard becomes the "right to life." More important is Albert Schweitzer's "Reverence for Life," which rests on the principle, "I am life that wills to live in the midst of life that wills to live." The will to live is important in questions regarding the quality of life.

Another area of increasing concern today, that of abortion, is being turned by the "Right to Life" movement into a question of life or death for a fetus, as though it were a viable human life. Legal definitions, medical criteria, and social thinking, as well as religious doctrine, all enter into the thinking on these matters.

Fetuses are not buried or given funeral or memorial services, although in some hospitals they are given the last rites of the Roman Catholic Church.

A question seldom faced by the liberal religious clergyman is that of the disposition of detached member portions of the body, such as a severed arm, leg, hand, foot, finger, or toe. Physicians tell me that some clergy conduct services for dismembered appendages of the body. This seems unnecessary as most hospitals have sanitary means available to them for the disposal of skeletal parts.

Medical science has long been concerned over the issue of bodies for research and study purposes, first to learn the workings of the human body, and then after progress was made, for the teaching of medical students. For many centuries the existence of veins, capillaries, and the diversified tissues, organs, nerve cells, and muscles were unknown. Servetus, the Unitarian Reformation leader, who was also a physician, drew a diagram of the concept of the circulation of the blood in 1540, but since the dissection and internal examination of the body was not then practiced, he did not take into account the veins, arteries, and heart mechanism. His was a first step along a long road that was not completed until after Andrea Vesalius published his treatise on the cutting of the human body in 1543. This monumental breakthrough made possible William Harvey's description of the circulation of the blood.

Still there was a lack of anatomical material, due to the strict religious taboos regarding the cutting of the dead human body, and the untold centuries of superstitions, fears of mysticism, and demonology, which stood in the way of those who wished to examine cadavers in order to learn how to administer to the sick and suffering. Even after the monumental works of Vesalius and Harvey there continued to be a lack of anatomical properties. As a result, and as the pressure for research and study built up, an eerie cult of "Resurrectionists" arose who would steal recently deceased bodies and sell them to reputable experimental physicians and surgeons. Out of this nefarious practice developed the magnificent discoveries of modern medicine.[6]

Gradually resistance to dissection ceased in Christian quarters, but it was not until 1747 that Prospero Lambertini, later Pope Benedict XIV, expressed the official attitude of the Catholic Church as favoring the practice for the advance of science. Today Canon Law prohibits the crime of desecrating graves and the theft of bodies but follows Lambertini in not opposing the dissection of the human body for medical ends. This was set forth in 1952 by Pope Pius XII as "In the domain of . . . science it is an obvious law that the application of new methods to living men must be preceded by research on cadavers or the model study and experimentation on animals."[7]

Thus the major religious restriction was at long last lifted from the use of the cadaver for research following death. However, the existence of sufficient cadavers for such study has always been inadequate, in spite of false rumors to the contrary. A few years ago, Dr. Melvin Knisely reported that the cadaver supply was barely enough in thirteen medical schools and insufficient in eleven others that he surveyed. He listed the following reasons as contributing to the shortage: Social Security laws, burial by charitable organizations, burial benefits of labor unions, increase of burial insurance, and lax laws or the lax administration of anatomy laws that make available to medical schools unclaimed bodies. Chiefly, however, is the lack of education and understanding of the need for such bodies, of the beneficial results to humanity, and of the advances in research and medical skills that result. The natural repugnance of religious piety preys upon all these reasons.[8]

Consequently, many persons today are beginning to consider the donation of the body to science and humanity. The accounts given elsewhere in this study, drawn upon the experience of the Demonstrators Association in Illinois and the account of Mrs. Harris who "gave herself away," illustrate the opportunity and procedures.[9]

Information on methods of donating are easily secured through the anatomy department of the nearest medical school, through your local physician, or through the organ and tissue banks maintained at most major medical facilities or general hospitals.

Many medical schools maintain consecrated ground, usually in a garden, in which, following cremation, the ashes of unclaimed cadavers are scattered. Such facilities are consecrated by clergymen of the major faiths. We have included above an account of the moving experience of the Reverend Francis Anderson[10] upon participating in the memorial service for such ashes in the grounds set aside by greater Boston medical schools.

Upon donating a cadaver to a medical school the next of kin usually fills out a form in which he or she indicates whether he or she wishes to be informed when the cadaver is cremated or not, and if he/she wishes to collect the ashes for personal disposal or to have the institution follow its own established procedure, which is always thoughtful and carried forward with dignity.

Families frequently hold a memorial service at the time of the death and announce that the body has been donated to science and humanity and so continues after death to serve constructive ends.

For many years now there have been bodily transplants of important organs. Most dramatic have been the successful transplants of the cornea of the human eye, restoring sight to the blind, of kidney transplants, and heart transplants. These donations perhaps adequately indicate the value of the human contributions that continue after death. In addition, a wealth of other tissues, organs, and bones may be transplanted, and many medical facilities maintain transplant banks where, under optimum conditions, various organs are preserved or made available for transplants. Many donors carry cards indicating their desire that organs be transplanted. Sometimes, since most people die in hospitals, the sensible arrangement is that whatever organs that hospital is prepared to use be donated. In my stepmother's case, the hospital in question had an ear disc transplant program and cooperated with the Institute for Sight Restoration, Inc., in New York City, so these two tissues were used.[11]

Since most deaths now have autopsies, it is a simple procedure for transplants to be made at that time or placed in a bank for future use. My family's experience just referred to was a highly comforting aftermath of a violent death by automobile accident and brought a measure of comfort and a sense of practical immortality for a dearly beloved person who restored sight and hearing to unnamed persons who continued to live more fulfilling lives.

In Appendix B will be found forms used by specific institutions that are samples any individual may use. These are basically similar to others and may be helpful in preparing for decisions regarding these issues.[12] These are merely offered as specimens, since each person is best advised to consult the nearest available medical institution.

The next issue to consider is made possible for the first time by modern technology. Persons since the dawn of written history imagined the day when they would return from the dead to see how their descendants had carried on and thus rejoin the earthly life again. From time to time one has read accounts of frozen animals preserved through eons of time. One such popular tale of the 1930s was of the discovery of the frozen body of a prehistoric mammoth, perfectly preserved in a Siberian glacier. It deteriorated rapidly after exposure to the air but, safe in its icy tomb, had withstood the ages since the glaciers descended.

Clarence Birdseye had discovered the quick-freeze method for the preservation of vegetables and flesh, changing the packaging and eating habits of modern man. He had demonstrated that rapid freezing prevented the breakdown of the cellular structure and the tendency for rancidity to develop. Was there something here for the preservation of the body? Some began to ask this question, and a new science of cryonics developed. Deep-frozen flesh should be maintained at a level of zero degree Fahrenheit ($-17°$ Centigrade) or lower until thawed.

By the late 1940s blood was stored for medical purposes by freezing. Experiments showed that fully 85 percent of all blood cells survived quick freeze, and the blood is fully usable upon thawing. In Europe various additional experiments with animals were carried forward: rodents, mice, embryos, a rabbit, and then, in Japan, a cat's brain were frozen and revitalized.

Successful experimentation of this type indicated that it was possible to freeze and then restore life to the living organism. The Russian report on experimentation with rabbits stated: "Post cooling could possibly prolong the period between the cessation of vital activity and loss of vitality, and so . . . increase the probability of body re-animation . . . after death."[13]

In the United States human and animal semen has been frozen in liquid nitrogen at 321 degrees below zero Fahrenheit and then used successfully. Cattle by the millions are so raised from implanted semen, and "test tube" babies are not unknown among humans today.

But this only suggests, it does not prove, the possibility of the deep freeze of human beings for restoration at a later time. According to cryobiologist, Dr. J. K. Sherman of the University of Arkansas School of Medicine,

"The dramatic, empirically derived success in banking spermatozoa for the animal-breeding industry . . . has been economically rewarding, but with the realization of this reward, research has receded to token interest.

"Unlike banks for frozen human spermatozoa, blood, and tissue culture cells, however, human body banks have not been qualified as 'proven.' That is to say, no frozen human body from such a bank has been thawed for evaluation of the functional and structural integrity of its cells and for comparison of its condition after thawing with that at the time of freezing."[14]

However, there are pioneering spirits who believe nothing along this line is impossible. Many regional organizations have been formed for the postmortal freezing of human bodies, and several have been so stored and are carefully preserved in deep freeze for eventual thawing when the time seems ripe to overcome the disease from which they died.

David Hendin, who has been the Science Editor of the Newspaper Enterprise Association (NEA), has included a chapter on these organizations in his book already referred to, *Death as a Fact of Life*. The first and most complete study of this subject is by Dr. Robert C. W. Ettinger, and his book is referred to as "the Bible of Cryonics" by those active in the field. He states: "Most of us now living have a chance for personal, physical immortality . . . . At very low temperatures it is possible, right now, to preserve dead people with essentially no deterioration, indefinitely . . . . If civilization endures, medical science should eventually be able to repair almost any damage to the human body, including freezing damage and senile debility or other causes of death."[15]

Cryonic believers look for a network of societies that will freeze such bodies. Today, these societies have arrangements whereby a life insurance policy of $10,000 is taken out on members, the income from which is used to cover the cost of freezing and perpetual control of the frozen cadaver until such time as it can be returned to life through reactivation.

The legal implications of this, of estates, of re-entry into life, and related factors are obviously complicated and unclear.

The human factors involved in returning in a later generation are not known. It may be a vast experience of loneliness and frustration, worse than the death that was escaped in an earlier day.

The possibility exists that it may be a vast, wasted technological effort that ends in death without restoration. The return to life remains an option that may fail, for such may be beyond control of the proponents of such expectations.

We have considered the issues concerning euthanasia, suicide, eugenics, abortion, anatomical transplants and donations, cryonics, finding new issues concerning death raised in each. Other areas pertain to legal problems and the ecology of death.

We shall deal with ecology in this chapter and legal aspects in the following chapter. The ecological issue concerning death deals with the means of disposition, which increasingly becomes a problem.

In Western society the traditional method of disposition has been in the burial ground or cemetery. As cities expand and the many urban centers become fused into a vast metropolitan area, the metropolis becomes a megalopolis, and the cemetery plots that were set aside for the dying become new problems for the living. Cemeteries standing in the paths of highways, transmission lines, sewer systems, create a repugnant problem if "progress" is to go forward. What are the rights, privileges, and options available to the deceased of former days?

In addition to legal questions, public opinion does not accept the desecration of graves or the bulldozing up of bodies, and so new cemeteries must be created to which the corpses of former days are moved. Indeed, some see this as an argument in favor of cremation, in which a small container of dust or ashes is all that must be disposed of.

However, ecologists often object to the scattering of the ashes, which appeals to the poetic nature of many (symbolic as it is of natural immortality), upon the pastures, beaches, water, or in the atmosphere from planes. Some burial grounds have regulations requiring the burial of the ashes or dust (euphemistically called "cremains" by the funeral industry) in containers. Some families have preferred to open the containers and pour the dust under the roots of a newly planted tree, bush, or flower garden, so that out of the old life emerges the new. This can be a most comforting idea. Elsewhere in the study is related the account of the lady who carried with her for years the ashes she was asked to dispose of in the Hudson River. Are the ecological objections reasonable?

With the exploding world population comes the consequent explosion of the demand for living space, followed by the subsequent demand for burial space. Is such land available?

Farsighted people have given concern to this matter. One California enterprise has proposed propelling the deceased by rocket into outer space. Yet there is already an awareness that outer space is becoming a junk yard of the discarded or faulty hardware of the space effort, of the falloff rockets and burned-out satellites that, bound in a gravity pattern, spin on forever through space. Should the deceased be added to this orbital junkyard?

Other West Coast firms fly the ashes out over the Pacific, beyond the national territorial limit, and scatter the ashes in the ocean. Cannot the oceans of the earth absorb the ashes of the deceased? The ancient biblical injunction, "Thus shall the body return to the earth," seeks fulfillment in one way or another, but permanent containers postpone this possibility.

In Tennessee a highrise apartment for the eternal care of the ashes or bodies of the dead has been built. Here, according to news accounts, in a highrise masoleum, one can purchase burial space on some twenty floors of a skyscraper where the ashes or caskets will be maintained at correct temperatures, air-conditioned and properly attended. This "vertical cemetery" is seen by its promoters as an answer to the horizontal burial grounds.

In view of the need for change and advances, many innovative efforts are being explored, some in the name of ecology, some in the name of technological progress, and some for the sake of expediting the American penchant for mass-production packaging and instant services. Among these is the unique service announced a few years ago by an Atlanta undertaker who created "a drive-in mortuary," which was described by the news items as a series of display windows on a circular driveway, each prepared to house on display the casket of the deceased person, now open for inspection. "So many people want to come by to see the remains of a relative or friend," the mortician said, "but they just don't have the time. This way they can drive by and just keep going." Another advantage, he explained, was that "The people won't have to dress up to view the remains." According to the news wire story carried in the *Boston Globe,* Hirshel Thomas had not only built a row of five drive-in windows, each six feet long, facing the driveway on a busy street, but "Each window contains a name plaque and has wall-to-wall carpeting and drapes." Thus, the last of the modern issues of death has been resolved by removing the inconvenience and time factor as the "mourner can drive by and just keep on going."

This, we expect, will remain an oddity rather than becoming the norm in the funeral practices we see around us.

The early biblical injunction, "The body shall return to the earth from whence it came" seems the ecological goal, but the perpetual maintenance of modern technology is a hindrance. Is there any higher goal than adjusting to the natural processes?

10

Legal Aspects of Dying

Our correspondents wrote:

I wish I could continue to support the church, but I find myself reduced to poverty since my husband's death. We know he wrote a will, but we cannot find it, and the courts have taken over his estate and advertised for all relatives to come forward. It appears that I, at the most, will only receive a small portion of the estate and his cousins, nephews, and nieces will benefit, altlhough they never bothered with him while he was living. I do not see the justice of this.*

When my husband died, the partnership of his brokerage business ceased, and for reasons not clear to me, his partner now owns the whole business. My husband and I worked for years to build it up and it seems I should have an equity in it.*

My sole support was my son who was killed in action in Vietnam. I never knew he was married, but since his death a Vietnamese girl has claimed his G.I. Insurance as his wife.*

I appreciate what you are trying to do in this study of death and grief, but there is another problem that caused me as much suffering as the emotional factors you are concerned about. I speak of the financial arrangements and disposition of property following death. First of all, we could not open my husband's safe-deposit box for five days following his death, and several officials from the government and bank were there to make an inventory. I had some heirloom jewelry there

116

that I never thought was particularly valuable, but the appraisers placed a value of thousands of dollars on it. Even though it was mine, not Harry's, the IRS is assessing me an inheritance tax on it because I have no way to prove it was mine, not his. In addition, we found that he owned a cemetery lot for which he paid $2,000. I never knew it and had already purchased another one through the funeral director, as the service was held on the third day following his passing, but the bank would not allow the vault to be opened until five days had elapsed.

Altogether all of his affairs are now out of my control, in the hands of the Court, since his brother, whom he listed as executor of his estate, has been dead three and a half years. I have spoken to a lawyer who tells me the Court will probably appoint the bank executor instead of me, although I have handled most of the family business for many years. But death, funeral arrangements, and wills had never been discussed by him. *

Anytime my husband and I talked about death, it was presumed it would be my death, since I have been in frail health for over twenty years, whereas Walter was robust, playing golf several days a week, and walking to work every day. It never seemed likely that he would have a heart attack and die instantly, whereas I have always been under a doctor's care. I always relied upon Walter as the strong, reliable partner who would support me and take care of me.

I did not know what to tell the hospital when he died, so they chose the funeral director. When they called me, they had already embalmed him, which made my son furious when he arrived because he believed his father wanted cremation, which surprised me.

I would advise everybody not to take anything for granted, and to find out early in life what should be done. *

There are two categories of legal aspects of dying: one pertains to a legal definition of death, and the second deals with the practical problems created by death with which the survivors must deal. We know in a general way some of the latter problems but are not prepared for specific applications concerning such matters as wills, joint bank accounts, ownership of property, transfer of property, etc.

The legal definition of death has become increasingly important in modern society. On the one hand, there is an increase in violent crime in which culpability is determined by the precise moment of death, and on the other hand, the question of when death occurs is raised due to the sophisticated technological instruments, now available in hospitals, that prolong "life" after normal processes cease functioning. When does death actually occur?

Traditional (as apart from legal) definitions of death describe it as a state that occurs either when breathing stops or when the heart stops beating. However, through respirators, breathing can be reactivated in many instances and, as every Boy Scout knows, even artificial respiration can induce breathing to begin again. In such instances was the patient dead and then restored to life?

Heart beats can be replaced by artificial hearts, by hand massage of the heart during surgery, transplants, and by artificial mechanisms.

Various states today have legislated that death occurs when motor activity in the brain has ceased. Due to modern medical apparatus, it is now possible to measure or denote any motor activity at all in the brain by registering electrical discharges. This is coming to be looked upon as the one evidence that some glimmer of life remains, and as long as such can be measured or registered, a person is not legally dead.

This became the issue around which the euthanasia case of Karen Ann Quinlan revolved in 1975 in New Jersey. This young woman's legal parents petitioned the Court to enjoin the physicians and hospital from maintaining her life artificially. Karen had been in a deep coma for many months, devoid of any muscular or conscious activity. Her weight had decreased drastically, and she had reverted to a fetal position in what, to all intents and purposes, was a sustained condition of borderline death, maintained only by the mechanical means of feeding and respiration. However, the hospital and physicians reported there was a slight registration of some mental waves so that the brain was not completely dead. The Court in this case ruled in favor of the brain waves and against the evidence on all sides that she could not sustain bodily functions on her own.

A somewhat similar question has been the subject of a few notorious criminal cases in which, after a person was apparently mortally wounded, brain activity continued until another type of accident or activity ended the life without recovery of consciousness. The courts in such cases are asked to rule that death was not from the bullet but from a subsequent cause.[1]

This legal question can touch anyone of us as individuals in euthanasia cases because it is conceivable that we might be called upon to face such decisions. Also another conceivable situation is the so-called death of partners in a common catastrophe. Whose will is then effective? If deaths occur minutes or hours apart, there is a transference from one to the other before his or her death, and so to the latter's legatees. The legal definition of death in the state involved can be all-important, even though both partners were killed in the same catastrophe, such as a fire, automobile accident, or airplane crash.

These may be esoteric considerations for most of us, but we must be concerned with the practical matters pertaining to survivor rights that may occur in any type of death. We will catalogue a number of these situations for which the survivor should be prepared. Indeed, even the decedent should be concerned and make proper preparations ahead of time. Most do, but there are times of discouragement, suffering, prolonged illness, or possible senility when legal arrangements are not kept in order; or, while such legal matters as wills are in order, business and financial matters are allowed to slide, which in the end require legal solutions.

There are states (when we use the word "state," it should be understood as applying to whatever jurisdiction has legal control: a state, province, or country) that by law specify that the next of kin has final authority over the disposition of the decedent's body. It is his or her choice whether burial, cremation, autopsy, transplants, or cadaver donation is made. It is a thesis of this study that each person has a right to say something about his/her desires in this regard. For this reason, it is always suggested that the next of kin sign or serve as witness to pre-arrangement forms, funeral contracts, donation cards, or memorial society documents. Witnessing the documents gives one an opportunity to share in what for some is a difficult subject to face; then, one is sure that the primary survivor knows one's wishes.

It is a major concern that spouses, parents, and offspring should communicate their thoughts concerning death arrangements, but we recognize how difficult it is to initiate such discussions. By witnessing the documents about the death situation, one then has an ideal opportunity to discuss one's expectations or to state one's reservations, so that a meeting of minds can take place.

Wills and trusts are the major legal documents of which most people think when the question of survivor's estates and arrangements come up. Generally, everybody should have a will so that their wishes regarding not only money, but real and personal property, may be distributed according to the decisions and wise management of their affairs, as they deem best.

As stated by some lawyers, there are circumstances in which wills are not necessary and prolong the period of personal transfer. An attorney is probably the best person to advise one on this. State laws, the number of potential survivors, the amount of property involved in the estate and family trusts are all considerations. If all property is already in the joint names of husband and wife or in a trust, and there are no other claimants, then a will may be unnecessary. In some states, however, the law specifically dictates that if a person dies without a will (intestate), there are specific procedures, or formulations, whereby a property is to be divided. If there is a spouse but no children, the spouse receives an amount up to a certain figure set by the state which holds jurisdiction (the amount varies from state to state and from time to time); above that, the spouse usually receives one-half if there are any other claimants, otherwise, all of it.

In referring to "children" in the foregoing paragraph we are less accurate than the law, which refers to "issue." One's issue is any person carrying on the direct bloodline of the decedent. This includes children, grand-children, great-grandchildren, etc. It also includes adopted children, but only immediately adopted children. That is, if one's son or daughter has adopted a child, that child is entitled to the stepperson's inclusion; however, if the parent predeceases the stepperson, then the adopted child has only such claims as are provided by specifically named legacies.

If there is no issue and no other claimants to the estate, the surviving spouse will receive the entirety of the estate, after taxes and court expenses are deducted.

If there is issue and no will, the spouse will receive one-third of the estate, with the rest being divided between issue and other claimants, which would include issue of the testator, such as children by previous marriages as well as present, and all other legal claimants. In some instances, a will may pro-vide less than the legal one-third to the spouse. In such cases the spouse may waive his/her rights under the will and claim the one-third that is his/her portion by law. In very large estates the survivor, having received the legal third, will be entitled to a proportion of the remainder funds according to the laws of the state having jurisdiction.

Most states provide for a "widow's allowance" or "survivor's allowance" from the estate while it is in probate, to assist either widow or survivors through the period prior to distribution of funds.

In general, a widow is best protected by a will and such is recommended, except in those situations provided for by trusts.

Trusts are created by the property holder in order to control the distribu-tion of his/her wealth and regulate the terms under which it is dispersed. Trusts are established in two major forms. The trust set up in one's lifetime that distributes the income to others while the benefactor is still living is the *inter vivos* trust, or the irrevocable trust, regulated by law. Once such a trust is set up, the funds involved have effectively been distributed by the owner under prescribed rules and regulations that have been set forth. Since it is a transference of capital funds from the owner to a legal entity that provides income to others, it is a donation and may be so claimed for tax purposes. This often works to the favor of the donor as well as the beneficiaries.

The second type of trust is the *in causa mortis* trust, created at the time of death, that transfers the income of controlled funds to another under spe-cific terms set forth in the instrument creating the trust. This is often the so-called "spendthrift trust," by which money is doled out in regular amounts over a period of time, possibly paid monthly, quarterly, or annually for a specified number of years. Laws nominally determine the maximum length of such trusts: usually, by the time a minor is either twenty-one or thirty-five, the trust is dissolved and the principal of the fund passes directly into the hands of the young person for whose protection it had been created in the first place. The "dead hand from the grave" is prevented from everlasting control of the living. A trust is frequently set up to provide an income to the spouse or parents so long as they live; then, upon the death of that person or persons, the trust is distributed to other heirs as specified.

Trusts and wills are frequently set up to be executed in states where favorable laws protect the integrity of the family fortune, if one can claim residence in such a state. At times residence is sought in such states for precisely this purpose. In general, however, wills should be prepared by a lawyer in the state in question, and it is hoped that this will be the state where the property exists and where death is likely to occur, so that there will be no problem with establishing the jurisdiction of the court. Courts have competed with one another for control of estates due to the inheritance tax claimed by specific states from certain estates. Such jurisdictional disputes can be costly to the estate, and hence to the amount of funds to be distributed to the heirs. Retirement homes are sometimes chosen as much for such legal advantages as for the climate and temperature. When one does so move upon retirement, the estate arrangements should be reviewed in relationship to the new place of residence.

We have stressed above the advisability of carefully selecting an attorney. One also is in a position to make the selection of the executor of the estate and should so designate the person desired. An administrator is appointed by the court if one dies intestate, or if there will be a prolonged period before the estate settlement is reached. Designation of the administrator is important. A letter or written statement that one desires a particular person to administrate the matters of intestacy will frequently be accepted by the court as conclusive. It is better if such a letter or statement is witnessed, however.

Many wills are written long before death and have various codicils, additional paragraphs listing further instructions concerning distribution, added to them. Each such codicil should be witnessed carefully, just as the original will had been. A will with codicils is in effect "a series of wills" and, frequently, contested cases arise out of the ambiguities found within the various documents.

One should always be reminded that every blood relative should be mentioned in the will, even if only for the proverbial one-dollar inheritance. The court is apt to look upon the omission of a single name as an oversight or typographical omission and recognize the claim of such unmentioned relatives as valid.

Most people choose as an attorney a respected senior member of their generation or the next older one. Those who live a long life frequently outlive the attorneys, the bankers, the potential trustees, and often family members cited for inheritance in the wills. Consequently, updating is desirable. Children and their spouses may now be divorced, creating new situations, and the concern over the blood issue (as descendants are called) of the grandparents may not be so easily located. There may be social and emotional problems to be taken into account as the years pass by.

There are important tax considerations insofar as inheritance is concerned, and to leave the entire estate to individuals may be an expensive means of remembering them. The inheritance tax laws of the United States create favorable conditions when a portion of the estate is given to a charitable, educational, or religious institution, so that the percentage of taxable income after such donations at time of death gives substantially more actual money to the individual inheritors than would be the case if the total estate went to them. As federal laws are changed from time to time, and state laws vary, the soundest advice is to seek periodic counsel from the legal counsel or deferred-giving department of the institution involved. Most universities, schools, churches, denominations, and charitable institutions have specialized information available that can guide the family, lawyers, and personal tax consultants.

It is important to note that wills should be accessible and in known places at the time of death. For many these are in a safe-deposit box, although frequently a copy is in the hands of the attorney or the next of kin who may not be immediately available. Traditionally, wills used to include burial (or cremation) instructions, but since wills are frequently kept in a safe-deposit box, this is not a helpful place for such information.

As we have noted, funeral or memorial arrangements must be made almost immediately. Frequently, a hospital or rest home urges that the body be removed within hours of death, and a funeral director who acquires possession of the body is apt to be a hard man with whom to bargain. Safe-deposit boxes in most states cannot be opened without an officer of the court present, as well as a representative of the Internal Revenue Service; thus, several days may be required before the vault can be opened and the contents made available for family inspection.

This raises or reminds us of other questions concerning immediate funds and necessary steps and arrangements for handling the family situation until legal arrangements can be worked out.

Most marriage partners seek to make such arrangements through their joint checking and savings accounts, but in some states these legally cannot be used after the death of a single member until legal approval has been secured. It is stated that frequently bank officials have overlooked this regulation, knowing the persons involved. However, for the elderly, who have outlived the employment days of the bankers with whom they did business, this is not always so easily arranged. They may find strangers a generation or more younger than they sitting in the banker's seat,who do not seem to comprehend the situation that applies. All of the elderly's former business and professional references from earlier days may also be retired or dead, so that they find themselves alone in a community where once they were well known. The time of death is a difficult moment without discovering this realistic truth. Thus, it is necessary to not only keep one's records and documents updated, but one's contacts as well.

Another situation involves insurance policies that were taken out years ago. Often the beneficiary outlives the agent upon whom they relied for guidance. A new person may sit in the agent's office, or perhaps the local agency is now dissolved, so that one must go directly to the home office of the insurance company. If not located in the local community, this can be done, of course, by letter or telephone. Policy number and the face names are necessary in such an event. Agents frequently can expedite the paperwork for securing immediate and quick settlements. It is stated that many life insurance policies are never collected due to neglect, loss, inertia, and forgetfulness. Life insurance is a source of untaxable inheritance, usually quickly available, which should be sought out and not let go by default.

Many families err in assuming that through a joint title to property the transference from one to the other is accomplished. This is not necessarily so, as many survivors learn to their sorrow. Consequently, the best advice is to seek competent legal counsel in estate planning. Whether joint tenancy is advantageous or not depends on many factors so that no general rule can be applied. Attorneys must take up each situation on its own merits.

There frequently are pension rights for widows or survivors at the place of employment that should be checked into. Usually, persons in the finance office of the company or institution will be most helpful to an inquiry and assist in the paper work that must be done.

Of course, if one was a veteran or government employee, there are government pension, burial, and death benefits that should be claimed. Most claim forms are not complicated and, in the case of government forms, help may not be readily forthcoming. The amount of paper work looms large. However, one simply needs to answer the questions one by one. By taking them gradually, checking on specific facts as found in other documents for dates and required details, the forms can be filled in by almost anyone.

New sources of assistance are becoming available through public service agencies for the elderly, organizations to which they belong, and the Social Security Administration.

Today most people are entitled to Social Security settlements, and these should be sought. The local Social Security office will be the best place to apply. It is necessary to have the social security number that will be found on a recent income tax form if not otherwise known.

In some instances automobiles may not have been registered in both names, so that property transfer of title is required. Most states have simplified the procedure for doing this, and usually a lawyer is not required.

Burial laws that regulate burial, cremation, embalming, the use of burial vaults, and other related topics vary widely between different states, and sometimes between counties or townships and municipalities. The Federal Trade Commission is seeking to unify all these confusing and difficult regulations so that a single standard will prevail. One of its regulations would require all funeral directors to make available a brief, easily understandable digest of such laws.

Some persons, in an effort to keep their affairs in order, maintain a "terminal file" in which all information that might be helpful is included. Also to be considered for such purposes is a listing of credit cards that should be cancelled. Many persons whose lives are subject to emergency situations, such as those in hazardous occupations, avocations, or who travel a great deal, look upon it as a matter of prudence to keep records in such condition that business and personal arrangements may be easily understood and expedited.

In recent, years, the procedure of issuing death certificates has come into practice since they are helpful for making claims for death benefits and for related legal matters, as indicated in the scope of concerns discussed in this chapter. Copies are usually available through the local Department of Public Health or Bureau of Vital Statistics.

Bills do go on; past due debts of the deceased must still be paid—they are not forgiven by death, and the survivor is required to place the financial house in order once again. In the meantime the estate, not a survivor, is responsible for the decedent's bills and debts. Ironically, bills include the medical and hospital bills for the fatal illness. Usually these are honored by the hospitalization and medical insurance plan carried (such as Medicare, Blue Cross, and Blue Shield), but it is wise to keep abreast of such bills as they come in during a prolonged or potentially fatal illness so that as many as possible have been processed prior to death. Such payments are not made voluntarily but must be claimed by the survivor. The survivor cannot be sued for the uncollected debts of the deceased, but his/her estate can be.

If there is a possibility of foul play or accidental cause of death, it is usual for there to be a police investigation. In all apparent industrial accidents federal investigators are apt to seek details for reports that are helpful in the legislative process and in monitoring industrial hazards. Cooperation is sought, is usually not taxing on one's health or time, and may be of benefit to others, as well as helpful in one's own situation.

The most important need of the survivors is to be prepared: to exercise caution in organizing the problems to be solved and seeking advice from trustworthy sources, often checking with a reliable attorney. Emotional overreaction is usually not helpful. Most commercial and business organizations have dealt with matters pertaining to death and have procedures that assist rather than hinder survivors. At times, one will feel that the unique factors applying to his/her situation need more than routine answers, and so, accordingly, one should quietly insist on special attention. Difficult problems can always be turned over to attorneys when one feels frustrated by responses received, but it is often best to make a personal effort to solve such.

A final word is in order: one should not hastily squander or expend the lump sums received because they are usually nonrecurring sums, and one must frugally budget for the remaining years. Investments should only be made through established institutions and well-known persons with whom they are connected, and it is well to shop around for the best available counsel before committing large investments or signing control over to third parties. Fortunately, today there are many consumer laws to protect the innocent, and it is best to check up on "get rich quick" investments that are offered (perhaps by those who follow the obituary notices). Before paying decedent's bills, be sure they were in fact incurred by him or her for the service rendered. Do not pay such bills out of personal income, but submit to the estate for settlement under the watchful eye of the court by the executor before taxes are deducted from the net amount payable to the government.

With so much to be concerned about it is wise that contingency arrangements be discussed in the quiet of family life long before drastic decisions are called for. Words out of youth experiences in scouting are well worth taking to heart: "Be prepared."

11

New Approaches
to Old Responses

Our correspondents wrote:

I will state my views briefly. The body is perishable; Hope says that the spirit is not. This is my creed. When the body and soul separate, Hope says that my soul will enter into a more exciting and satisfactory sphere. The body, bereft of spirit, will return to the ecosphere from which it was derived. The less processing and preserving the better. It cannot be, but I would like to be interred in a place of the living—a forest? Perhaps, someone would be kind enough to place a seedling oak on the ground above it. The elements of my body would again have life and seek the heavens and This. Perhaps, the oak would show some kindness to those who follow. *

Therefore, in the case of my sister who suffered immense emotional problems for nine months while enduring malaise of undiagnosed origin (which was confirmed to be a malignancy only three days before death), the family was faced with such very big unanswered questions that a memorial service served mainly to close with dignity an episode which was filled with such traumatic upheaval and indignity.

In my own reactions to the whole subject of what to do at the time of death, I am prompted by my strong aversion to the "worship" of a body without life, and to the use of valuable land that could serve the living being used for endless rows of monuments. I believe strongly that the most worthwhile monument is the positive remembrance of and perpetuation of ideals of the deceased. *

Any funeral service has always seemed an awful experience for those closest, and at best more an outlet for personal emotions and fears for the other attendants.

What my son calls a marble orchard seems a great waste of beautiful land.

When the temple of my soul has become useless, I'd be happy if the resulting ashes from its purification could join some good, rich earth in a hole deep enough to plant a tree or shrub.

I'd like to see a memorial society set up that could purchase a fine big park in which such plantings could be made.

However, my dream park would be picnic grounds where members' dues and paying guests would make its upkeep feasible.

Then, instead of flowers, picnic tables, old-fashioned wooden swings, yes, even a slide and sandpile for the children could be provided.

Here families could gather for fun and good discussions, surrounded by natural beauty.

I call that my impossible dream.

Next best idea would be a wildlife preserve where such plantings would be allowed. *

TO REMEMBER ME . . .

The day will come when my body will lie upon a white sheet neatly tucked under four corners of a mattress, located in a hospital busily occupied with the living and the dying. At a certain moment a doctor will determine that my brain has ceased to function and that, for all intents and purposes, my life has stopped.

When that happens, do not attempt to instill artificial life into my body by the use of a machine. And don't call this my deathbed. Let it be called the Bed of Life, and let my body be taken from it to help others lead fuller lives.

Give my sight to the man who has never seen a sunrise, a baby's face, or love in the eyes of a woman. Give my heart to a person whose own heart has caused nothing but endless days of pain. Give my blood to the teenager who was pulled from the wreckage of his car, so that he might live to see his grandchildren play. Give my kidneys to one who depends on a machine to exist from week to week. Take my bones, every muscle, every fiber and nerve in my body and find a way to make a crippled child walk.

Explore every corner of my brain. Take my cells, if necessary, and let them grow so that someday, a speechless boy will shout at the crack of a bat and a deaf girl will hear the sound of rain against her window.

If you must bury something, let it be my faults, my weaknesses, and all prejudice against my fellow man.
Give my sins to the devil. Give my soul to God.
If, by chance you wish to remember me, do it with a kind deed or word to someone who needs you. If you do all I have asked, I will live forever.[1]

In a sense, this chapter may almost be considered an appendix to the first ten chapters because here we are presenting practical examples of the approaches, attitudes, and ideas that we have discussed. Much has already been put into practice by others, and we may profit by noting what and how they did it. Beyond this illustrative material is the practical guidance of a consumer nature, showing how in any community a few people may band together to form a memorial society, and we will offer their suggestions and show their pre-arrangement forms, which may prove helpful in more ways than one.

After the in-depth study carried forth in this volume, the author's earlier Death and Grief Survey, and in practical experience as a minister and counselor on death and grief, it is a conclusion hard to avoid that almost any contemporary church may, and should, act for its own membership as a memorial society. After all, it is a main function of the church to give solace and comfort at the time of death; its ministry is trained in counseling and in the practice of the compassionate assistance to all who turn to either the institution or the personal leader for help. What better way to serve the living than to lead them in times of strength and vitality to reflect upon the arrival of death, and then to actively put down in writing what should be done?

Memorial societies are handicapped because the funeral directors look upon memorial societies as economic threats, that is, as competitors and advocates of alternative ways of doing business. Morticians, too, often tend to assume that to assist a memorial society is commercial suicide. This undoubtedly should change when the Federal Trade Commission has issued its binding guidelines for funeral practices. But any church may prepare its own pre-arrangement forms, setting forth in a preamble the religious principles that its members adhere to in regard to death arrangements. Funeral directors tend to respect religious principles while they resist economic coercion.

There is a creativity, freedom, and joy possible in a memorial service that commemorates the deceased when it is not related to the disposal of the body, which has already been taken care of quickly and simply. Some years ago Marshall Schacht, a not inconsequential poet, died. His brother, a Unitarian minister, followed his wishes and sent out the following memorial letter to his many friends and literary associates who were scattered far and wide.

MARSHALL WEBSTER SCHACHT
1905–1956

Marshall Schacht died about 8:30 on the morning of November 21, after experiencing about fifteen minutes of breathing difficulty. He knew he had leukemia and had, roughly, six months to three years to live. Probably the immediate cause of his death was a "heart attack."

When he learned of his fatal illness last September, he thought it exciting news and a real adventure. His life's horizon had simply come nearer and more definite. No longer did he have to worry about buying more clothes, going to the dentist, and all the uncertainties of an indefinitely prolonged life. Importantly, too, he had been able to save enough money to see him through. Now he could cease from a "bread and butter" occupation to apply his full time to the creative writing he loved. He did not wish to travel abroad or any such thing—just to enjoy his apartment "home," his intimate friends, his music, and have those occasional visits to the countryside he loved, and with family and friends whose comradeship he cherished.

He had responded well to X-ray treatment earlier in the fall, and already felt he belonged to and with his fellow cancer patients at the clinic. He was utterly unfearful of death and ready for it whenever it was to be. He was grateful for having been spared pain, and hopeful of not being a bother and burden to others. He hoped some of his savings would be left to go to his sister for her comfort and needs.

His quiet slipping out of this world is characteristic of his modesty. "No fuss and feathers." Yet this statement must not belie the fact that he loved life and lived it with a kind of zestful adventure. He enjoyed his years of teaching English, especially in extension courses at the College of the City of New York, and many of the different forms of employment in which he did well and saved wisely, since his childhood heart condition precluded obtaining life insurance. But at heart he was always the poet, seeing life-situations through a sensitivity to the sufferings and frustrations of the downtrodden, through his hate of sham and pretense, through his love of music, and the beckoning beauties he found everywhere in the country, especially the New England countryside.

Never formally religious but highly sensitive to suffering and injustice, his poetry of the '30s identified his deep sympathy with the unemployed, the foreigner, and the other "outcasts" of that time. Their anguish was his anguish. Also, he did not fail to see the beauty and rhythm in modern architecture and some engineering developments which sang to him as modern symphonies. To him, poetry always had "to sing," and his basic relation to life was to catch the lyrical interpretation of every aspect of life and put it into singing words of color, emotion, and rhythm so as to be able to celebrate it and share it with others.

He knew he ws not a great poet, but he knew he was a real one, and some of his verse outstanding. It all started back in his Brookline High School days.

The year he graduated from high school the editor of a nationwide book of secondary school verse included more of his poetry than of any student in the country. At Dartmouth College, where in his senior year, 1927, he was editor of the literary magazine *The Tower,* he was producing more and better verse. While there he won the New England Golden Rose Poetry Prize. After college he had a little travel abroad—by cattleship and back!—and attempted to exist in such manner that he could make poetry his life-work. But, like so many other poets and artists, he found this could not be so. He obtained in 1930 an M.A. at Harvard and hoped for a suitable teaching or writing career. The Great Depression and other circumstances prevented this realization. Consequently, he did some library work in a settlement house, some store work, house-organ writing for a business firm, copy-reading, etc.—all things for "bread and butter" so he could satisfy in some measure his "drive" to write the poetry in his soul.

Probably winning the Twayne Poetry Prize in 1949 and having so good a selection from among his poems published as a book, *Fingerboard,* and the most gracious and understanding foreword written by Prof. F. O. Matthiessen of Harvard, have been the high water mark of his public recognition and personal satisfaction. It appears to have been a truly happy and deserved recognition.

Of course he had appeared publicly in other ways: *Poetry, The New Yorker, The American Mercury, Commonweal, New Masses, The Dial,* Oscar Williams' *A Little Treasury of Modern Poetry,* Geoffrey Grigson's British anthology *The Year's Poetry,* 1940, the 1949 edition of *Bartlett's Quotations,* as well as Louis Untermeyer's *Yesterday and Today.* Another special pleasure had been going, by invitation, to Dartmouth College a few years ago to give a reading of some of his poetry.

And then came the news last September of a definitely "limited horizon." We have already mentioned the keen anticipations this gave him. Yet he would be the first to know and tell us of the many uncertainties and sudden changes in life's mysterious ways, so why should one worry about them and make a fuss? Such worry and fuss do no one any good.

He would like us to share his own songs of courage, acceptance, and endurance of what life requires, and non-acceptance of the evil and ugly which man can do something about. He would like us to enjoy his memory and his writings as they move us and help us.

He felt quite deeply that death is probably an adventure into complete non-existence; yet there was always the possibility it might be some form of personal survival. If the latter proves true, we may find he has some wonderful poetry awaiting us when we all take the same journey for ourselves.

With many of his best friends at considerable distance from New York City, and with his indifference to formal religious services, his sister and I have thought this "memorial communication" might be the most meaningful "formality" we could devise. Through it we all share the same basic content; and by it each of us can add his own personal thoughts as his own heart and knowledge prompt him. There is no expense of travel, time, or flowers involved (all of which Marshall would certainly cheer!)—just the loving thoughts of family and friends who really knew him and care.

Cremation has taken place.

His sister and brother are grateful for the relatives and friends who have known and loved Marshall and contributed joy to his life. We send our affectionate greetings to you, one and all!

Robert H. Schacht[2]

In like manner, we faced a somewhat similar situation when my stepmother died following an automobile accident in a state in which she did not live, and, needless to say, where her friends were not present. In addition, in retirement she no longer lived where her friends of a lifetime lived, nor where she had family. Consequently, my brothers and I felt it proper to follow her wishes for immediate cremation and then send out a memorial letter to all of her known friends and relatives. We found her small address book most helpful in this endeavor. We sent the following letter, which brought us a wealth of responses that were a joy to read over the difficult passing months and added many forgotten incidents, unknown kindnesses, and appreciated acts which she had done for others. Our memorial letter follows

"IN MEMORIAM"

MARGARET REGAL MARSHALL (Mrs. J. Wallace)

July 10, 1894–July 14, 1963

This Memorial Letter is written to the friends, relatives, and correspondents of Margaret, many known to us, and others simply names listed in her address book who somehow, for some reason, were on her personal list. For whatever reason you knew her, we are sending this letter.

In our complex world of today, we live and travel far and wide so that there is no place that is like the old homestead where family and friends may be brought together. There is, therefore, no suitable location where a Memorial Service bringing all of Margaret's friends and relatives together could be held. Any such service would be representative of only a tiny segment of family and friends. We know this, and so did Margaret. Accordingly, it was planned and agreed that a family Memorial Service would be held, with cremation and farewell combined. This has been done in Montclair, New Jersey, and this Memorial Letter is our second step in widening the circumference of sorrowing remembrance to include her friends and associates.

This letter is written by one of "the boys," Rev. George N. Marshall, who conducted the Service, and had the good fortune to visit her a number of times in very recent weeks, so that I can report to all of you that up to the time of her fatal accident she was in the best of health, with her jaunty, vigorous step unimpaired, her delighted eyes bright with interest and humor in the events about her, and her mind alive with the keen sensitivity that made us all marvel at her knowledge and wisdom. I, for one, remember her as "the most intellectual woman I knew," and yet she was a very warm, emotional woman too, and her deep affection for us was an enriching experience in all our lives.

Margaret Marshall worked at the Eye Clinic of the Union Health Center in NYC up until the very end. One of her vacation weeks had come, and she and her dear friend, Margaret Chesser, planned some day trips to visit the countryside outside New York City. It was on one of these trips, the day after her birthday, that Margaret, laughing and happy at the close of the trip, was in one sudden violent moment propelled from consciousness to unconsciousness. From Thursday evening until Sunday morning she lay in a coma while the most advanced medical methods were used in an attempt to save her life. She died from skull injuries received when the car in which she was riding was struck by an oncoming vehicle. She was an inspiration to both doctors and nurses in the way her body rallied again and again in spite of the unconsciousness of the mind. Some consolation comes in the knowledge that she was spared conscious suffering. Always in good health, indeed, one who made a point of it, she knew not the slow attrition of the years. In the hospital I noticed particularly the skin without wrinkles and the body without blemish of one who had not really aged, and therefore had not known its infirmities. This was a blessing.

In keeping with the thoroughly rational life she lived, her eyes were donated to the Eye-Bank for Sight Restoration and they wrote us on July 15 that, "Through this generous act today two people will be restored to normal active lives." Let us hope that they will see the beauty and wonder of life as she saw it, without prejudice and with clarity. Also, the small temporal bone in each ear (the size of a dime) was transplanted to restore hearing to two deaf persons through the Deafness Research Foundation. May they hear the wonders of music and human joy as did she. Indeed, here is one type of immortality— one which Margaret really believed in.

Memorial gifts may be sent to CARE in her name, through your local post office, or to the United Nations Children's Emergency Fund.

Thus, her life is consistent to the end.

(Signed by the three stepsons)

Another flexible and exhilarating possibility arises in a nontraditional memorial service. Often family or friends wish to say a few words, and one example that shows how well a memorial service commemorates the life, rather than dwells upon the death, is found in these words of a young son, married with one child and another on the way, as he spoke at his father's memorial service. He had jotted down a miscellaneous collection of remembrances that brought his father back into a living reality for all of us. John wrote and said:

TRIBUTE TO DONALD SIMPSON BY HIS SON, JOHN

I want to thank you for coming here today. I could never understand why Dad chose to retire to a narrow little valley in a landlocked state when he had spent his life up to that time overlooking the sea or up on a hillside. He loved Vermont, though, and spent many happy days driving back roads and exploring the convolutions of the terrain. Some of you may have noticed the "251 Club" sticker on the rear window of the car. This club must be unique in America, for its sole reason for being is to see if its members can visit all 251 towns in our state! I think it says something about Dad that he and Mother managed to visit all of the tiny, obscure, and distant towns in their travels, while some of the more obvious places are still not checked off.

One of Dad's other long-term interests **was** photography. He has taken pictures for as long as I can remember, but his recent work with birds and flowers reveals an artistic talent none of us ever thought existed. Sometimes having your picture taken by Dad could be an exasperating experience with nonflashing bulbs and malfunctioning cameras, but when it really mattered—like at Nancy's and my wedding and Aunt Dot and Uncle Sherb's fiftieth anniversary—he got all the shots people wanted to look at long after the event was over.

Dad's days in Vermont were also devoted in part to the community. He was a substitute RFD mailman for a while and really received an education—who gets what in his mailbox, how to untangle the generations and stepgenerations of some of our illustrious families and what some people are still wearing at 1:00 in the morning. He served on the library board and was Quartermaster of both the local barracks and State Chapter of the Veterans of World War I. I just don't know what they will do without him. He was the most able and competent member and one of the few with a sense of humor.

But most of all, retirement in Vermont meant a mellowing and strengthening of a marriage that was already strong and warm. It was a comfortable life highlighted by a never-ending schedule of events, trips, and visits that kept him hopping certainly, but never permitted vegetation or a trace of senility to interfere with his enjoyment of life. Retirement can be a deadly experience for many people as busy as Dad was with his work. He and mother knew how to have fun, though. I think the mill for him was a frustrating place he had to be between weekends. What fun he had. I remember him pulling a double to right with the bases loaded in a church picnic softball game. I remember the day he climbed the three thousand-foot Pico Peak in Vermont with a whole bunch of us and suddenly felt old at sixty. I remember him painting our house in Needham and teaching me some few words when a bucket of paint went off the ladder. I remember Dad and his boats. He was in a play once that was some kind of silly comedy, as I recall. Speaking of comedy: there he and mother did not see eye to eye. She likes subtle, low-key wit. He liked Laurel and Hardy and a room full of pies. He was a wonderful gardener. He had an acre during World War II that he and Mother did themselves. This year he was really going to get a head start, and his tomato plants are two feet high indoors right now. He liked people when he got to know them. He loved the cocktail hour ritual when friends were in and was always ready for a debate. It was indicative of his interest in current affairs that Nancy and I had been unable to argue politics with him since the Watergate hearings. We just found we had everything in common!

I could go on and on. He loved life. He loved my mother. He loved Nancy and me. Garrie was a joy to him and he was thrilled to hear that we will have a second. It seems a shame he had to leave before he finished all he wanted to do. But I don't think the day would ever come when he wouldn't look forward to the next.[3]

Everybody cannot do this for their father or a loved one. The voice may crack and tears blind the eyes, but there are some who, regardless of the deep emotion felt, need to give audible, public expression, and their grief is released in the tension of the moment, as is that of the small company gathered together. The nation saw this happen on television at the memorial service in Riverside Church for Nelson Rockefeller some while back. The heroic in human nature must emerge, and both family members and friends joined the clergy in honoring the life of a person respected by many.

How to plan a memorial service? A funeral director is not necessary, nor is a cleric, but they help—at least one. We suggest the clergy since, in all probability, the mortician's work of disposal of the body has already been done. Almost any setting is to be preferred to a "funeral home" for a life celebration. After all, the major reason for utilizing the undertaker's services is to dispose of the body.

The material in the *Church of the Larger Fellowship Handbook* gives a practical guide for a do-it-yourself method of planning a memorial service,[4] and the St. Francis Burial Society of Washington, D.C., even goes further, offering shrouds and ready-to-build coffins at reasonable prices for plain pine boxes.[5]

The *C.L.F. Handbook,* following the example of the Community Memorial Society of New York City, recommends:

WHAT TO DO WHEN DEATH COMES

1. BE PREPARED, IF POSSIBLE. Make your preparations in advance. We encourage you to talk over with your dear ones, and to *write down* your desire and make your arrangements in advance. The CLF provides a special form to be filled in and signed by you and two witnesses. This form should be prepared in triplicate, with one copy placed with your nearest kin, one with your important papers, that is with the papers which will be turned to immediately upon death, or a fatal illness. The advantage of having family sign as witnesses, insures that they know what you have set down.

2. THE FUNERAL DIRECTOR. Choose him, if possible, in advance, and make your arrangements with him. Indicate in your memo who he is. Consult him and others ahead of time if you have any doubts. Discuss with him the cost of their services. Generally speaking, more satisfactory and less expensive services may be obtained from Funeral Directors with whom you have talked ahead of time. "Shop around." Ask the nearest Unitarian Universalist minister of his experience, if possible. Be practical.

3. WHAT TO ASK FOR.

(a) First choice is probably immediate cremation, without embalming, with a plain pine casket. If burial is desired, and a casket thus required, extreme simplicity is recommended. Immediate burial is desirable, without embalming. The body need not be at a funeral or Memorial Service. It need not be "viewed" and can be buried *before* services.

(b) State that you want friends to come, not to a funeral, but to a memorial service to be held later. Taking leave of the remains should be immediate and private, so that even if it is to be burial instead of cremation, no elaborate preparation is necessary.

(c) State where you want the memorial service held. Check to see if your choice of a minister is available at the desired time. Ask him to call soon and take charge of the service, in consultation with the family.

(d) Notices may then be sent to the newspapers. See below.

4. PREPARING THE MEMORIAL SERVICE

Place: Preferably your home, or some setting more meaningful than a strange funeral parlor. We suggest the home as the most suitable place generally.

Time: If not immediately, then perhaps a week or two after death, while memory is still green. Some prefer a little later when fresh grief has passed. A late afternoon or evening hour may be convenient for most. The nearest weekend may be desirable for visiting family or friends.

Newspaper notices: These should state, along with name of deceased, "Cremation (or burial) private: friends are invited to a memorial service at .... on .... (day) .... (hour). Instead of flowers, deceased requested that memorial gifts be made to .... (name, fund or cause.)" The same information would be given in making phone calls. If date and place of memorial service are not settled when notice is given, state "Time and place of memorial service will be announced later."

Decorations: Friends or family may make the place chosen for the service as beautiful with floral or other decorations expressing their own taste and sentiment as they may desire.

Music: Minister, musicians and family should plan the music together. In so doing it may fit the service material used and be truly meaningful to family and friends, rather than traditionally emotional or inappropriate to the taste of the deceased.

Service Material: Ordinary funeral service material may not voice the faith of the deceased, and is generally more concerned with the flesh and sad farewells than ongoing life, thanksgiving, and the sense of the continuing presence of those we love. Material should be selected by the minister in conference with the family. It should emphasize appreciation of the values the deceased sought to live by. CLF material on services will be helpful to many of our people.

Specifically, we suggest a service no longer than half an hour, to consist of a fifteen minute musical prelude, meditative in nature; other selections as desired to fit the readings, prayer and other material used by the minister; a short postlude, affirmative in mood. The purpose of the whole service should be not to revive sorrow but to inspire. It should send people away strengthened and uplifted.

The Pre-Arrangement Forms referred to earlier, primarily in chapter 7, as used in this handbook are roughly similar to those used by many memorial societies. However, in the second paragraph of the preamble the C.L.F. form states: "We accordingly request Funeral Directors to respect our religious convictions . . . " whereas memorial societies rely upon the economic argument. Readers not in a church or religious fellowship able to act in this manner are advised to communicate with the Continental Association of Funeral and Memorial Societies[6] concerning the nearest memorial society or assistance in organizing one locally.

PRE-ARRANGEMENT FORM FOR FUNERAL OR CREMATION

The undersigned, as a member of the Church of the Larger Fellowship, Unitarian Universalist, joins with thousands of fellow members around the world in seeking rational and simple funeral arrangements in keeping with the ethical and religious insight of Unitarian Universalism.

We feel that many customs and practices relating to funerals and burials emphasize the mortal and material rather than the triumph of the human spirit. They often impose an unjustifiable emotional strain, are vain, and too extravagant. We therefore favor simple and economical funeral arrangements, which can be planned ahead of time.

We, accordingly request Funeral Directors to respect our religious convictions in this matter as Unitarian Universalists. We offer these five principles for their guidance. (Members have complete freedom of choice as noted in Instructions.)

1. That simple funeral procedures are desirable and adequate.
2. That Memorial Services be held at a convenient time and place following disposition of the body. (If the family desires to hold an intimate family gathering before burial or cremation, it should be private, brief, without elaborate formalities.)
3. That the showing of the corpse be omitted, and that the body be disposed of, wherever possible, without embalming and that the use of costly caskets be avoided.
4. That both cremation and burial without embalming are acceptable means for the disposition of the body, the method chosen being a personal decision.
5. That sympathy may best be expressed by some gift to a fund or cause in which the deceased had an active interest.

My Instructions for Funeral Arrangements
1. I prefer immediate cremation ...., immediate burial ...., other form .... I prefer a service without embalming .... (write "yes" or "no.").
2. I suggest that the ashes (cremation) or the remains (burial) be disposed of as follows:...
....
3. Donation of eyes, body, tissue, vessels, bone, cartilage, or skin to science and humanity. Directions:...
....
4. Preference for Funeral Director .... Talked with him? ....
5. I prefer a Memorial Service held later ...., no Memorial Service ...., Other..
6. I would like the Memorial service held at .... and, if possible, conducted by .... (or his successor)
7. If possible, I would like the following readings to be read: .... Music:..
8. Other than a Memorial Service, please hold..............................
....
9. Instead of flowers, memorial gifts should be sent to the following: ....
....

Other Instructions (other side may be used for fuller instructions)
....
....

Date ....   *Signed*.............................

(Avoid Safe-Deposit Box)   *Witnessed*.........................

Witnessed.........................
Additional copy of this form is available at CLF office.

According to Federal Trade Commission findings in the spring of 1979, there are nearly 2 million funerals in the United States each year at 22,000 funeral homes at a cost of $6.4 billion. A funeral is the third most expensive consumer purchase after buying a home and a car. Before the 1979 inflationary spiral, the average funeral cost was $2,400. However, half of the population has only had to arrange for a funeral once, and a quarter of the population has never had to buy one. Accordingly there is a lack of acute awareness of the tremendous cost and financial involvement.[7] At the time the Federal Trade Commission had modified its earlier proposed "funeral trade regulation rule," removing some of the industry's major objections.

The FTC pointed out that the funeral industry needed regulation because people who arrange funerals are particularly vulnerable and suggestible due to bereavement, guilt feelings, time pressures, and general lack of knowledge about funeral transactions.

Funeral directors usually use "lump sum" prices and refuse to quote prices over the phone, so that comparison shopping is not possible. Itemization of costs making up the funeral is avoided.

In consequence, costly merchandise, neither needed or desired, is often purchased due to lack of specific information. Such services as embalming, often not required by state law, caskets for burning in a crematory, and special funereal clothing are examples of such unnecessary purchases that oftentimes put a grieving family in debt.

Some funeral directors have used unfair and improper tactics to hinder consumers or competitors from providing alternative funeral arrangements, such as cooperating with memorial societies in preplanned funerals or memorial services.

In consequence of these abuses and excesses by the funeral industry, the FTC proposed four central rule provisions:

Price disclosures. Itemized price information must be provided on request over the telephone as well as in person. Consumers must be provided with itemized price lists before being shown the merchandise so that they are aware of the cost of each item, including the various styles of caskets and burial containers.

Misrepresentations. The FTC rule would prohibit the funeral directors from misstating either laws or cemetery requirements. Also, there is a prohibition against suggesting that embalming, caskets, or burial vaults can preserve the body for an extended period of time.

Unfair practices. The rule would prohibit embalming without permission from family members. It would prohibit undisclosed padding of prices on items purchased on behalf of the customer from other persons (i.e., percentage markups as the agent for purchasing other services such as florists, obituary notices, organist and clergy services, etc.). Finally, it prohibits funeral directors and crematories from requiring caskets for cremations.

Interference with free market. The FTC would prohibit the use of boycotts, threats, disparagement, and similar tactics to prevent persons from starting up competing businesses (e.g., immediate cremation, disposal services for ashes, etc.). It would also prohibit interference with the operation of memorial societies (groups arranging pre-planned funerals) or similar consumer groups.[8]

Whether or not this rule becomes operative in 1981 following nearly four years of research, testimony, and review by the Federal Trade Commission, the fact is overwhelming that based on their impartial study, such controls are needed in order to protect the consumer from exploitation. The danger of congressional rejection, based on the opposition of the powerful funeral industry lobby, still hangs heavily over the prospects as we go to press. In that case, stronger state regulation will be necessary.

A further concern is the arrangement with medical schools for cadavers as a necessary alternative that serves the needs of humanity and science. Such donations should be unencumbered by obsolete laws like those in Massachusetts, where four prominent medical schools—Harvard, Tufts, Boston University, and the University of Massachusetts—all make major contributions to science, humanity, and educational advances. The law in this state specifically bans the medical schools from cremating the remains after the schools are through with the cadavers; thus, burial is required. This is precisely what many donors of their bodies wish to avoid. In each state one should inquire of the medical colleges or friendly legislators what the law is and whether it may be repealed or updated to conform to modern expectations.

As we have previously stated, either the anatomy departments of the medical schools or the organ and tissue banks at metropolitan hospitals (i.e., the nearest major medical facility) are usually able to give guidance on procedures for body or organ donations or transplants. In states such as Massachusetts, just cited as backward in regard to the cremation of medical school cadavers, a progressive law now allows all automobile drivers' licenses to indicate whether the holder is a universal transplant donor. Thus, if such a universal donor dies in an automobile accident, the nearest hospital may immediately perform the life-affirming transplants for the benefit of the living.

Death remains an unclosed book, and through the constructive, meaningful utilization of this opportunity we can help erase the grief often attendant upon the unprepared death.

A final consolation may be found in the passage previously quoted,[9] of David Livingstone who, in the jaws of a lion, experienced the loss of fear, pain, and anguish at his seemingly inevitable death, leading to his subsequent theory that death is not a frightful experience, but is as though a mechanism switches on to carry one forward in tranquillity.

If so, this explains why it is not the dead who suffer but we the living. Thus we must offer consolation for the living, not the dead, and deal creatively with the issues of grief which remain. For this we are the better.

APPENDIX A

Orthodox Jewish Practices[1]

Much the most complete pattern of time-limited mourning still observed . . . is that followed by the Orthodox Jews; since it is so sharply contrasted with most contemporary practice it seems worthwhile outlining rather summarily the enjoined behavior.

Unless death occurs after sunset on Friday, in which case the burial is postponed until the Sunday, an Orthodox Jew should be buried within twenty-four hours of death, and, the more honored the person, the quicker will be the burial. While the body is in the house it should not be left unattended; ideally, the sons or other near relatives should keep the vigil, the body having a candle at its head and feet; relatives are available, professional watchers are called in.

The rabbi is sent for as soon as death occurs; and he returns to the house of mourning about an hour before the funeral is due to start. All the closest relatives of the dead person should be gathered there, wearing some old garment—such as a jersey—from which a piece is ritually cut by an official of the burial group; this rent garment should be worn continuously during the seven days of sitting *shiveh* (*shiveh* is the Hebrew for seven) of intensive mourning. The rabbi says special prayers at the house, mentioning the deceased by name and hoping that "he/she has found his/her heavenly world and is happy." The same prayers are used during the *shiveh* period.

After these prayers the coffin is carried out, and all the mourners should follow on foot. If the cemetery is beyond ordinary walking distance, the mourners should walk quite a way—say, half a mile—before getting into conveyances.

The body is taken into a special room, serving the same function as a funeral chapel, at the cemetery; the mourners wait outside until it is placed in the center of the room; then (in those groups where both sexes attend the funeral) the men stand on the left and the women on the right. Prayers and psalms are recited, and a panegyric of the dead person's virtues is declaimed by the rabbi and also frequently by a lay friend.

The coffin is then carried to the grave, followed by the mourners. All the sons and brothers of the dead person shovel some earth on to the coffin. All the relatives of the dead person then line up by the grave; and all the visitors walk down the line of mourners, shake them by the hand, and say in English, "I wish you long life." This phrase is only used in this context; it is also written in letters of condolence by people who have not been present at the funeral. After the burial, the special prayer for the dead, *kaddish,* is recited for the first time by the sons and brothers of the dead person.

The funeral party then returns to the house where the death has occurred (or occasionally to the house of a near relative). The closest relatives of the dead person sit on special low mourning stools (these can be borrowed from the synagogue) wearing their rent garment and special slippers without any leather in them. For the whole seven-day period the mourners should sit, thus dressed, on the low stools, unwashed and unshaven and the women without make-up, from sunrise to sunset. They should move as little as possible and do no work at all.

On the return from the cemetery, a meal is provided of eggs, salt-herrings and circular rolls, bagels. The mourners should not feed themselves; it is a good deed to feed the mourners. After this ceremonial meal the visitors go home.

During the seven days of intensive mourning, prayers for the dead are said every morning by the men, every evening by the men and women, and at any other time during the day when ten males over the age of thirteen are gathered in the room to compose a *minyan.* The mourners are meant to do nothing and in theory only to eat the food that the visitors bring them.

The ritual for women ends with this seven-day period; men should not cut their hair or shave for thirty days; and for eleven months the sons or other mourners should go twice daily to the synagogue to say *kaddish.* At the end of these eleven months the gravestone is erected and the period of mourning is over; but four times a year prayers for the dead are said at the synagogue, which should be repeated meticulously, since "the souls of the dead are said to be nearest the earth," and at every anniversary of the death (counting by the Jewish calendar) the grave should be visited and prayers recited in which the names of all surviving relatives and descendants are mentioned and memorial lights should be lit in the home.

All the informants agree that they found this very concentrated and overt mourning therapeutic; the fact that they could hide neither their grief nor their mourning made it easier for them.

As far as my knowledge goes, there is no Christian practice which regulates the behavior of the mourners to anything like the same extent.

Reform Jewish Practices[1]

The customs and rules governing mourning are numerous. Reform Judaism, in accordance with its principles of adjusting and adapting older customs to modern needs, has simplified many of the older practices and has abolished others which were found to be no longer helpful or valid.

The following practices prevail today among Reform Jews:

Viduy — It is proper, as death approaches, to pray for forgiveness of sins. This is called Viduy or confession.

Mourning — Mourning is observed for parents, husband, wife, son, daughter, brother and sister. Mourning is not observed for an infant less than thirty days old.

Shiv'ah — The first week after the death of a dear one is the period of intense mourning. It is proper to absent oneself from usual occupations during that week. The customs of "sitting low" and of not wearing shoes during Shiv'ah have been discontinued.

Year of Mourning — Mourning for any dear one in the above list is observed for twelve months. One should not indulge in any frivolous or gay pursuits during that period.

The wearing of black is not required, but subdued colors are generally worn.

Light — As soon as a death occurs a light is kindled in the home of the deceased and is kept burning continuously for seven days after the burial. Thereafter a light is kindled annually in the home of every mourner on the Yahrzeit date. (See below under "Yahrzeit.")

Post-Mortem Examination (Autopsy) — Reform Judaism holds that there is no religious objection to post-mortem examinations or autopsies. It is for the family to decide whether or not an autopsy or post-mortem examination should be performed.

Funeral Dates — Funerals are not permitted on the Sabbath, on Rosh Hashanah (which is observed on the day only), on Yom Kippur, on the first day of Pesach or Sukkos, and on Shovuos (which, also, is observed on the day only).

143

Burial — Reform Jewish practice does not hasten burial. Usually burial takes place on the third day after death.

Embalming — Embalming is permitted and is generally practiced.

Casket — The type or kind of casket or coffin to be used is entirely a matter of family choice.

Burial Garments — In the Reform Jewish practice the body of the deceased need not be garbed in a shroud (tachrichim). The body is usually clothed in whatever garments the family chooses.

Covering of Mirrors — This practice does not exist among Reform Jews.

Keriah or Tearing of Garments — The ancient practice of tearing the garments as a mark of grief, and the recent practice in America of substituting a black ribbon attached to the outer garments for purposes of Keriah, has been dispensed with in Reform Judaism.

Flowers — Flowers are permitted to be placed on and about the casket or coffin, and graves may be beautified with plants, shrubs and flowers.

Cremation — Cremation is permitted by Reform Judaism, and the ashes are permitted burial in a Reform Jewish cemetery.

Minyan — Many Reform Jewish families observe the old custom of having kinfolk and friends assemble at the home of the deceased or any other member of the family for evening worship during the week of Shiv'ah. The number of nights on which such worship-services are held varies from one to three. A special ritual is used for such services. (See *The Mourner's Service* by Rabbi Abraham J. Feldman.) Such services are not held on the Sabbath and festivals since the mourners are expected to attend the worship in the Synagogue.

Visiting the Graves — It is not customary to visit the grave of one recently deceased until after thirty days from the day of burial have elapsed.

Visiting the cemetery on the Sabbath and festivals is not permitted.

One may visit the cemetery at all other times.

Kaddish — Mourners are required to recite the Kaddish in the Temple for a period of twelve months from the day of burial. Thereafter it is recited at the recurring anniversaries of the death (Yahrzeit). Kaddish is recited by women and men alike.

Inasmuch as the Kaddish is always recited standing up, it is proper for all the members of the family of the deceased to rise during the saying of the Kaddish (grandchildren, son-in-law, daughter-in-law, nephew, niece, all who are saddened by the particular death) on the ground that the sorrow or grief of any member of a family is the grief or sorrow of all the members.

In many Reform congregations it is customary for the whole congregation to rise when Kaddish is said, the mourners because of their loss, the rest of the congregation out of sympathy with the bereaved in their midst.

> It is a prayer which overarches the ages of Jewish history and links all the generations of Israel. We, and they who have crossed from life known to life unknown, through the Kaddish become as one, representing an unbroken continuity of devotion to God . . . We and they are united as we proclaim the certainty of the coming of God's kingdom with a confidence that is as daring as it is warranted by reason and sentiment and faith.

Monuments — A monument or other memorial marker is placed over the grave of the deceased usually within the year of mourning. It may be dedicated ("unveiled") at any time during the year, at the convenience of the family.

Mausoleums are permitted by Reform Judaism.

Yizkor—Yizkor or memorial services in Reform Temples are held only on Yom Kippur afternoon and at the morning service of the Seventh Day of Pesach.

Yahrzeit—The annual anniversary of the death of one is observed on the date of death (not the date of burial). Some observe the Yahrzeit in accordance with the Jewish calendar, others do so in accordance with the civil calendar. Whichever calendar is followed, it should be done by agreement with all the members of the family, so that all observe the Yahrzeit at the same time.

On the eve preceding the date of the Yahrzeit, a light is kindled in the home of every mourner, and is kept burning for twenty-four hours. It need not be a candle or an oil lamp. Any type of light is acceptable provided it is in addition to whatever lights are used for illumination.

Where no daily services are held in Reform Temples the Yahrzeit-Kaddish is said on the Sabbath following the anniversary date. Some Reform Temples have the practice of doing this on the Sabbath nearest the Yahrzeit (i.e., sometimes preceding, sometimes following the actual date).

Roman Catholic Practices[1]

The Roman Catholic view of man is not a pessimistic one; on the contrary, it holds that man can attain a destiny of glory. Yet, as one examines the funeral rite of a few years ago, one would wonder if indeed the church had faith in the Resurrection. The priest, vested in black; the crossbearer; the somber chants; the texts of readings as well as of the antiphons were fearsome tales of the fire and brimstone variety.

Through contemporary liturgical change, one is more readily able to see that the church's funeral ritual is built on faith in resurrection from the dead, i.e., that life "is changed, not taken away" (Preface from the time of his Baptism, at which time he begins his new life in Christ, the life that is to be his unending existence [Rom. 6:9–11]).

The new Roman Catholic funeral rite stresses this Baptismal life, that is, the *new life* of the Christian, in many symbolic ways, such as, the use of white vestments by the priest and placing of a white cloth over the casket. The cloth is a replica of the Baptismal robe, and white vestments are a sign of joy. The paschal candle is carried in procession, reminding the community of the Resurrection of Christ and that, through Baptism, the Christian participates in the risen life of Christ. During the rite, at special times, holy water is sprinkled; again to recall the water of Baptism and to symbolize the "washing clean" and the new life.

In Baptism, the new Christian is made a member of a living organism, the corporate body of Christ. He lives in Christ and Christ in him and with Christ and his members forms the "new creation." Each Christian is meant to contribute to the development of this new creation; at the same time, each Christian as an individual should grow to the full stature of Christ. Christian Baptism is an entry into a *new people or community,* the Church. In Christ's own teaching, Baptism is described as a new birth; and this new life, to which the Christian is called and into which he is emerged as he comes from the Baptismal water, is a *participation in the risen life* of the glorified Christ. Finally, the ceremony of Baptism indicates that the baptized person is undertaking a vocation that continues Christ's own messianic role. Baptism is a commitment of oneself to Christ in the mystery of the church.

Life, however, is not an easy affair and though Baptism implies a fundamental self-commitment, man knows moral weakness. Frequent infidelity to his Christian vocation is a sad and disconcerting experience for every Christian. By his Baptism, he is committed to working with Christ in the struggle against evil; and yet, his capacity to do so is hampered by his own sinful involvement in the very evil he should be combating. So, while the community does have faith in the promise of Christ that all who die with him shall live with him, there is the realization that all fail and are in need of forgiveness. This is manifest in the several pleas for deliverance and mercy which are voiced in the psalms and prayers of the funeral service.

In addition, these same prayers remind the community of mourners that they too will pass from this life and will once again be reunited with the one whose loss they mourn. With all its emphasis on new life and resurrection and a view of death as change rather than cessation of life, the church has never discounted the *loss* element inherent in death. There is separation, at least a physical absence, which is painful and heartbreaking on the human level alone; and so, the funeral rite includes the words of comfort which reaffirm the promise of fullness of life which is open to the person who has passed through death.

In life now, death always remains somewhat a mystery but the Christian's faith tells him that in the fullness of time there will also be fullness of understanding.

The Roman Catholic Church expresses all this in terms of three services in connection with a funeral or Rite of Christian Burial: 1) a Wake service; 2) a Funeral service, usually a Mass and 3) a Cemetery service. Traditionally, the funeral Mass is an ordinary Mass with the theme being set by the use of special music, lessons, prayers and preface . . . . It should be kept in mind that every Mass celebrates the death and resurrection of Jesus Christ.

The distinction between a Solemn High, a High, and low Mass is essentially a matter of elaboration of the Mass including the number of celebrants, that is, priests, or bishops, leading the worship.

APPENDIX B

HARVARD MEDICAL SCHOOL

**INFORMATION REGARDING DONATION OF BODY AFTER DEATH
TO THE HARVARD MEDICAL SCHOOL[1]**

Immediately after death the attending physician should be asked to make arrangements with a local undertaker to deliver the body, unembalmed, to the Harvard Medical School's Department of Anatomy, and the undertaker should be asked to call the Department of Anatomy at the School so that preparations may be made for its reception. There should be no hospital autopsy.

Should death occur within the Commonwealth of Massachusetts, the Harvard Medical School will be pleased to pay transportation expenses to transfer the body to the School. However, should death occur outside of the Commonwealth, it will be necessary for the next of kin to underwrite the expenses involved in delivering the body to the School.

A body may be kept by the School for as long as a year. If the relatives wish to have the remains returned, at their own expense, for cremation or burial in a family plot, they should designate the undertaker who is to be notified when the School has completed its studies. Unless otherwise directed, the School will bury the remains at no expense to the family in a marked grave in Pine Hill Cemetery maintained by the School in Tewksbury, Massachusetts. A committal service will be conducted by a priest or minister of the faith of the deceased.

148

INSTRUMENT OF ANATOMICAL GIFT
FOR A MASSACHUSETTS MEDICAL SCHOOL[1]

Being of the age of eighteen or over and of sound mind, I hereby give my body, after death, for purposes of education, research and advancement of medical or dental science to:

_____Boston University School of Medicine

_____Harvard Medical School

_____Tufts University School of Medicine

_____University of Massachusetts Medical School

The selected medical school may, however, in its sound judgment transfer my body to one of the other listed medical schools where it would be more useful for the purposes stated. I understand that NO AUTOPSY should be performed, NO EMBALMING be done, and that acceptance of my body is based on the need of the medical school at the time of my death. I authorize and request the person making final arrangements to call the Office of the Coordinator of Anatomical Gifts to determine if a medical school is able to accept my body. If so, a funeral director should be notified to transport my body to the selected medical school. I understand that the designated school will bear the cost of transportation from the place of death to the medical school if death occurs within Massachusetts. If death occurs outside Massachusetts, the medical school will bear the cost of that portion of the transportation which is within Massachusetts.

I further direct that after studies are complete, the designated medical school shall:

_____Bury my remains at the expense of the medical school in the Pine Hill Cemetery in Tewksbury, Massachusetts in a registered grave_____with services (   ) _____with no religious services
                 denomination

OR

_____Release my remains to my executor or next of kin for private burial or cremation at the expense of my estate.

Having read this instrument in full and understanding its content and legal effect, I hereby sign it in the presence of the undersigned witnesses:

Name of Donor (Please Print)

Signature of Donor

Address

Social Security Number   Date of Birth

City   State   Zip code

Date

WITNESSES ATTESTATION
Signed in our presence and we hereby subscribe our names as witnesses:

1)

2)

Signature of witness

Signature of witness

Name of witness (Please Print)

Name of witness (Please Print)

Address

Address

City   State   Zip code

City   State   Zip code

NEXT OF KIN OR EXECUTOR

Name (Please Print)

Relationship to Donor

Address

Telephone Number

City   State   Zip code

INSTRUCTIONS AT TIME OF DEATH OF DONOR

1. Donor cannot be a carrier of any infectious disease at death.

2. No AUTOPSY or EMBALMING should be done.

3. If Donor is also an EYE DONOR immediately call the New England Eye Bank (617) 523-7900 Ext. 567.

4. Acceptance of an anatomical gift is contingent upon the need of the medical schools at the time of death of the Donor. Donors should have made alternate arrangements in the event that their gift cannot be accepted. The person responsible for making final arrangements should call the Office of Coordinator of Anatomical Gifts for appropriate instructions COLLECT (617) 856-2458.

5. Body must be delivered to school within 24 hours after death unless other arrangements are made. Instructions for acceptance of donations by medical schools can be made by calling the Office of Coordinator of Anatomical Gifts.

THE MEMORIAL SOCIETY[1]

Dedicated to Simplicity,
Dignity and Economy
in Funeral Arrangements

Because death is a universal human experience and because it has a profound emotional and social impact on the survivors, the customs and practices associated with it are very important.

We have learned by experience that a simple, dignified service held with a closed casket or, better yet, in the form of a memorial after the body has been removed, can effectively emphasize the deeper meaning of the occasion and, by stressing the enduring values of the life which has passed, bring inspiration and comfort to the survivors.

Also important, this simple procedure can ease the financial burden. Instead of $1,500 or more, including cemetery costs, a dignified and satisfying service may be had for a fraction of that amount.

Because simplicity in funeral arrangements tends to be contrary to prevailing custom, families often have difficulty in knowing where to turn or how to proceed in order to get either simplicity of service or the moderate costs which properly should go with such simplicity.

The Memorial Society is organized to provide guidance and moral support in this matter to such families as desire it. The Society is a non-profit organization, democratically controlled by its members. Its officers serve without pay. The following pages will give you further information about the Society and about the simplicity which it advocates.

THE NEED FOR ADVANCE PLANNING

The custom of displaying dead bodies in an elaborate and costly routine is taken for granted in most places. Families wishing to follow this custom need no advance planning. When death occurs they need only call a reputable funeral director to take care of all arrangements.

Any departure from this custom should be planned in advance. When death occurs in a family in which there has been no planning, the survivors, under pressure of grief and shock, find themselves virtually helpless in the face of entrenched custom.

Advance planning is needed, not only in making arrangements with funeral directors, but for working out understanding within the family. Death, like marriage, affects a wide area of human relationships. Like marriage, its observance requires sympathetic acceptance by an entire family if it is not to become a source of discord.

Advance planning with the help of a memorial society, done at a time when the family is not under emotional stress, costs little and is very simple, yet it can minimize suffering and expense. No family genuinely desiring simplicity should neglect such planning.

SITUATIONS DIFFER

No two families are alike; each should get the service which best meets its needs and preferences. Some prefer an elaborate service and willingly accept the cost; others, regardless of economic status, want simplicity. A few may want no commemorative service at all. Each should be encouraged to take account of its own religious ideals and customs. The important thing is that each family be free to get the kind of service it wants, without pressure from any organization or business.

ABOUT CREMATION

Modern cremation is a clean, orderly process for returning human remains to the elements. With the rising cost of land burial it is finding increased use. Many people prefer it, and specify that their own remains be ultimately disposed of in this way. Orthodox Jews, however, tend to consider cremation as a desecration of the body, which they regard as a temple. The Catholic prohibition against cremation, on the other hand, is not absolute and arises not so much from opposition to the burning of the remains as from a concern that this may be considered a religious (or anti-religious) rite.

SPECIAL NEEDS AT TIME OF DEATH

Memorial societies recognize that at a time of death the survivors have deep emotional and social needs. Failure to meet these needs can lead to unnecessary suffering and even, in some cases, to nervous disorder. The normal person experiences shock and grief, together with a sense of loneliness and insecurity tinged with feelings of guilt.

Through the warm consideration of friends and the careful planning of a memorial service, grief and loneliness can be eased, the sense of security restored and feelings of guilt gently lifted. Procedures in each case should relate directly to the religious or philosophical outlook of the family.

In some situations help can be extended by friends, in such matters as child care, meal preparation and hospitality for out-of-town relatives.

MEMORIAL SERVICES AND MEETINGS

Whether the service is held in the presence of the body, or subsequently in the form of a memorial meeting, its form and content are important. This is the time when the survivors must accept the finality of the physical loss and, with the moral support of their friends, begin a new life which will be somehow different from the old.

The reality of death and the experience of grief should not be avoided, but should be accepted honestly and with dignity and made an occasion for drawing the survivors closer to one another in love and fellowship. Death provides an occasion also for serious heart-searching and meditation on the meaning of life, and the strengthening of personal dedication. It should be an occasion therefore, not just for grief, but for looking to the future with fresh courage and hope. This positive emphasis is sometimes easier to achieve in a memorial meeting, centered on the life of the departed, than in a service held in the presence of the body.

In addition to the above functions the memorial service can help remove the normal feeling of guilt so generally experienced by the survivors. This may be done by providing an occasion for a re-affirmation of values, a strong sense of identification with the deceased and what he stood for, and an opportunity for an expression — by means of their presence — of the warm solidarity of friends. It should also be the occasion for such formal religious observances as are appropriate to the individual.

BEQUEST OF BODIES TO MEDICAL STUDIES

There is, in many areas, a serious shortage of bodies for education and science. This is the result of more doctors in training and fewer unclaimed bodies. The deficit must be made up by the bequeathal of bodies by individuals who wish to perform this service for humanity. Each memorial society has on file, for the use of its members, complete information about which medical schools need bodies, and the procedures to follow with each. Such bequeathal, by the way, often eliminates funeral expenses entirely. Bodies may only be given; they may not be "sold."

THE EYE BANKS

An estimated 10% of all blind persons in America, about 35,000, are capable of having their sight restored through corneal transplant. Eye-Banks have been widely established through which persons may leave their eyes, after death, to provide corneas to relieve the blindness of others. This has become one of the great altruistic movements of our time. All memorial societies have the necessary information on file.

CONCERNING FUNERAL DIRECTORS

This necessary but overcrowded profession gets a lot of criticism. Its ethical level is probably as high as that of most other businesses, but the circumstances in which it operates make some abuses almost inevitable. Nearly half the morticians in America handle less than one funeral per week. To make ends meet they must charge the expense of days and sometimes weeks of costly overhead to a single funeral. This they can do because competition does not exist in their business the way it does in others. (What grief-stricken widow goes shopping for a funeral?)

Trimmings have developed; elaborate caskets with inner-spring mattresses and plexiglas handles, guaranteed to remain air-and-water tight for "eternity." We can hardly blame the funeral director for putting forward his best merchandise, nor can we altogether blame him if he sometimes takes a dim view of memorial societies!

AN INTERNATIONAL MOVEMENT

The Memorial Societies in Canada and the United States form a broad and growing movement and, with a few exceptions, are affiliated in such a way that a member of one society may transfer to another without the payment of an additional fee. Furthermore, should a member of one society die while travelling or visiting in the territory of another society, his family will receive the same assistance and cooperation that is accorded local members.

Each Memorial Society undertakes to keep on file an up-to-date directory of all other reciprocating societies, with information on the types of service offered by each. This is done through the Continental Association of Funeral and Memorial Societies, 1828 L Street, N.W., Washington, D.C. When a family plans to move, or in the event of a death away from home, the home society is contacted by the family to obtain the name and address of the organization and receives whatever assistance is normally given by that society to its own members.

A few large societies employ paid secretaries. Many more depend on the work of unpaid volunteer secretaries; a housewife, minister or retired lawyer. All are non-profit service organizations supported by membership fees and contributions. Some societies have comprehensive contracts with funeral directors; others serve only in an advisory capacity, furnishing helpful information as to where the desired type of service may best be obtained. Whatever the organizational arrangement or type of service offered in a particular city, if there is a Memorial Society there, friendly help will be forthcoming.

When transferring membership to a reciprocal society a family is not required to duplicate the usual one-time membership fee, regardless of the amount involved. It will, however, be expected to accept the same terms and prerogatives of membership which the new society offers to its other members.

A DIRECTORY OF FUNERAL & MEMORIAL SOCIETIES

BELONGING TO THE CONTINENTAL ASSN. OF FUNERAL & MEMORIAL SOCIETIES AND THE MEMORIAL SOCIETY ASSOCIATION OF CANADA

CANADA

ALBERTA: CALGARY: Calgary Co-op Memorial Society, Box 6443, Sta. D   T2P 2E1   403-243-5088
EDMONTON: Memorial Society of Edmonton & District, 5904 109 B Ave. T6A 1S8 403-466-8367
GRANDE PRAIRIE: Mem. Soc. of Grande Prairie, P.O. Box 471   T8V 3A7
LETHBRIDGE: Mem. Soc. of Southern Alberta, 634 15th St. South   T1J 2Z8
MANITOBA: WINNIPEG: Funeral Planning & Memorial Society of Manitoba, 709 Banning St., R3E 2H9
NEW BRUNSWICK: FREDERICKTON: Memorial Society of New Brunswick, P.O. Box 622 E3B 5A6
NEWFOUNDLAND: ST. JOHNS: Memorial & Funeral Planning Assn. of Newfoundland, Box 9183   A1A 2X9
NOVA SCOTIA: HALIFAX: Greater Halifax Memorial Society, Box 291, Armdale P.O. B3L 4K1   902-429-5471
ONTARIO: GUELPH: Memorial Society of Guelph, P.O. Box 1784   N1H 7A1   519-822-7430
HAMILTON: Hamilton Mem. Soc., P.O. Box 164 L8N 3A2   416-549-6385
KINGSTON: Memorial Society of Kingston, P.O. Box 1081   K7L 4Y5
KITCHENER: Kitchener-Waterloo Memorial Society, P.O. Box 113 N2G 3W9 519-743-5481
LONDON: Memorial Society of London, P.O. Box 4595 Station C   N5W 5J5   519-472-0670
OTTAWA: Ottawa Memorial Society, 62 Steeple Hill Crescent, R.R. 7   Nepean   K2H 7V2 613-836-5630
THUNDER BAY: Memorial Society of Thunder Bay, P.O. Box 501   P7C 4W4   807-683-3051
TORONTO: Toronto Memorial Society, Box 96, Station "A" Weston   M9N 3M6   416-241-6274
WINDSOR: Mem. Soc. of Windsor & Dist., Box 481   N9A 6M6   519-969-2252
QUEBEC: MONTREAL: Memorial Association of Montreal, P.O. Box 85, Dorion Vaudreuil J/V 5V8   514-455-4670
SASKATCHEWAN: LLOYDMINSTER: Lloydminster, Vermillion & Districts Memorial Society, 4729 45th St.   S9V 0H6
SASKATOON: Mem. Soc. of Saskatchewan, P.O. Box 1846   S7K 3S2

UNITED STATES

ALABAMA: MOBILE: Baldwin-Mobile Funeral & Memorial Society, P.O. Box U1178, University P.O.   36688   205-344-0122

ALASKA: ANCHORAGE: Cook Inlet Memorial Society, P.O. Box 2414   99510   907-272-7801
ARIZONA: PHOENIX: Valley Mem. Soc., Box 15813   85060   602-956-2919
PRESCOTT: Mem. Soc. of Prescott Inc., Box 190   86302   602-445-7794
TUCSON: Tucson Memorial Society, P.O. Box 12661   85732   602-323-1121
YUMA: Memorial Society of Yuma, P.O. Box 4314   85364   602-783-2339
ARKANSAS: FAYETTEVILLE: Northwest Arkansas Memorial Society, 1227 S. Maxwell 72701   501-442-5580
LITTLE ROCK: Memorial Society of Central Arkansas, 12213 Rivercrest Dr.   72207   501-225-7276
CALIFORNIA: ARCATA: Humboldt Funeral Society, 666 11th St.   95521   707-822-1321
BERKELEY: Bay Area Funeral Society, P.O. Box 264   94701   415-841-6653
FRESNO: Valley Memorial Society, P.O. Box 101   93707   209-224-9580
LOS ANGELES: Los Angeles Funeral Society Inc., P.O. Box 44188, Panorama City   91412 213-786-6845
MODESTO: Stanislaus Mem. Soc., P.O. Box 4252   95352   209-523-0316
PALO ALTO: Peninsula Funeral Society, 168 S. California Avenue, 94306   415-321-2109
RIDGECREST: Kern Memorial Society, P.O. Box 2122   93555
SACRAMENTO: Sacramento Valley Memorial Society Inc., Box 161688, 3720 Folsom Blvd. 95816   916-451-4641
SAN DIEGO: San Diego Mem. Soc., P.O. Box 16336   92116   714-284-1465
SAN LUIS OBISPO: Central Coast Mem. Soc., Box 679   93406   805-543-6133
SANTA BARBARA: Channel Cities Mem. Soc., Box 424   93102   805-962-4794
SANTA CRUZ: Funeral & Memorial Society of Monterey Bay Inc., P.O. Box 2900   95063 408-462-1333
STOCKTON: San Joaquin Mem. Soc., P.O. Box 4832   95204   209-462-8739
COLORADO: DENVER: Rocky Mountain Memorial Society, 4101 East Hampden   80222 303-759-2800
CONNECTICUT: GROTON: Southeastern Branch of Greater New Haven Memorial Society, Box 825   06340   203-445-8348
HARTFORD: Memorial Society of Greater Hartford, 2609 Albany Ave., West Hartford   06117 203-523-8700
NEW HAVEN: Greater New Haven Memorial Society, 60 Connelly Parkway, c/o Co-op, Hamden   06514   203-288-6436   203-865-2015
SOUTHBURY: Southbury Branch of Greater New Haven Memorial Society, 514A Heritage Village   06488   203-264-7564

STAMFORD: Council Mem. Soc., 628 Main St. 06901 203-348-2800

WESTPORT: Mem. Soc. of SW Conn., 71 Hillendale Rd. 06880 203-227-8705

D.C.: WASHINGTON: Memorial Society of Metropolitan Washington, 16th and Harvard Sts., NW 20009 202-234-7777

FLORIDA: COCOA: Brevard Mem. Soc., P.O. Box 276 32922 **305**-783-8699

DeBARY: Funeral Society of Mid-Fla., P.O. Box 262 32713 305-668-6587

FT. MYERS: Mem. Soc. of SW Florida, P.O. Box 1953 33902 813-936-1590

GAINESVILLE: Mem. Soc. of Alachua Co., Box 13195 32604 904-376-7073

JACKSONVILLE: Jacksonville Memorial Society, 6915 Holiday Rd. North 32216 904-724-3766

MIAMI: Community Funeral Society, P.O. Box 7422, Ludlam Branch 33155 305-898-3621

ORLANDO: Orange County Memorial Society, 1815 E. Robinson St. 32803 305-898-3621

ST. PETERSBURG: Suncoast-Tampa Bay Memorial Society, 719 Arlington Avenue North 33701 813-898-3294

SARASOTA: Mem. Soc. of Sarasota, P.O. Box 5683 33579 813-953-3740

TALLAHASSEE: Funeral & Mem. Soc. of Leon Co., Box 20189 32304

TAMPA: Tampa Memorial Soc., 3915 N. "A" St. 33609 813-877-4604

WEST PALM BEACH: Palm Beach Funeral Society, P.O. Box 2065 33402 305-833-8936

GEORGIA: ATLANTA: Memorial Society of Georgia, 1911 Cliff Valley Way, NE 30329 404-634-2896

HAWAII: HONOLULU: Funeral and Memorial Society of Hawaii, 200 N. Vineyard Blvd., Suite 403 96817 808-538-1282

ILLINOIS: BLOOMINGTON: McLean County Branch of Chicago Memorial Society, 1613 E. Emerson 61701 309-828-0235

CARBONDALE: Memorial Society of Carbondale Area, 1214 W. Hill St. 62901 618-549-7816

CHICAGO: Chicago Mem. Assn., 59 E. Van Buren St. 60605 312-939-0678

ELGIN: Fox Valley Funeral Assn., 783 Highland Ave. 60120 312-695-5265

PEORIA: Memorial Society of Greater Peoria, 908 Hamilton Blvd. 61603 309-673-5391

ROCKFORD: Mem. Soc. of N. Illinois, P.O. Box 6131 61125 815-964-7697

URBANA: Champaign County Memorial Society, 309 W. Green St. 61801 217-328-3337

INDIANA: BLOOMINGTON: Bloomington Memorial Society, 2120 N. Fee Lane 47401 812-332-3695

FT. WAYNE: Northeastern Indiana Memorial Society, 306 W. Rudisill Blvd. 46807 219-745-4756

INDIANAPOLIS: Indianapolis Memorial Society, 5805 E. 56th St. 46226 317-545-6005

MUNCIE: Memorial Society of Muncie Area, 1900 N. Morrison Rd. 47304 317-288-9561 (evenings) 317-289-1500

VALPARAISO: Memorial Society of N.W. Indiana, 356 McIntyre Ct. 46383 219-462-5701

WEST LAFAYETTE: Greater Lafayette Memorial Society, Box 2155 47906 317-463-9645

IOWA: AMES: Central Iowa Memorial Society, 1015 Hyland Ave. 50010 515-239-2421

CEDAR RAPIDS: Memorial Option Service of Cedar Rapids, 600 3rd Ave., S.E. 52403 319-398-3955

DAVENPORT: Blackhawk Memorial Society, 3707 Eastern Ave. 52807 319-326-0479

IOWA CITY: Memorial Society of Iowa River Valley, 120 N. Dubuque St. 52240 319-338-1179

KANSAS: HUTCHINSON: Mid-Kansas Mem. Soc., Box 2142 67501

KENTUCKY: LOUISVILLE: Memorial Society of Greater Louisville, 322 York Street 40203 502-585-5119

LOUISIANA: BATON ROUGE: Memorial Society of Greater Baton Rouge, 8470 Goodwood Ave. 70806 504-926-2291

MAINE: PORTLAND: Memorial Society of Maine, 425 Congress St. 04111 207-773-5747

MARYLAND: BALTIMORE: Memorial Society of Greater Baltimore, 3 Ruxview Ct., Apt. 101 21204 301-486-6532 301-296-4657

COLUMBIA: Howard County Memorial Foundation, c/o Suite 100 Wilde Lake Village Green 21044 301-730-7920 301-997-1188

GREENBELT: Maryland Suburban Memorial Society, c/o Bruce Bowman, 14Z3 Laurel Hill 20770 301-474-6468

MASSACHUSETTS: BROOKLINE: Memorial Society of New England, 25 Monmouth Street 02146 617-731-2073

ORLEANS: Mem. Soc. of Cape Cod, Box 1346 02653 617-255-3841

NEW BEDFORD: Memorial Society of Greater New Bedford Inc., 71 Eighth St. 02740 617-994-9686

SPRINGFIELD: Springfield Memorial Society, P.O. Box 2821 01101 (evenings) 413-567-5715

MICHIGAN: ANN ARBOR: Memorial Advisory & Planning Service, P.O. Box 7325 48107 313-663-2697

BATTLE CREEK: Memorial Society of Battle Creek, c/o Art Center, 265 E. Emmett St. 49017 616-962-5362

DETROIT: Greater Detroit Mem. Soc., 4605 Cass Ave. 48201 313-833-9107

EAST LANSING: Lansing Area Memorial Planning Society, 855 Grove St. 48823 517-351-4081

FLINT: Mem. Soc. of Flint, G-2474 S. Ballenger Hwy. 48507 313-232-4023

GRAND RAPIDS: Memorial Society of Greater Grand Valley, P.O. Box 1426 49501 616-459-4032

KALAMAZOO: Mem. Soc. of Greater Kalamazoo, 315 W. Michigan 49006

MT. PLEASANT: Memorial Society of Mid-Michigan, P.O. Box 313 48858 517-772-0220

MINNESOTA: MINNEAPOLIS: Minnesota Memorial Society, 900 Mt. Curve Ave. 55403 612-824-2440

MISSISSIPPI: GULFPORT: Funeral and Memorial Society of the Mississippi Gulf Coast, P.O. Box 265 39501 601-435-2284

MISSOURI: KANSAS CITY: Greater Kansas City Memorial Society, 4500 Warwick Blvd. 64111 816-561-6322

ST. LOUIS: Memorial and Planned Funeral Society, 5007 Waterman Blvd. 63108 314-361-0595

MONTANA: BILLINGS: Memorial Society of Montana, 1024 Princeton Avenue 59102 406-252-5065

MISSOULA: Five Valleys Burial-Memorial Assn., 401 University Ave. 59801 406-543-6952

NEBRASKA: OMAHA: Midland Memorial Society, 3114 Harney St. 68131 402-345-3039

NEVADA: RENO: Memorial Society of Western Nevada, Box 8413, University Station 89507 702-322-0688

NEW HAMPSHIRE: CONCORD: Memorial Society of New Hampshire, 274 Pleasant St. 03301 603-224-0291

NEW JERSEY: CAPE MAY: Memorial Society of South Jersey, P.O. Box 592 08204 609-884-8852

EAST BRUNSWICK: Raritan Valley Memorial Society, 176 Tices Lane 08816 201-246-9620 201-572-1470

LANOKA HARBOR: Mem. Assn. of Ocean County, P.O. Box 173 08734

LINCROFT: Memorial Association of Monmouth County, 1475 W. Front St. 07738 201-741-8092

MADISON: Morris Memorial Society, Box 156 07940 201-540-1177

MONTCLAIR: Mem. Soc. of Essex, 67 Church St. 07042 201-746-9352

PARAMUS: Central Mem. Soc., 156 Forest Ave. 07652 201-265-5910

PLAINFIELD: Memorial Society of Plainfield, P.O. Box 307 07061

PRINCETON: Princeton Mem. Assn., P.O. Box 1154 08540 609-924-1604

NEW MEXICO: ALBUQUERQUE: Memorial Association of Central New Mexico, P.O. Box 3251 87190 505-299-5384

LOS ALAMOS: Memorial & Funeral Society of Northern New Mexico, P.O. Box 178 87544 505-662-2346

NEW YORK: ALBANY: Albany Area Memorial Society, 405 Washington Avenue 12206 518-465-9664

BINGHAMTON: Southern Tier Memorial Society, 183 Riverside Dr. 13905 607-729-1641

BUFFALO: Greater Buffalo Memorial Society, 695 Elmwood Ave. 14222 716-885-2136

ITHACA: Ithaca Memorial Society, P.O. Box 134 14850 607-272-5476

NEW HARTFORD: Mohawk Valley Memorial Society, 28 Oxford Road 13413 315-797-1955

N.Y.C. Community Funeral Society, 40 E. 35th St. 10016 212-683-4988

N.Y.C. Consumers Memorial Soc., 309 W. 23rd St. 10111 212-691-8400

N.Y.C. Memorial Society of Riverside Church, 490 Riverside Dr. 10027 212-749-7000

ONEONTA: Memorial Society of Greater Oneonta, 12 Ford Ave. 13820 607-432-3491

PAINTED POST: Memorial Society of Greater Corning Area, P.O. Box 23 14870 607-962-2690

POMONA: Rockland County Mem. Soc., Box 461 10970 914-354-2917

PORT WASHINGTON: Memorial Society of Long Island, Box 303 10050 516-627-6590

POUGHKEEPSIE: Mid-Hudson Memorial Society, 249 Hooker Ave. 12603 914-454-4164

ROCHESTER: Rochester Mem. Soc., 220 Winton Rd. S 14610 716-461-1620

SYRACUSE: Syracuse Memorial Soc., P.O. Box 67 13214 315-474-4580

WELLSVILLE: Upper Genesee Memorial Society, 4604 Bolivar Rd. 14895 (in process of joining) 716-593-1060

WHITE PLAINS: Funeral Planning Assn. of Westchester, Rosedale Ave. & Sycamore Lane 10605 914-946-1660

NORTH CAROLINA: ASHEVILLE: The Blue Ridge Memorial Society, P.O. Box 2601 28801

CHAPEL HILL: Triangle Memorial & Funeral Society, Box 1223 27514 919-942-4427

CHARLOTTE: Charlotte Memorial Society, 234 N. Sharon Amity Rd. 28211 704-597-2346

GREENSBORO: Piedmont Memorial & Funeral Society, Box 16192 27406 919-674-5501

LAURINBURG: Scotland County Funeral & Mem. Soc., Box 192 28352

OHIO: AKRON: Canton-Akron Memorial Society, 3300 Morewood Rd. 44313 216-836-8094

CAMPBELL: Memorial Society of Greater Youngstown, 75 Jackson Dr. 44405 216-755-8696

CINCINNATI: Memorial Society of Greater Cincinnati Inc., 536 Linton St. 45219 513-281-1564

CLEVELAND: Cleveland Memorial Society, 21600 Shaker Blvd. 44122 216-751-5515

COLUMBUS: Memorial Society of the Columbus Area, P.O. Box 14103 43214 614-267-4696

DAYTON: Dayton Memorial Soc., 665 Salem Ave. 45406 513-274-5890

ELYRIA: Memorial Society of Lorain County (branch of Cleveland Memorial Society) 226 Middle Ave. 44035 216-323-5776 ext. 441

TOLEDO: Memorial Society of Northwestern Ohio, 2210 Collingwood Blvd. 43620 419-475-4812

WILMINGTON: Funeral & Memorial Society of Southwest Ohio, 66 North Mulberry St. 45177 513-382-2349

YELLOW SPRINGS: Yellow Springs Branch of Memorial Society of Columbus Area, 317 Dayton St. 45387 513-767-2011

OKLAHOMA: OKLAHOMA CITY: Memorial Society of Central Oklahoma 600 NW 13th St. 73103 405-232-9224

TULSA: Mem. Soc. of E. Oklahoma, 2952 S. Peoria 74114 918-743-2363

OREGON: PORTLAND: Oregon Memorial Association, 5255 Southwest Dosch Rd. 97201 503-283-5500

PENNSYLVANIA: BETHLEHEM: Lehigh Valley Memorial Society, 701 Lechauweki Ave. 18015 215-866-7652

ERIE: Thanatopsis Society of Erie, P.O. Box 3495 16508 814-864-9300

HARRISBURG: Memorial Society of Greater Harrisburg, 1280 Clover Lane 17113 717-564-4761

PHILADELPHIA: Memorial Society of Greater Philadelphia, 2125 Chestnut St. 19103 215-567-1065

PITTSBURGH: Pittsburgh Memorial Society, 605 Morewood Ave. 15213 412-621-8008

POTTSTOWN: Pottstown Branch of Philadelphia Memorial Society, 1409 N. State St. 19464 215-323-5561

SCRANTON: Memorial Society of Scranton-Wilkes-Barre Area, 303 Main Ave., Clark's Summit 18411 717-587-5255

RHODE ISLAND: See Massachusetts for New England Memorial Society

SOUTH CAROLINA: CHARLESTON: Memorial Society of Charleston, 2319 Bluefish Circle 29412

CLEMSON: Clemson Funeral Society, P.O. Box 1132 29631

MYRTLE BEACH: Memorial Society of Eastern Carolina, P.O. Box 712 29577 803-449-6526 803-449-3064

TENNESSEE: CHATTANOOGA: Memorial Society of Chattanooga, 1108 N. Concord Rd. 37421 615-267-4685

KNOXVILLE: East Tenn. Mem. Soc., P.O. Box 10507 37919 615-523-4176

NASHVILLE: Middle Tennessee Memorial Society, 1808 Woodmont Blvd. 37215 615-383-5760

PLEASANT HILL: Cumberland Branch of East Tennessee Mem. Soc., P.O. Box 246 38578 615-277-3795

TEXAS: AUSTIN: Austin Mem. & Burial Info. Soc., P.O. Box 4382 78765

BEAUMONT: Golden Triangle Mem. Soc., Box 6136 77705 713-833-6883

COLLEGE STATION: Memorial Society of Bryan-College Station, P.O. Box 9078 77840 713-696-6944

DALLAS: Dallas Area Memorial Soc., 4015 Normandy 75205 214-528-3990

HOUSTON: Houston Area Memorial Society, 5210 Fannin St. 77004 214-526-1571

LUBBOCK: Lubbock Area Mem. Soc., P.O. Box 6562 79413 806-792-0367

SAN ANTONIO: San Antonio Memorial Society, 777 S.A. Bank & Trust Bldg., 771 Navarro 78205

UTAH: SALT LAKE CITY: Utah Memorial Association, 569 S. 13th East 84102 801-582-8687

VERMONT: BURLINGTON: Vermont Memorial Society, P.O. Box 67 05401 802-863-4701

VIRGINIA: ALEXANDRIA: Mt. Vernon Memorial Society, 1909 Windmill Lane 22307 703-765-5950

ARLINGTON: Memorial Society of Arlington, 4444 Arlington Blvd. 22204 703-892-2565

CHARLOTTESVILLE: Memorial Planning Society of the Piedmont, 717 Rugby Road 22903 703-293-3323

OAKTON: Fairfax Memorial Soc., P.O. Box 130 22124 703-281-4230

RICHMOND: Memorial Society of Greater Richmond Area, Box 180 23202 804-355-0777

ROANOKE: Memorial Society of Roanoke Valley Inc., P.O. Box 8001 24014 703-774-9314

VIRGINIA BEACH: Memorial Society of Tidewater Virginia, 2238 Oak St. 23451 804-428-1804

WASHINGTON: SEATTLE: People's Memorial Association, 2366 Eastlake Avenue East 98102 206-325-0489

SPOKANE: Spokane Memorial Assn., P.O. Box 14701 99214 509-926-2933

WISCONSIN: RACINE: Funeral & Memorial Society of Racine & Kenosha, 625 College Ave. 53403 414-634-0659

RIVER FALLS: Western Wisconsin Funeral Society, 110 N. 3rd 54022 715-425-2052

STURGEON BAY: Memorial Society of Door County, c/o Hope United Church of Christ 54235 414-743-2701

GUIDELINES TO CONSIDER WHEN ORGANIZING
A MEMORIAL SOCIETY: AS ADOPTED JUNE 22, 1974

Certain Basic Guidelines have been adopted by CAFMS and MSAC as requirements for accepting new societies as members. These Basic Guidelines and the Suggested Guidelines that follow are based on long experience with the special needs and problems of memorial societies.[2]

A. **Democratic Control.** The membership through annual meetings and an elected board of directors must have ultimate authority over all phases of the society's operation. This authority must be recognized and followed by the elected leadership. The society must remain free of any control by any member of the funeral industry.

B. **Open Membership.** Membership must be open to all persons unrestricted by race, creed, or national origin.

C. **Non-profit.** The society must be non-profit and no benefits may accrue to any private individual or group of individuals in ownership, operation, or in dissolution. On dissolution, or in case a society, without formal dissolution, becomes inactive, the Society should provide for the servicing of its members and for the distribution of its assets. The By-Laws of the Society should provide that in either of these events the responsibility for servicing its members, together with its remaining assets, should be transferred to a neighboring society which is a member or which is eligible to become a member of CAFMS, or MSAS. In the event that a society is unable to find a society which is willing and qualified to service its members, the by-laws should provide that its remaining assets should be transferred to CAFMS, MSAC, or some other non-profit corporation serving similar purposes duly qualified under Section 501 (c) (4) of the Internal Revenue Code, or equivalent law.

D. **Service Voluntary.** No director, trustee, or policy-making officer may receive compensation for services, although, when feasible, actual out-of-pocket expense may be reimbursed. Members paid as staff may not serve as directors, trustees, or policy-making officers, either locally or on the CAFMS or MSAC boards while in the employment of any local memorial society or either of the national organizations.

E. **No Proxy Voting.** Because attendance at membership meetings of memorial societies is often low, and since a small group could, by the solicitation of relatively few proxies, take over the society, proxy voting is not permitted.

F. **Provision for Amending By-Laws.** By-Laws of a memorial society may be amended only by a vote of the members of the Society present at a legally called meeting at which a quorum is present, and providing adequate prior written notice of the meeting, including the proposed By-Laws changes, has been furnished to the membership. These are simply customary parliamentary procedures and serve to protect the membership from changes imposed without their knowledge.

G. **All Members Must Be Direct Members of the Memorial Society,** with full privileges and responsibilities, even when regarded as branch members.

(Comment: This is not intended to preclude the possibility that at some future time suitable arrangements might be evolved for a society, CAFMS, or MSAC to enroll an entire consumer organization, labor union, or other interested group on some type of limited group basis. This is not now being done, and any such plans should be carefully considered on the local and national level.

H. **Reciprocity among societies.** The benefits of membership will be extended to a member of any member-society of CAFMS or MSAC when death occurs in the service area of any other member-society.

I. **Transfers among societies.** A member moving from the service area of one member-society of CAFMS or MSAC to the service area of another member-society shall be welcome as a member upon request of the transferring member, who may be required to pay a transfer fee to the receiving society to cover costs where necessary.

Suggested Guidelines

Unlike the Basic Guidelines, which are required for acceptance into membership, these Suggested Guidelines are merely the outgrowth of many societies' experiences, and represent suggestions to new societies. The decision of an individual society on each of these ideas is to be a free choice, based on the society's determination of the applicability of the idea to its society. The decision of an individual society not to follow one or more of these would not be cause for refusing that society membership in CAFMS or MSAC. Frequently, when processing applications for membership, the CAFMS or MSAC board will offer suggestions such as these to help strengthen a new society's organizational structure or procedures, as one of the major purposes of the national organizations is to help develop strong, viable local societies.

A. **Naming the Society and Area to be Served.** This should be considered carefully. Certainly a major factor would be the existence of a nearby memorial society. Where a number of societies exist within a state or province, it is important to delineate together those areas that can best be served by each society. Even if there is presently no other society in the state, it is better to designate an area that can be served than to undertake grandiose plans that cannot realistically be fulfilled, and that might possibly prevent the organization of memorial societies in other areas.

Newly-organizing societies should be careful not to adopt a name so all-inclusive as to include areas which may be served by another society. It is also a good idea to choose a name beginning with "Memorial Society of . . . ", as this will make it easier for potential members to locate your society in the telephone listings. Even though your society will serve an area larger than the corporate limits of a large city, use of this city's name makes for ready identification of the territory you serve. Frequently just adding the word "area" after the city's name or "greater" before it will indicate the scope of your service area. In order that a non-geographical name not be duplicated, it is suggested that you first look over the names other so-cieties have selected (in the listing to be found in the Manual).

B. **Incorporate.** By incorporating as a non-profit organization, you limit the personal liability of members involved and give a degree of permanency to the society. It is certainly wise to work closely with an attorney. Hopefully, you either have or can recruit one who will serve without compensation, or at least for a minimum charge, and will make his or herself available for consultation. Since financial assets of the society are minimal in the begin-ning, be sure to have a prior understanding as to what fee, if any, the attorney will charge.

C. **Apply for Federal Tax Exemption.** After you are organized and incor-porated, an application should be filed to obtain United States Federal Income Tax Exemption, although obtaining exemption does not eliminate the need for filing tax reports. There is a complete discussion of this in the section on Legal and Legislative Matters. (Not applicable to Canada. Con-sult MSAC on this matter.)

D. **Enrollment Fee.** The most satisfactory basis for the lifetime membership fee has been found to be on an individual adult basis, with minor children being covered by the adult's membership. Death, divorce, transfers and separations all tend to complicate record-keeping on a family basis. Mail-ings may, of course, be done on a family basis to save mailing expense.

E. **Quorum.** Most societies have a quorum for board meetings of a majority of the board. For membership meetings, 10 to 25 members (according to the society's size) or 10% of the total membership, whichever is less, has been found to be a workable quorum.

F. **Limit Terms of Office.** Many societies avoid perpetuating any person or persons governing the affairs of the society by limiting terms of directors or trustees to not more than two consecutive terms of three years each. This usually does not preclude their being re-elected to the board after an inter-val of time. Usually it is not a good idea to extend this provision to offices requiring certain skills which may be difficult to replace. A society tends to benefit by the continuing addition of new members into leadership positions.

G. **Nominating Committee.** Usually a three-member Nominating Committee is appointed by the president in consultation with the board. Only one mem-ber of this committee should be from the board and the other two from the membership. Nominating committees are also sometimes elected by the membership. In any case, the committee should meet in sufficient time to report its nominations for inclusion in the written notice of the membership meeting at which the election will take place. It is recommended that By-Laws provide that nominations from the membership not be accepted from the floor but rather be submitted in writing and received by the nominating committee chairman at least three days before the meeting. This allows time to inquire whether the person is willing to serve and acts as a safety check against the takeover of the organization by persons inimical to our purposes, while providing for legitimate expression of democratic rule by the members.

H. Records Change. Many societies find that a lifetime membership fee is used up over a period of time, even with careful management, because of the increasing costs of mailings, printing, and other basic expenses. The use of a Records Charge, which is described more fully in the section on finances, meets the need for sound long-term financing because it is a continuing source of income. (Comment: Even though new societies do not usually feel the need for this additional source of financing in the early stage of their development, it is wise to project ahead and to include provision for such arrangements in negotiating contracts or agreements with morticians. Some societies feel that a records charge as described under the section on finances is useful for their societies. Other societies oppose this charge as unwise. Each society will make its own *free choice* on this idea.)

CONFIDENTIAL

Personal Data of_____

Use a separate form for each individual

PUTTING MY HOUSE IN ORDER
Foreword

This form is published by the Continental Association of Funeral and Memorial Societies, Inc., 1828 L St. N.W., Washington, D.C. 20036 for use by its member societies and their members.

The following factual data is to provide survivors with a guide for attending to the legal, tax, funeral, obituary and other matters after your death. Omit items that do not apply. Additional sheets may be added to complete information. This form should be brought up-to-date at each important change that occurs and reviewed at least once each year. Revisions can be more readily made if pencil is used in filling in the items subject to change.

This is **NOT A WILL** and does not govern the disposition of your property after death as that is the main purpose of your **WILL.** You may wish to consult your attorney and arrange to execute a will in event you have not done so.

Section I contains information that is **needed immediately** and should be kept readily available in case of need. Section II contains items needed later and should be filed with your Will and other valuable papers.

*   *   *

SECTION I   Keep this sheet readily available.
The person named below has consented to help in making arrangements after my death and to comply with my wishes: (usually a close and trusted friend, perhaps your Executor).

Name _____Phone _____

Address_____

I am a member of the following memorial society and I wish to have my remains cared for through arrangements that have been made by them:

Society's Name _____Phone_____
For prompt assistance after my death call:

Mortuary _____ Phone_____

Address_____

DATA FOR DEATH CERTIFICATE: The doctor in attendance is officially required to prepare and file a death certificate. The following personal data is usually required:

Name _____
           First   Middle   Last

Address _____
                          Street

_____
    City   County   State   Zip Code

Resided in this location since (state year) City____: County____; State____
Residence is: Inside city limits – Yes____: No____
             On a farm – Yes____; No____
Sex: Male____; Female____ Color or race____ Place of birth _____
Marital Status: Never Married____   Separated____   Widowed____
              Married____   Divorced____   Remarried____
Date of Birth:_____
Citizen of what country: _____My Social Security No. is _____
My Father's full name _____
My Mother's maiden name _____
Served in U.S. Armed Forces? Yes____: No____ State War and dates _____

FUNERAL ARRANGEMENTS   I prefer: Cremation____ Burial____ Bequeathal____

Method	Type		Place		Name & Location of Place
Dispose of cinerary	Urn in niche	____	columbarium	____	_____
(cremated) ashes by:	Urn Burial	____	cemetery	____	_____
	Urn entombment	____	mausoleum	____	_____
	Scatter	____	(where permitted)		_____
Body to receive	Earth burial	____	cemetery	____	_____
	Entombment	____	mausoleum	____	_____

If niche, lot or mausoleum is owned or otherwise provided list details separately.

TYPE OF SERVICE: Memorial (body not present)____; Conventional (casket open____, closed____;
    FOR: Friends and relatives____; Private____; Other _____
    AT: Church____; Funeral Home____; Our Home____; Other _____
NAME & ADDRESS OF   If church show denomination
PLACE TO BE HELD: _____
TO CONDUCT SERVICE: Soloist,
Clergyman, or other: _____ if any _____
Favorite hymns/music _____
LIMIT EXPENSE TO: Minimum____; Low average____; Average____; Immaterial____

REMEMBRANCES to church or favorite charity. To those wishing to aid the "Memorial Way" movement you may name Continental Association or your local Memorial Society.

Send remembrances to: _____

MY SAFE DEPOSIT BOX is Number_____, in _____Bank,

_____Branch, in_____, key is located _____

Contents of box belonging to others, explain: _____

Name others that have access to box _____

LAST WILL & TESTAMENT   I have no Will:____ On (date)_____I executed a Will;

Location of my Will is_____

(Attach the following data on separate sheet or sheets)

OTHER INFORMATION FOR NEWSPAPERS: Time lived in this community, occupation, employer's, organizations of which you are a member, schools attended and degrees or honors received, military service showing honors or decorations, other items of interest as well as names of those that would survive you as of this date. (Don't be bashful, tell about your life, it will be a big help to your survivors.)

PEOPLE TO BE NOTIFIED: (List names, addresses and phone numbers).

PROFESSIONALS THAT ASSIST ME: (Show profession, name, address and phone). My attorney, accountant, banker, investment counselor, life insurance agent, casualty insurance agent, auto insurance agent, doctor, dentist, etc.

FAMILY DATA: Date and place of marriage to present spouse; domicile on date of marriage to present spouse; children by present marriage: (Name, sex and birthdate, if children married state married name also). Previously married? Yes___; No____. If yes, indicate following: termination date, by death, divorce, annulment; name of former spouse (before marriage to you); children by former marriage (Name, sex and birthdates — if children married state married name also).

BUSINESS OR OCCUPATION: (If retired show former occupation.) Business or Industry; business address, if in business for yourself show your employer Social Security number, if any.

HEIRS: Next of kin, devisees, and legatees (only five principal ones required. Show their names, relationship (if related) and complete addresses.

END OF SECTION I—Additional data is filed with my valuable papers in Section II.

Additional copies of this form may be obtained from either of the following sources by enclosing 40¢ per set; 3 sets for $1.00 with your request.

**Continental Association of Funeral
and Memorial Societies, Inc.**
  1828 L Street N.W., W
  Washington, D.C. 20036

Signature _____

Address_____

Date compiled ____   My phone is _____

(change as revised)

SECTION II

CONFIDENTIAL

Personal Data of_____

This form for an individual or couple. Use H for Husband; W for Wife, where applicable.

SECTION II   Keep this section with your Will and other valuable papers.

YOUR WILL – Everyone should have a Will, if you have not made one we urge you to do so promptly, and then bring it up-to-date as conditions change, it avoids much delay, expense and doubt. It also provides for you to distribute your estate in the manner **YOU** desire. You will obtain satisfaction and be aiding the cause of the non-profit "Memorial Way" movement if you are able and include in your Will a bequest either to the Continental Association or your local Memorial Society.

SURVIVORS DEATH BENEFITS: Many death benefits are unclaimed as the survivors are not informed of their availability. Some of the sources are listed below, check the ones you are entitled to receive. Details as to source and amount where known.

Social Security lump sum benefit____; most covered workers are entitled to benefits under varying conditions. Is your job normally covered under State Workman's Compensation Insurance?____. Employers'?____; Fraternal organizations?____; religious groups?____; trade unions?____; death benefits included in life, health and accident insurance policies?____; other possible sources_____

_____Are you currently covered under Medicare? Yes____; No____.

Veterans of U.S. Armed Forces in certain cases are entitled to death benefits. Are you a veteran of the U.S. Armed Forces? Yes____; No____. If yes, state your service serial number_____,

branch of service_____Dates served_____,

peace time_____; war time_____; Are you now receiving a service pension? Yes____;

No____. If yes, is pension for disability____; length of service____; other _____

* * *

The following items make up a **check list** of the information your Executor, Lawyer, Accountant and family will need answers to after your death. Many items will not apply to most persons. Where they do apply to you a sheet should be made up with the information and attached to this form on all items to which your answer is Yes or which need space to explain in detail.

RENTS, PENSIONS, ANNUITIES   Do you own any property upon which you receive or are entitled to rent or royalties? Yes____; No____. If yes, describe your property rights, lease, contract or royalty source and basis of amount of income derived.

SOCIAL SECURITY BENEFITS Do you now receive S.S. benefits for Old Age? – Yes____; No____; Survivors? – Yes____; No____; Disability? – Yes____; No____

If Yes—state monthly amounts $_____. Do you contribute toward a pension fund (thru your employer) other than for Social Security? Yes___; No___; If yes, explain. Do you now receive an annuity from your employer or insurance company? Yes___; No___. If yes, show Company, address and amount. Did you contribute toward the above annuity? Yes___; No___. Is any continuing annuity payable to spouse or other survivors? Yes___; No___. Where are policies or contracts located? _____

OUT OF STATE PROPERTY   Do you own property in any other state or country? Yes___; No___.

GIFTS AND/OR TRANSFERS   Have you made any gifts or transfers of the value of $5,000 or more during your lifetime without an adequate and full consideration in money or money's worth? Yes___; No___.

TRUSTS   Have you created any trusts or any trusts created by others under which you possess any power, beneficial interest, or trusteeship? Yes___; No___.

LIFE INSURANCE ON YOUR LIFE   Show name of insuring company and address, also name and address of local agent, policy numbers, face amount, beneficiary, who pays the premiums and location of policies. Explain any policy loans you may have.

HEALTH AND ACCIDENT INSURANCE   Same general data as for life insurance.

AUTO INSURANCE AND CASUALTY CONTRACT   Same data as for other insurance and also show what property the insurance covers or what other risk covered.

REAL ESTATE   Separate property owned by married persons should be clearly indicated. Jointly owned property (other than with spouse) should be indicated and fully explained giving names, addresses and interest of each joint owner. For each parcel of property show: description of property, deed in name of___, location of deed, date acquired, how acquired? Purchase___; gift___; other___. Cost___. Mortgaged—Yes___; No___. Leased— Yes___; No___. If real estate contract still owing show name, address and balance owed to contract holder.

STOCKS, MUTUAL FUND SHARES OWNED   Show number of shares owned, type of shares, name of company or Mutual Fund, your Mutual Fund account number, certificate numbers, location of certificates and name of your broker and the brokerage company he represents.

BONDS AND DEBENTURES   Same general data as for stocks and add face amount of the bond, interest rate, and type of bond or debenture.

MORTGAGES AND/OR PROMISSORY NOTES OWNED Show original amount, date made, name and address of maker, collateral, interest rate, location of documents, assignments or co-signers, etc.

CONTRACTS TO SELL REAL ESTATE OWNED Full price, down payment, date of contract, name and address of purchaser, interest rate, location contracts, balance as of what date $_____ ___/___/___

CASH- CHECKING-ACCOUNTS Show name and branch name, and address of bank, your account number, list names of other signers on account.

CASH ACCOUNTS WITH CREDIT UNIONS, SAVINGS BANKS, & SAVINGS & LOAN ASSOCIATIONS: Show name, branch and address of each depository, your passbook number, type of deposit, rate of interest currently paid, other signers on the account, location where passbooks are kept. Explain any interest of others in any balance.

MISCELLANEOUS PROPERTY OWNED Check only the items you own or in which you own interest and give full details. Interest in a copartnership___; interest in life insurance on life of another___; interest in an unincorporated business___; debts owed to me by others___; amounts due me from claims___; rights___; royalties___; leaseholds___; judgments___; remainder interests___; shares in trust funds___; farm products___; growing crops___; livestock___; farm machinery___; autos___; other _____

LIABILITIES Check only the items that you owe as of this date: Real Estate mortgages___; Real Estate Contracts___; Notes Payable___; Bank Loans___; Credit Union Loans___; Finance Company Loans___; personal loans from friends___; personal loans from relatives___; time payment accounts (where not paid in full each month)___. On all of the above liabilities checked indicate where the documents are located, and attach details.

LAWSUITS Are there now pending any lawsuits against you? Yes___; No___. Explain.

CLAIMS Are there any claims against you which you consider invalid? Yes___; No___. Explain in detail.

END OF SECTION II—Additional data is filed where readily available, in Section I.

**Continental Association of Funeral
and Memorial Societies, Inc.**
 1828 L Street N.W., W
 Washington, D.C. 20036

Signature _____
Address_____
Date compiled ____　My phone is _____
(change as revised)

A Proposed Pronouncement on
THE RIGHT TO DIE

Recommended by the Council for Christian Social Action to the Ninth General Synod of the United Church of Christ, meeting in St. Louis, Missouri, June 22–26, 1973, for adoption as a Pronouncement.

"A pronouncement is a declaration of Christian conviction on a matter of social principle, approved by the General Synod and directed to the churches and to the public." (63 GS 18)

Submitted to the churches, the Conferences and the delegates to the Ninth General Synod for study and comment.

Medical science has made tremendous progress in the last half century. Killing epidemics are virtually unknown in this land. Illnesses are usually overcome and injuries repaired with relative ease. The life span has been lengthened with new medicines and treatment for famous killers such as heart failures and pneumonia. Diseases normally producing death in a short time have been replaced by long chronic illnesses such as cancer, heart diseases and emphysema. As the end of life approaches, new means have been found to keep the body functioning through resuscitation, intravenous feeding, stimulants, oxygen tanks, respirators, heart pumps, drainage tubes and similar devices.

We are grateful for enhancement of God-given life. Sometimes, however, patients irreversibly and terminally ill have been made to continue functioning organically for a substantial period of time through artificial and very expensive means. Often such patients have suffered pain and loss of dignity and sometimes are semi-conscious or even comatose.

These newly won technical abilities have outstripped the categories of conventional medical ethics. We must now struggle anew with such questions as: What is death and how can we determine when it has occurred? Are there distinctions to be made between prolonging life and artificially delaying death? Are there occasions when affirmative steps should be taken to hasten death as a way of relieving suffering? To whom do we turn for answers?

The Religious Perspective

Informed by our Hebrew-Christian tradition, we affirm God as the source of all life. In creating us, He has endowed us with privileges as well as responsibilities; we are both creature and creator. In embracing our full humanness we acknowledge our limitations and seek to exercise our freedom responsibly. With the awesome increase in medical technology, we recognize that we must always guard against undisciplined use of our knowledge and power.

At the same time we recognize that our religious heritage has always stressed reverence for human life—personhood as well as biological vitality. Thus the enhancement of life—responsible stewardship of our role as creator—required equal regard for both aspects of our human existence. Accordingly, over-regard for the body, without proper concern for the needs of the person, or the human spirit, can become a kind of biological idolatry. What is required is a balanced appreciation of the whole person.

The basic tenets today are to have faith in God's word, a belief in Jesus Christ and the way of life which He taught. This means that we try to have love and respect for each other—for our well being, quality of life, personality, dignity, self-possession. We are concerned with each other's mental and physical health, comfort and personal growth. This includes growth of a healthy body but does not necesarily mean that the body must be kept alive as long as scientifically possible, regardless of the circumstances. That depends on what is best for the person, on his or her well being.

The supreme value in our religious heritage is placed on the person in wholeness, the person in freedom, the person in integrity and dignity. When illness takes away those abilities we associate with full personhood, leaving one so impaired that what is most valuable and precious is gone, we may well feel that the mere continuance of the body by machine or drugs is a violation of the person.

Also relevant is our view of death. Death for an older person should be a beautiful event. There is beauty in birth, growth, fullness of life and then, equally so, in the tapering off and final end. Transformation from life on this earth to life in the hereafter of the Lord is a fulfillment. The acceptance of death is our witness to faith in the resurrection of Jesus Christ (Romans 8). We can rejoice.

The Ethics in Life-Death Decisions

We will consider three areas of decision making. In two of them, we have reached a conclusion, but in this third area, we have not reached a conclusion.

(1) Consider the ethical decision involving the patient who decides that he or she does not want the drugs or treatment recommended by the doctor as requisite to continued life. Generally a patient has the right to refuse operations and treatments, even if the refusal is expected to lead to death. (Normally written consent is required.)

Nothing in Jewish or Christian traditions presumes that a physician has a mandate to impose his or her wishes and skills upon patients for the sake of prolonging the length of their dying where those patients are diagnosed as terminally ill and do not wish the interventions of the physicians. People who are dying have as much freedom as other living persons to accept or to refuse medical treatment where that treatment provides no cure for their ailment. Thus the freedom of the patient to choose his own style for the remainder of his life and the method and time for dying is enhanced. This is distinguished from suicide where the person makes the decision to die. Here the illness, or, depending on one's theology, God, has already made death imminent.

Some people realize that when the time comes for a specific decision in their terminal illness they may be comatose and unable to make their wish known. To prepare for this contingency while still in good mental health, they may sign a "living will," or a document like a will in its formalities, or a formal direction to a guardian or committee appointed to represent them while non compos mentis, expressing their desire or stating their orders that they may not be kept alive by artificial means or "heroic measures" and requesting that drugs be administered to alleviate terminal suffering even if they hasten the moment of death.

We believe it is ethically and theologically proper for a person to wish to avoid artificial and/or painful prolongation of a terminal illness and for him or her to execute a living will or similar document of instructions.

(2) In another situation the patient may be in an irreversible terminal illness, perhaps with substantial pain or physical distress, but in no condition to give instructions and without a previously made living will or document of instructions. Again, death itself is no longer a question. The only question is "when." These are patients who would die reasonably soon if given only painkilling treatment but whose body could be kept alive, or at least with functioning organs (heart, lungs) by artificial means. The question is whether these extraordinary measures should be used or whether the patient should be allowed to complete his or her natural death.

Every day in hospitals across the land, these decisions are made clinically. Too often they are made covertly. Too many hospitals, doctors and relatives feel vulnerable when facing the issue and so refuse to have the decision-making process open. Some are torn over their own motivation. Some fear they may be violating the will of God. Some fear malpractice suits by a money-seeking heir or ambitious prosecuting attorney.

We believe there comes a time in the course of an irreversible terminal illness when, in the interest of love, mercy and compassion, those who are caring for the patient should say: "Enough." We do not believe the continuance of mere physical existence is either morally defensible or socially desirable or is God's will.

(3) There are also situations where the patient is mentally competent and irreversibly and terminally ill but where death is not imminent. There may be years of insurmountable financial obligations (all too frequently a heavy private burden), suffering by the family and friends and a clearly expressed desire by a competent patient to be released from this life. Some adults, suffering varying degrees of pain, indignity or meaninglessness, but knowing what they are doing, do ask their physicians to help them go, quickly and painlessly. What principles should guide medical and legal authorities and law makers in deciding whether to grant the patient's request?

Christian teaching does not require that mere physical existence in itself be preserved in all circumstances. Important criteria on the continuance of life are the desire of the person and the quality and wholeness of the life in question. The approach must be one of concern and love for the person's entire being and not for the mere functioning of the body. Although Paul admonishes us to appreciate suffering and some Christians make their witness through suffering, that does not justify society in forcing people to suffer against their will.

We are unable to reach a conclusion about the issue of actively intervening to end a life in these circumstances but realize that it is none the less a real and pressing dilemma for those faced with this decision.

A Challenge

The progress of medical technology has developed new possibilities and new problems in the care and perpetuation of human bodies. New conditions inevitably raise new ethical and religious questions. They call for fresh deliberations and possibly new answers.

We call upon the members in the United Church of Christ to recognize the new problems, consider the principles set forth above, and to seek to determine, with tolerance and prayer, the Will of God in today's world. We encourage the Church, and lay persons, to stand with those who face these decisions.

For Freedom of Choice: A Guide to Funeral Planning[1]

Plan Your Funeral with the People You Love

- Let your funeral reflect the person you are and the way you want to be remembered.
- Understand costs of merchandise and services you want to purchase.
- Feel a sense of relief and peace of mind.
- Let your family and friends know what you want.
- Save them unnecessary expense and guilt when you die.

---

1. Read this entire guide once; it is designed to help you plan the funeral of your choice. It gives you basic costs, options and general information to complete each step of the planning process.

2. Discuss your plans with those who are close to you (family, friends, advisor or clergy). Consider their ideas and let them know your wishes.

3. Choose one basic funeral plan, according to your preference. Some basic types of funerals are listed on the next page. Decide which type you prefer and provide guidelines for arrangements related to it.

All choices include these basic services provided by the funeral director: removal from place of death within a 25-mile radius; clearing of papers and permits; notifying newspapers; simplest, lowest priced casket; arranging cemetery/crematory details, and delivery to cemetery/crematory within a 25-mile radius.

Basic Types of Funerals[2]

The price ranges given are "average low" to "moderate" prices, *not* least expensive to most expensive.

Simple Burial $400 to $760   Includes: basic services; assisting cemetery personnel with lowering into grave.

Simple Jewish Burial $700 to $900   Includes: basic services; arranging for rabbi to officiate; arranging for Watchers of the Dead; ritually correct shroud and casket; assisting cemetery personnel with lowering into grave.

Simple Cremation $475 to $750   Includes: basic services; cremation fee; scattering in undeveloped cemetery property or delivery of ashes to next-of-kin.

Average Complete Adult Funeral $1100 to $1400   Includes items in Simple

Burial or Simple Cremation plus: embalming; preparation for viewing; viewing hours; use of funeral home chapel for services; use of limousine for family.

Bequeathal of Body to Medical School $45 to $125   Medical school pays for almost all costs.

Newspapers: Placing death notices in newspapers is part of the basic services that funeral directors provide. However, you must pay the cost of the notices charged by the newspapers. These charges can be surprisingly high depending upon the newspaper and length of your notice. When you select the papers in which you want notices to appear, you may also want to check on their costs.

Cremation is an increasingly common means of disposition. It is less expensive than burial, particularly if the ashes are scattered. Remains may also be stored in a simple urn, buried in a cemetery or placed in a columbarium, an area with niches for this purpose.

Bequeathal should be arranged well in advance of death. Types of bequeathal are explained below.

Organ Donation is most practical when death occurs in a hospital. You can bequeath your kidneys, eyes or other organs. In many states, the Registry of Motor Vehicles provides Uniform Donor Cards on which you can indicate what organs you wish to donate. For more information, contact: The Kidney Foundation, the Eye Bank, or similar organizations in your state.

Post Mortem Examination (autopsy) may greatly benefit your family and society by adding to the knowledge of disease. There is no charge when the examination is requested by the attending physician and when death occurs in the hospital where the examination is performed. It does not interfere with organ donations or the funeral director's preparations. It does make the body unsuitable for bequeathal.

Bequeathal of Your Body to a Medical School is a worthy consideration. However, it is wise to make alternate plans in case the circumstances at death make donation impossible. If desired, bodies accepted by a medical school can be buried without charge in the cemetery maintained by the schools.

4. Add to your basic plan as you desire. The choices and prices in Step 3 cover the simplest, lowest priced merchandise and basic services from a funeral director. If you want others, the cost of your funeral will increase accordingly, for example: Finished and lined casket: $295 and up; Urn or container for ashes: $60 and up; Embalming: $95 to $150 and up; Additional limousine: $55 to $80; Flowers: $25 and up; Use of funeral home chapel; $50 to $190 and up; Viewing: $50 per hour (average)[3]

5. Contact the cemetery of your choice. In most cases, cemeteries will give all necessary information, including prices, by telephone. Average low to moderate cemetery charges for burial include:

Plot for 1 or 2 caskets buried at different depths: $165 to $540; Opening and closing fee during working hours: $225 to $750.

Cemetery charges for cremation include:

Burial site for 1 urn or 2 urns buried at different depths: $150 to $425; Opening and closing fee for urn site: $25 to $115; Niche in columbarium: $200 to $1600.

Cremation fees ($105 to $115) usually are billed to the funeral director who, in turn, bills you. Although *concrete grave liners* ($75 to $125) are required in many cemeteries to prevent the land from caving in, they are not required by law. Other cemeteries may be found that do not require this expense. Perpetual care is usually included in the price of a plot, urn site or niche, but be sure to ask about this.

6. Plan your services to give the living an opportunity to honor your life and mourn your death. Ceremonies may be public or private, religious or secular. You may even prefer to have no services at all. There are three basic types:

Funeral services are usually held in a church or funeral home with the body present in an open or closed casket. They may be preceded by visiting hours.

Committal services are held at the graveside immediately before burial or in a crematory chapel prior to cremation.

Memorial services do not include the presence of the body and can be held whenever and wherever you wish. Appropriately planned, they can be both meaningful and economical.

In planning, you may wish to consider:
Participants: clergy, family, friends, others
Attendance: family, friends, public or private
Place: church, synagogue, home, funeral home, other
Contents: music, prayers, readings, scriptures, other
Memorial gifts: flowers, donations to charity, other
Viewing: public, private; closed or open casket; no viewing

7. Understand the law. While the law varies from state to state, the next-of-kin usually has control over the body's disposal, although in some states instructions left by the deceased are binding. In addition the following usually will be established by local state law:

- A physician's death certificate will be required;[4]
- Transportation of the body may be limited to a licensed funeral director or in a specifically licensed vehicle;
- A permit required for burial;

- Legally, the term "casket" applies to any suitable container, which may include a cardboard, fiberboard or wooden box;
- A 48-hour delay may be required between death and cremation;
- Cremated remains may be transported by anyone and sent by parcel post in a cardboard box.

Embalming is *not* required by law except when the cause of death is deemed highly contagious and dangerous to the living by the State Department of Public Health. However, funeral directors may advise or "require" it in some circumstances. Public viewing presumes an embalmed body.

8. Get help if you need it. Write ahead of time to the nearest Memorial Society.[5] These societies are non-profit organizations which provide information on funerals. The National Association of Funeral and Memorial Societies can furnish information on the nearest Memorial Society to your locale. Its address is given at the end of this guide. A Directory of Local Societies is available on request.

9. Choose a funeral director. Before deciding, consider the director's business reputation, his rapport with you, and the cost of services and merchandise offered. If you are not satisfied, "shop around" for another.

To avoid misunderstandings, have someone else present for discussions, be specific about arrangements and ask for an itemized list giving prices of services and merchandise selected.

10. Consider all costs of your funeral. If the total seems high, you may wish to reconsider your plans. A dignified funeral can also be economical.

Pre-payment: As of 1979, there is no law protecting the consumer in pre-paid financial arrangements with funeral directors. Therefore, such agreements are not recommended. Pre-payment for cemetery sites can save money only if you are absolutely sure you will not move or change your funeral plans. Cemeteries usually do not buy back or re-sell sites.

Benefits: Most people qualify for death benefits which help pay funeral costs. Social Security pays $255. Veterans may receive $300 for a funeral and $150 for burial. Pension plans or insurance policies may also provide help.

11. Gather information needed by your next-of-kin or funeral director to file for death benefits and to complete the death certificate:

- Name of funeral director (and cemetery)
- Your place and date of birth, marital status, occupation and type of business, social security number, military service information, veteran's number, insurance company, doctor, etc.
- Your spouse's full name, date and place of birth

- Your parents' names, your mother's maiden name, places and dates of birth
- Biographical information for your death notices

12. Write your funeral plans, using Steps 3 through 7 as a guide. Be sure to sign and date them. **Send copies** to your funeral director, your next-of-kin and/or the person who will carry out your plans, and the Memorial Society if you are a member. Keep a copy for yourself where it can be found easily. *Don't* put it with your will or in your safe deposit box.

13. Up-date your plan any time. If and when you need to change your plan, sign and date the changes and send copies to everyone who has the original version.

If you need **legal assistance or information,** or if you suspect unfair or illegal practice by a funeral director or cemetery, contact: Department of the Attorney General, Consumer Protection Division (of your state); Consumer Affairs Office (of your city or county); your Memorial Society; or write for help to the Continental Association of Funeral and Memorial Societies, Suite 1100, 1828 L Street NW, Washington, D.C. 20036.

Notes

Note to Prefacing Letters to Each Chapter:

*Throughout this volume I shall share with you, the readers, the experiences related in the continental research survey of death and grief, which was conducted a few years ago. These intimate, personal disclosures, attached to a scientific sampling, remain anonymous in keeping with a pledge of confidentiality. Therefore, the names and localities of the sources of these letters from the author's personal research project will not be disclosed in the printed text. Similar quotations will be found as opening passages of each chapter.

Preface

1. Marshall, George N., "Funeral and Memorial Services: A Study of the Comparative Values of Traditional Funerals and Modern Memorial Services to Determine the Potentialities for Enhancing the Death and Grief Situation," 1975, Ann Arbor, Michigan 48106, University Microfilms International, 300 North Zeeb Road. (Available in either bound volumes or on microfilms.)

1—A Rendezvous with Death

1. See chapter 9, "Modern Issues concerning Death," pp. 98–115. For a fanciful reconstruction of this cryonic theory, or deep-freeze thaw of a human body preserved accidentally in a glacier, see the opening chapters of the novel by Ben Sapir, *The Far Arena* (New York: Simon & Schuster, Seaview Books, 1978).

2. George N. Marshall, *An Understanding of Albert Schweitzer* (New York: Philosophical Library, 1966), pp. 6–11.

3. George N. Marshall and David Poling, *Schweitzer, A Biography* (New York: Harcourt, Brace, Jovanovich, Inc., Pillar Books, 1975), p. 307.

4. Plato, *Apology* (abridged).

5. Robert Louis Stevenson, "Requiem," in many volumes.

2—The Fellowship of Grief

1. John Brantner, M.D., "Proceedings," in *Death and Attitudes Toward Death,* ed. Stacy B. Day (Minneapolis: University of Minnesota Medical School, 1972). (See Bibliography.)

2. Edgar N. Jackson, "Grief," in *Concerning Death,* ed. Earl A. Grollman (Boston: Beacon Press, 1974), p. 2.

3. Lily Pincus, *Death and the Family* (New York: Pantheon Books, 1974), p. 123.

4. Lynn Caine, *Widow* (New York: William Morrow and Co., 1974), p. 90.

5. John Donne (1573-1631), "Devotions XVII," in *Bartlett's Familiar Quotations,* 15th ed. (Boston: Little, Brown & Co., 1972).

6. Caine, *Widow,* p. 90.

7. Jackson, "Grief," pp. 9-12.

8. John Hinton, *Dying* (Baltimore: Penguin Books, 1967), p. 88.

9. Jackson, "Grief," pp. 9-12.

10. Ibid., p. 11.

11. Geoffrey Gorer, *Death, Grief and Mourning* (New York: Doubleday & Co., 1965), p. 129.

12. Bernardine Kries and Alice Pattie, *Up From Grief* (New York: The Seabury Press, 1969), p. 9.

13. Sarah Morris, *Grief and How to Live With It* (New York: Grosset & Dunlap, 1972), p. 8.

14. Ibid., pp. 18 f.

15. Ibid., pp. 12 f.

16. Pincus, *Death and the Family,* p. 115.

17. Jackson, "Grief," p. 10.

18. Hinton, *Dying,* p. 184.

19. Edgar N. Jackson, *The Christian Funeral* (New York: Channel Press, 1966), p. 8.

20. Gorer, *Death, Grief and Mourning,* p. 63.

21. Hinton, *Dying,* p. 8.

3—The Travail of Dying

1. Herman Feifel, *The Meaning of Death* (New York: McGraw-Hill Book Co., 1959, 1965), p. 126.

2. Hinton, *Dying,* p. 23.

3. Ibid.

4. Elisabeth Kübler-Ross, *On Death and Dying* (New York: Macmillan paperback, 1970), pp. 38-41. Quotations in this paragraph from these pages.

5. Ibid.

6. William Cullen Bryant, "Thanatopsis," in various anthologies and collections of poetry, including *CLF Service Handbook,* ed. George N. Marshall (Boston: Church of the Larger Fellowship, Unitarian Universalist Association, 1972), p. 34.

7. Feifel, *Meaning of Death,* p. 127.

8. Dylan Thomas, *The Collected Poems of Dylan Thomas* (New York: New Directions, 1957).

9. Edwin O'Connor, *The Last Hurrah* (Boston: Little, Brown & Co., 1959), final page.

10. See Kübler-Ross, *On Death,* pp. 67-69, 82-86, also pp. 110-144 ff., for a more detailed exposition.

11. Ibid., pp. 82 ff.

12. Ibid., pp. 85 f.

13. See Hinton, *Dying,* pp. 93–95, 100, also pp. 16 ff.

14. See Kübler-Ross, *On Death,* pp. 112 f.

15. See Hinton, *Dying,* pp. 103–105; p. 64.

16. See Kübler-Ross, *On Death,* p. 177.

17. Ibid., pp. 25, 119.

18. Ibid., pp. 138–141.

19. Kübler-Ross, *On Death,* pp. 5, 7.

20. Hinton, *Dying,* p. 30.

21. Feifel, *Meaning of Death,* p. 115.

22. Kübler-Ross, *On Death,* pp. 31, 246 f.

23. Hinton, *Dying,* pp. 134–138.

24. Joseph Fletcher, "The Patient's Right to Die," in *Euthanasia and the Right to Die,* ed. A. B. Downing (Los Angeles: Nash Publishing, 1969), p. 64.

25. Robert Fulton, "Proceedings," in *Death and Attitudes Toward Death,* ed. Stacy B. Day (Minneapolis: University of Minnesota Medical School, 1972), p. 28.

26. Hinton, *Dying,* pp. 132 f.

27. Ibid., pp. 133 f.

28. Ibid., p. 133.

29. Gorer, *Death, Grief and Mourning,* pp. 3 f.

30. Kübler-Ross, *On Death,* p. 29.

31. Ibid., pp. 36 f., 116, 30.

32. Elisabeth Kübler-Ross, *Questions and Answers on Death and Dying* (New York: Macmillan, Collier Books, 1974), p. 3.

33. Gorer, *Death, Grief and Mourning,* pp. 44, 65, 79, 80.

34. Norman Cousins, *The Celebration of Life* (New York: Harper & Row, 1974).

35. Kübler-Ross, *On Death,* p. 268.

4—Funeral Practices from Prehistory to Today

1. This eyewitness account of the funeral of King Faisal of Saudi Arabia following his assassination in 1975 was reported in a letter by an American temporarily employed in that country.

2. Gorer, *Death, Grief and Mourning,* p. 47.

3. Edgar N. Jackson, *The Christian Funeral, Its Meaning, Its Purpose, and Its Modern Practice* (New York: The Channel Press, 1966), pp. 9–10.

4. René Dubos, *A God Within* (New York: Charles Scribner's Sons, 1972), pp. 60 f.

5. R. S. Solecki, "Shanidar" (New York: Knopf, 1971), as quoted by René Dubos, *A God Within,* p. 257.

6. Kathleen Kenyon, *Archeology and the Bible* (New York: Praeger, 1962).

7. See photograph section for pictures I took on location of one such Jericho cave.

8. G. Ernest Wright, *The Bible and the Ancient Near East* (New York: Doubleday & Co., 1961), pp. 63 ff., 77, 103; also, Dubos, *A God Within,* p. 119.

9. See photograph section.

10. Richard A. Martin, *Mummies* (Chicago: Field Museum of Natural History, 1969).

11. Philippe Aries, *Western Attitudes Toward Death,* trans. Patricia Ramun (Baltimore: Johns Hopkins University Press, 1974; paperback edition, 1975).

12. Philip Hewett, "The Joy of Rehearsing Your Funeral," in CLF Sermon Series, April, 1976, *CLF News Bulletin,* 25 Beacon Street, Boston, MA 02108, p. 4.

13. Ibid., p. 3.

14. Gorer, *Death, Grief and Mourning,* p. 128.

15. Ibid., pp. 63 f.

16. Hinton, *Dying,* pp. 183-185.

17. Morris, *Grief and How to Live with It,* pp. 56-59.

5 – Physicians and Funeral Directors

1. Kübler-Ross, *On Death,* pp. 5-7.

2. Bonaro Overstreet, *Brave Enough for Life* (New York: Harper, 1941), pp. 64-65.

3. Gorer, *Death, Grief and Mourning,* pp. 4-5.

4. Kübler-Ross, *On Death,* p. 246.

5. Ibid., p. 247.

6. Ibid., pp. 246 f.

7. Hinton, *Dying,* p. 69.

8. Kübler-Ross, *Questions,* p. 94.

9. Ibid., p. 95.

10. Ibid., p. 118.

11. Ibid., p. 130.

12. As stated earlier, confidentiality of respondents to our survey is protected.

13. Hinton, *Dying,* pp. 134-138. The reader may wish to review physicians' responses to dying, presented in chapter 3, pp. 59-62.

14. LeRoy Bowman, *The American Funeral* (Washington, D.C.: Public Affairs Press, 1959), p. 81.

15. Commonwealth of Massachusetts, *Rules, Regulations and Laws,* chapter 112, as amended by chapters 13, 160, 232, 407, 491, 569.

16. Bowman, *American Funeral.*

17. Association of Better Business Bureaus, Inc., *Facts Every Family Should Know about Funerals and Interments* (New York: Association of Better Business Bureaus, 1973), pp. 1 and 4.

18. Ibid.

19. Bowman, *American Funeral,* p. 86.

20. Frank O. Holmes, *Funeral and Memorial Services in Liberal Churches* (Oklahoma City: First Unitarian Church, 1964), pp. 15-16).

6 – The Church and the Clergy

1. Kahlil Gibran, *The Prophet* (New York: Knopf, 1955).

2. A Unitarian Universalist minister.

3. Hinton, *Dying,* pp. 8, 184.

4. Gorer, *Death, Grief and Mourning,* p. 128.

5. Ernest Morgan, ed., *A Manual of Death Education and Simple Burial,* 6th ed. (Burnsville, N.C.: The Celo Press, 1973), p. 6.

6. Holmes, *Funeral and Memorial Services,* pp. 3-5.

7. Jackson, *Christian Funeral,* p. 3.

8. Roger D. Blackwell and W. Wayne Talarzyk, in Jackson, *Christian Funeral,* p. 8. For an overall evaluation of the scientific reliability of these reports, refer to the Federal Trade Commission, U.S. Government Printing Office, Report of the Presiding Officer on Proposed Trade Regulation Rule concerning Funeral Industry Practices (16 C.F.R., Part 453, Public Record 215-46), July 1977.

9. Gorer, *Death, Grief and Mourning,* pp. 126, 128.

10. Ibid., p. 79; Hinton, *Dying,* p. 22.
11. Ralph W. Emerson, *Self-Reliance.*
12. Hinton, *Dying,* p. 138; Kübler-Ross, pp. 246 f. See chapter 3, pp. 22-31; chapter 5, pp. 42-52 of this book.
13. Kübler-Ross, *On Death,* p. 254.
14. Ibid.
15. Gorer, *Death, Grief and Mourning,* p. 36.
16. Holmes, *Funeral and Memorial Services,* p. 14.
17. Memorial letter sent to Mrs. Marshall's friends and distant relatives will be found in chapter 11.
18. See chapter 11.
19. Rev. Francis C. Anderson, in the *Braintree Sunday Observer Forum,* 7 November 1971.

7 – The Service: How Traditional?

1. "Death on Parade," *Reader's Digest,* April 1949, p. 90.
2. Gorer, *Death, Grief and Mourning,* p. 128.
3. Robert Fulton, *Death and Identity* (New York: John Wiley and Sons, 1965), p. 334.
4. Jackson, *Christian Funeral.*
5. Ibid., p. 32.
6. Herbert S. Patchell and Robert B. Wentworth, *The Facts of Death* (Boston: Commonwealth of Massachusetts, Department of Education, 1970), p. 57.
7. Adapted from the booklet by Dr. Frank O. Holmes, *Funeral and Memorial Services,* pp. 7 f.
8. Robert W. Haberstein and William Lamars, *Funeral Customs around the World* (Milwaukee, Wis.: National Funeral Directors Association, 1960), pp. 729 ff.; Jessica Mitford, *The American Way of Death* (Greenwich, Conn.: Fawcett, 1963, pp. 56 ff.
9. Edward C. Johnson, "Embalming," *Encyclopaedia Britannica,* vol. 8 (Chicago: Encyclopaedia Britannica, Inc., 1973), p. 307.
10. Continental Association of Funeral and Memorial Societies, *Funeral and Memorial Societies,* 1975 pamphlet, published at their address, 1828 L Street, N.W., Washington, D.C. 20036.
11. Holmes, *Funeral and Memorial Services,* p. 7.
12. A boat – not a person – Ed.
13. Bill Downey in Santa Barbara, California, *News-Press,* Wednesday, 14 March 1973.
14. The Demonstrators Association of Illinois, 2240 West Filmore Street, Chicago, Illinois 60612 (telephone: (312) 733-5283). A sample registration form follows in Appendix B.
15. Elizabeth T. Harris, "On Giving Oneself Away," *Harper's Magazine,* December, 1964.
16. J. D. Ratcliff in *Reader's Digest,* August, 1961.
17. Harris, "Giving Oneself Away," pp. 99-101.
18. See footnote 10 above for address of the continental organization that can direct the inquirers to nearest memorial societies. A sample pre-arrangement form supplied by this organization will be found in Appendix B.

8 – Children and Death

1. John Gunther, *Death Be Not Proud* (New York: Harper, 1949).
2. Lois E. Flanagan, "The Death of Two Sons – How I Survived," *St. Francis Burial Society Quarterly* 1, no. 2 (fall 1975):6.

3. Dalia Keyser, "Tears and Protest — A Mother Remembers," in *Children and Dying,* ed. Sarah S. Cook (New York: Health Sciences Publishing Co., 1974), p. 56.

4. Ibid., pp. 57 f.

5. Ibid., p. 58.

6. See George N. Marshall, *Buddha, The Quest for Serenity* (Boston: Beacon Press, 1978) for the author's study of Buddha's confrontation with suffering as the central problem of human life.

7. See Marshall and Poling, *Schweitzer, A Biography* (New York: Doubleday, 1970), currently available through CLF Book Service, 25 Beacon Street, Boston, MA 02108 for Dr. Albert Schweitzer's lifetime concern with suffering and of "the fellowship of those who bear the mark of pain."

9 — Modern Issues concerning Death

1. This letter was part of the correspondent's testimony in October 1971 to the delegates to the Montana Constitutional Convention.

2. Camden, N.J., *Courier-Post,* 3 February 1976. Copyright © 1976 by Litton Industries, Inc., published by Medical Economics Company, a Litton Division at Oradell, N.J. 07649. Reprinted by permission.

3. Euthanasia Society, 250 West 57th Street, New York, N.Y. 10019. Contributions for copies are invited.

4. As stated earlier, confidentiality of respondents to our survey is protected.

5. Lael T. Wertenbaker, *Death of a Man,* Introduction by Dr. Joseph Fletcher (Boston: Beacon Press, 1974), pp. v, viii, x.

6. Oliver P. Jones, Ph.D., M.D., *Cadavers, Autopsy and Transplantation* (Chicago: National Society for Medical Research, National Conference on the Legal Environment of Medical Science, 27 May 1959).

7. Ibid.

8. Ibid.

9. See chapter 7, p. 77 above; also, Harris, "Giving Oneself Away," p. 79ff.

10. See account on page 64, chapter 6.

11. See chapter 6, p. 63. The local hospitals or major medical facilities will be able to guide one to the nearest available institution.

12. Many states now provide for a universal donor identification on driver's licenses upon request. Since traffic deaths offer a major supply of healthy organs, this program is very valuable.

13. David Hendin, *Death as a Fact of Life* (New York: W. W. Norton, 1973; New York: Warner paperback, 1974), Warner edition, p. 163.

14. Ibid., p. 164.

15. Robert C. W. Ettinger, *The Prospect of Immortality* (New York: Doubleday & Co., 1964), p. 3. Attention is called to footnote 2, chapter 1, Sapir, *The Far Arena,* pp. 3–39, 150–160.

10 — Legal Aspects of Death

1. See the *Boston Herald American* and *Boston Globe,* Friday, 21 May 1976, p. 1, account of a "landmark case" involving Siegfried Golsten in the clubbing death of Ronald J. Salem. Jury ruled brain death occurred before respirator was unplugged; hence, he had been murdered although bodily functions were maintained by so-called "heroic measures."

11 – New Approaches to Old Responses

1. This statement was copied from the weekly newsletter of All Souls Unitarian Church, New York City, 28 May 1978. In keeping with our custom, we have omitted the author's name.

2. Permission to reprint the Memorial Letter for Marshall Webster Schacht was given by his brother and its author, the Rev. Robert H. Schacht, late of Providence, R.I.

3. Permission to reprint the Tribute to Donald Simpson was given by his widow, Mrs. Nancy Simpson and her son, John, the author.

4. Published by Church of the Larger Fellowship, Unitarian Universalist, 25 Beacon Street, Boston, Massachusetts 02108. More detailed forms prepared for Memorial Society use will be found in Appendix B.

5. St. Francis Burial Society, P.O. Box 9727, Friendship Heights Station, Washington, D.C. 20016.

6. Continental Association of Funeral and Memorial Societies, Inc., Suite 1100, 1828 L Street N.W., Washington, D.C. 20036. See forms in Appendix B, including list of local societies and guidelines.

7. *Washington Post,* Friday, 29 June 1979, page E3.

8. Fact Sheet, Proposed FTC Funeral Rule, Federal Trade Commission, Washington, D.C.

9. See chapter 8, p. 93.

Appendix A

Orthodox Jewish Practices

1. The material for this section came from the following sources: Earl A. Grollman, ed., *Concerning Death* (Boston: Beacon Press, 1974), chap. 7, pp. 119ff. and Geoffrey Gorer, *Death, Grief and Mourning* (New York: Doubleday & Co., 1965), pp. 76-81. See also, Earl A. Grollman, ed., *Explaining Death to Children* (Boston: Beacon Press, 1967), chap. 9, p. 233ff.; Abraham J. Feldman, D.D., *In Time of Need* (Hartford, Conn.: Weinstein Funeral Home, 1946).

Reform Jewish Practices

1. Rabbi Abraham J. Feldman, D.D., *In Time of Need* (Hartford, Conn.: Weinstein Funeral Home, 1946), pp. 7-12. Copyright © by Rabbi A. J. Feldman, 1946, used with permission.

Roman Catholic Practices

1. The current situation and attitude regarding the Roman Catholic service was described for an extension course of the Massachusetts Department of Education, Bureau of Adult and Extended Services and is reproduced here as an example of contemporary Catholic thinking on this subject. The material was written by Sister Rosaria Salerno, O.S.B., of the Fenway Center, Archdiocese of Boston.

Appendix B

Information Regarding Donation of Body – Harvard Medical Schools

1. The reader's own choice of medical school will furnish its own information.

Instrument of Anatomical Gift — Massachusetts Medical Schools

1. The reader's nearest medical school can undoubtedly furnish similar forms.

The Memorial Society

1. For further reference, see *A Manual of Death Education and Simple Burial* (64 pp.) by Ernest Morgan. $4.50. This standard reference work, frequently revised, is used by all memorial societies and includes full information about the Continental Association, discussion of the philosophy and practice of simplicity in funeral arrangements, advice on procedures at time of death, suggestions for memorial services, directories of memorial societies, of cooperative mortuaries, of medical schools, of eye banks, and of temporal bone banks, and many other useful data.

2. CAFMS is the acronym for the Continental Association of Funeral and Memorial Societies, and MSAC is the acronym for Memorial Society Association of Canada.

For Freedom of Choice

1. From a guide produced by the Consumer Funeral Information Project, which was supported by Grant No. 90-A-1816, awarded by the Department of Health, Education and Welfare, OHD Administration on Aging. You are invited to reproduce this material for use in church bulletins, senior citizen newsletters, adult classes and consumer education programs. Printed 2/15/80.

2. Sources of cost information: cemetery cost ranges were compiled from a 1979 survey of fifteen cemeteries in Boston, Somerville, Cambridge, and Brookline. Other prices were compiled from a 1979 survey of funeral directors in Boston, Cambridge, Somerville, and Brookline, from consultation with a funeral director who serves the Memorial Society of New England, and from a 1978 survey conducted for the National Funeral Directors Association of the United States, Inc. Similar costs may be found locally through consumer protection organizations.

3. In addition, viewing requires embalming, which is an added expense.

4. A death certificate usually requires the name and place of birth of the parents of the deceased, as well as the full name and birth date of the deceased. Consequently, this information should always be made available ahead of time and should be easily accessible in available family records.

5. The Continental Association (CAFMS) will furnish a directory of local societies.

Glossary

1. Not a safe-deposit box, since this cannot be opened immediately at the time of death.

Glossary

A few specialized words used in the text of the study in connection with funerals and memorial services are listed here so that there will be no confusion in subsequent references.

BEREAVEMENT. The condition of suffering that a person is in at the time of mourning. These terms are sometimes used interchangeably, but this study will seek to differentiate between the different processes or conditions involved.

CASKETS, COFFINS. Interchangeable terms for the container in which the body is buried.

COFFINS. *See* CASKETS.

COMMITTAL SERVICE. The service held at graveside following the funeral. It is usually a brief service of prayer, committing the body or ashes to the earth.

COOPERATIVE FUNERAL SOCIETIES. Somewhat similar to memorial societies but usually employ their own funeral director or undertaker. (*See* MEMORIAL SOCIETIES)

CREMATION. The process of consuming the body by fire or heat.

EMBALM. To prepare the body for burial through a process of draining off blood and body fluids and injecting a preservative, usually a solution of formaldehyde. Usually, if the body is to be viewed, cosmetic adornment of the body for visual display is a part of the task.

EMBALMER. The person licensed to embalm a body. In all fifty states, all funeral directors are required to be embalmers but may employ others to actually perform the task.

FUNERAL DIRECTOR, UNDERTAKER, OR MORTICIAN. Interchangeable terms for the licensed person authorized by law to provide funeral services and to perform or oversee the embalming of the body. Which term is used is merely a matter of local convention or preference.

FUNERAL PRACTICES. The related matters, such as embalming, cosmetic preparation of the body for viewing, floral arrangements, placing newspaper notices, arranging for the funeral procession, the opening of the grave or cremation preparations, and the filing of all legal papers appertaining thereto.

FUNERAL SERVICE. The actual service that takes place when the people are assembled before a burial or cremation, usually with the body present, at which time a traditional service recognizes the death of the deceased. The service is usually held in a funeral home, a church, or the home.

GRIEF. The emotional state, with varying degrees of shock, emotional incapacity, and loss of energy and will, that settles over one (lethargy) at the time of a death and persists for sometime thereafter, until one has reorganized his or her life and can face the future again.

MEMORIAL SERVICE. A simple, modern service for the deceased, without the body present, where the main emphasis is on the value of his life rather than a concern over the nature of death. It is a more flexible service in content, timing, and place, since there is no necessity to dispose of the body, which usually has already been done.

MEMORIAL SOCIETIES. Non-profit, local groups of people who have banded together in a voluntary society to assist one another in pre-arranging simple, rational, and economical services. They will contact funeral directors and know which ones are cooperative. They frequently are able to negotiate prices for simple burials or cremations, without embalming, subject to a cost of living index factor.

MODERN SERVICE. A memorial service.

MORTICIAN. *See* FUNERAL DIRECTOR.

MOURNING. The process of grieving through which one passes, generally involving the three stages of shock, suffering, and recovery, requiring both time and hope to assist in readjusting one's life.

PRE-ARRANGEMENT FORMS. Available through memorial societies and some ministers. Funeral directors may have a form of a somewhat more commercial nature for those who go directly to them. On the pre-arrangement form, one checks or notes his/her wishes for the disposition of the body and for service arrangements, in a period of good health, when one is free of tension and can make rational decisions devoid of the emotional pressures that surround the time of death. These forms are then distributed to the most likely persons involved in making final arrangements, such as the next of kin, minister, family doctor, medical file, legal papers,[1] and memorial society file. The funeral director will have a copy in his file.

TRADITIONAL SERVICES. The conventional, or traditional, funeral.

UNDERTAKER. *See* FUNERAL DIRECTOR.

Bibliography

Anderson, The Rev. Francis C. In the *Braintree Sunday Observer Forum,* 7 November, 1971.

Aries, Philippe. *Western Attitudes Toward Death.* Translated by Patricia Ramun. Baltimore: Johns Hopkins University Press, 1974, 1975 (paperback edition).

Association of Better Business Bureaus, Inc. *Facts Every Family Should Know about Funerals and Interments.* New York: Association of Better Business Bureaus, Inc., 1973.

Blackwell, Roger D., and Talarzyk, W. Wayne. *American Attitudes Toward Death and Funerals.* Columbus, Ohio: Casket Manufacturers Association of America, Inc., 1974.

Boston Globe or *Boston Herald American.* Friday, 21 May 1976.

Bowman, LeRoy. *The American Funeral.* Washington D.C.: Public Affairs Press, 1959.

Brantner, John, M.D. "Proceedings." In *Death and Attitudes toward Death.* Edited by Stacy B. Day. Minneapolis, Minn.: University of Minnesota Medical School, Bell Museum of Pathology, 1972.

Caine, Lynn. *Widow.* New York: William Morrow, 1974.

CLF (Church of the Larger Fellowship). *See* Marshall.

191

Consumer Reports, eds. *Funerals, Consumers' Last Rights.* Consumers Union Report. New York: W. W. Norton & Co., 1977.

Continental Association of Funeral and Memorial Societies. *Directory of Funeral and Memorial Societies.* Washington, D.C.: Continental Association of Funeral and Memorial Societies, Suite 1100, 1828 L St., N.W. 20036, 1975.

Cook, Sarah, S. R. N. ed. *Children and Dying.* New York: Health Sciences Publishing Co., 1974.

Courier-Post, Camden, N.J., 3 February 1976. Copyright © 1976 by Litton Industries, Inc., published by Medical Economics Co., a Litton Division at Oradell, N.J. 07649.

Cousins, Norman. *Anatomy of an Illness.* New York: Random House, 1979.

————. *The Celebration of Life.* New York: Harper & Row, 1974.

Day, Stacy B., ed. *Death and Attitudes Toward Death.* Minneapolis, Minn: University of Minnesota Medical School, Bell Museum of Pathology, 1972.

Demonstrators Association of Illinois, 2240 W. Fillmore St., Chicago, Ill. 60612.

Donne, John. *Devotions, XVII.* Quoted in Bartlett's *Familiar Quotations.* 15th ed. Boston: Little, Brown & Co., 1972.

Downey, Bill. In Santa Barbara, Calif., *News-Press,* Wednesday, 14 March 1973.

Dubos, René. *A God Within.* New York: Charles Scribner's Sons, 1972.

Ettinger, Robert C. W. *The Prospect of Immortality.* New York: Doubleday & Co., 1964.

Euthanasia Society, 250 West 57th St., New York, N.Y. 10019.

Feifel, Herman. *The Meaning of Death.* New York: McGraw-Hill Book Co., 1959, 1965.

Feldman, Abraham, J., D.D. *In Time of Need.* Hartford, Conn.: Weinstein Funeral Home, 640 Farmington Ave., 06105, 1946.

Flanagan, Lois E. "The Death of Two Sons—How I Survived." *St. Francis Burial Society Quarterly,* vol. 1, no. 2, fall 1975.

Fletcher, Joseph. "The Patient's Right to Die." In *Euthanasia and the Right to Die,* edited by A. N. Downing. Los Angeles: Nash Publishing, 1969.

Fletcher, Joseph . Foreword to *Death of a Man,* by Lael Tucker Wertenbaker. Boston: Beacon Press, 1974 edition only.

Fulton, Robert. *Death and Identity.* New York: John Wiley & Sons, 1965.

————. "Proceedings." In *Death and Attitudes Toward Death,* edited by Stacy B. Day. Minneapolis: Univ. of Minnesota Medical School, 1972.

Gibran, Kahlil. *The Prophet.* New York: Knopf, 1955.

Gorer, Geoffrey. *Death, Grief and Mourning.* New York: Doubleday & Co., Inc., 1965.

Grollman, Earl A., ed. *Concerning Death.* Boston: Beacon Press, 1974.

————. *Explaining Death to Children.* Boston: Beacon Press, 1967.

————. *Living When a Loved One Has Died.* Boston: Beacon Press, 1978.

Gunther, John. *Death Be Not Proud.* New York: Harper & Row, 1949.

Haberstein, Robert W., and Lamars, William. *Funeral Customs Around the World.* Milwaukee, Wis.: National Funeral Directors Association, 1960.

Harris, Elizabeth T. "On Giving Oneself Away." *Harper's Magazine,* December, 1964.

Hendin, David. *Death as a Fact of Life.* New York: W. W. Norton Co., Warner Paperback Library Edition, 1973, 1974.

Hewett, Philip. "The Joy of Rehearsing Your Funeral." In *CLF News Bulletin.* CLF Sermon Series. Boston: CLF, 25 Beacon St., Boston, MA 02108, April, 1976.

Hinton, John. *Dying.* Baltimore: Penguin Books, 1967.

Holmes, Frank O. *Funeral and Memorial Services in Liberal Churches.* Oklahoma City, Okla.: First Unitarian Church, 1964.

Huxley, Thomas H. "Letter to Charles Kingsley." Quoted in *The Practical Cogitator.* Boston: Houghton Mifflin Co., 1950.

Jackson, Edgar N. *The Christian Funeral.* New York: Channel Press, 1966.

————. "Grief." In *Concerning Death,* edited by Earl A. Grollman. *See* Grollman, Earl A.

————. *Understanding Grief.* Nashville, Tenn.: Abingdon Press, 1957.

Johnson, Edward C. "Embalming." *Encyclopaedia Britannica,* vol. 8. Chicago: Encyclopaedia Britannica, Inc., 1973.

Jones, Oliver P., Ph.D., M.D. *Cadavers, Autopsy and Transplantation.* Chicago: Society for Medical Research, National Conference on the Legal Environment of Medical Science, 27 May 1959.

Kenyon, Kathleen. *Archaeology and the Bible.* New York: Praeger, 1962.

Keyser, Dalia. "Tears and Protest—A Mother Remembers." In *Children and Dying,* edited by Sarah S. Cook. New York: Health Sciences Publishing Co., 1974.

Kries, Bernardine and Pattie, Alice. *Up from Grief.* New York: The Seabury Press, 1969.

Kübler-Ross, Elisabeth. *On Death and Dying.* New York: Macmillan Company, 1970.

————. *Questions and Answers on Death and Dying.* New York: Macmillan Company, Collier Books, 1974.

Marshall, George N. *Buddha, The Quest for Serenity.* Boston: Beacon Press, 1978.

————. "Funeral and Memorial Services: A Study of the Comparative Values of Traditional Funerals and Modern Memorial Services to Determine the Potentialities for Enhancing the Death and Grief Situation," 1975, Ann Arbor, Michigan 48106, University Microfilms International, 300 North Zeeb Road. (Available in either bound volumes or on microfilms.)

————, ed. *CLF Service Handbook for Members.* Boston: Church of the Larger Fellowship, Unitarian Universalist Association, 25 Beacon St., 1972.

————. *An Understanding of Albert Schweitzer.* New York: Philosophical Library, 1966.

————, and Poling, David. *Schweitzer, A Biography.* New York: Doubleday, 1970.

Martin, Richard A. *Mummies.* Chicago: Field Museum of Natural History, 1969.

Massachusetts, Commonwealth of. *Rules, Regulations and Laws.*

Mitford, Jessica. *The American Way of Death.* Greenwich, Conn.: Fawcett World Library, 1963.

Morgan, Ernest, ed. *A Manual of Death Education and Simple Burial.* 6th edition. Burnsville, N.C.: Celo Press, 1973.

Morris, Sarah. *Grief and How to Live with It.* New York: Grosset & Dunlap, 1972.

O'Connor, Edwin. *The Last Hurrah.* Boston: Little, Brown & Company, 1959.

Overstreet, Bonaro. *Brave Enough for Life.* New York: Harper & Row Publishers, 1941.

Patchell, Herbert S., and Wentworth, Robert B. *The Facts of Death.* Boston: Commonwealth of Massachusetts, Department of Education, 1970.

Pincus, Lily. *Death and the Family.* New York: Pantheon Books, Inc., 1974.

Plato. *Apology* (abridged).

Ratcliff, J. D. "Let the Dead Teach the Living." *Reader's Digest,* August, 1961.

McClusky, Thorp. "Death on Parade." *Reader's Digest,* April, 1949.

St. Francis Burial Society, *Quarterly* (Washington, D.C., 3421 Center St., N.W., 20010).

Salerno, Sister Rosaria, O.S.B. Material for extension course, Massachusetts Department of Education, Bureau of Adult and Extended Services.

Sapir, Richard Ben. *The Far Arena.* New York: Simon & Schuster, Seaview Books, 1978.

Solecki, R. S. "Shanidar." In *A God Within,* by René Dubos. New York: Knopf, 1971.

Start, Clarissa. *On Becoming a Widow* (original title: When You're a Widow). New York: Family Library, Pyramid Publications, 1973.

Thomas, Dylan. *The Collected Poems of Dylan Thomas.* New York: New Directions, 1957.

Wertenbaker, Lael Tucker. *Death of a Man.* New York: Random House, 1957; reissued, with an Introduction by Joseph Fletcher, hardcover and paperback editions. Boston: Beacon Press, 1974.

Wright, G. Ernest. *The Bible and the Ancient Near East.* New York: Doubleday & Co., 1961.

U.S. Government, Federal Trade Commission, Report of the Presiding Officer on Proposed Trade Regulation Rule Concerning Funeral Industry Practices (16 C.F.R., Part 453, *Public Record* 215–46), July, 1977 (subsequent reports issued 1978, 1979, etc.).

Index

Victorian, 59, 107
Walker, Mr., 6
War examples, 3
Weinstein Funeral Home, xi

Wertenberger *(Death of a Man),* 106
White, Paul Dudley, M.D., 23
Widows, 120
Wills, viii, 116ff.